100 THINGS YELLOW JACKETS FANS SHOULD KNOW & DO BEFORE THEY DIE

100 THINGS
YELLOW
JACKETS FANS
SHOULD KNOW & DO
BEFORE THEY DIE

Adam Van Brimmer

Foreword by HOMER RICE

TRIUMPH
BOOKS

Triumph Books and colophon are registered trademarks of Random House, Inc.

Library of Congress Cataloging-in-Publication Data

Van Brimmer, Adam
    100 things Yellow Jackets fans should know & do before they die / Adam Van Brimmer.
        p. cm.
    Includes bibliographical references.
    ISBN 978-1-60078-574-0
    1. Georgia Institute of Technology—Football—History—Miscellanea.
    2. Georgia Tech Yellow Jackets (Football team)—History—Miscellanea.
    I. Title. II. Title: One hundred things Yellow Jackets fans should know & do before they die.
        GV958.G43.V34 2011
        796.332'6309758231—dc23

                                                                2011029352

This book is available in quantity at special discounts for your group or organization. For further information, contact:

Triumph Books
542 South Dearborn Street
Suite 750
Chicago, Illinois 60605
(312) 939-3330 | Fax (312) 663-3557
www.triumphbooks.com

Printed in U.S.A.
ISBN: 978-1-60078-574-0
Design by Patricia Frey
Editorial production by Prologue Publishing Services, LLC
All photos courtesy of Georgia Tech Sports Information unless otherwise specified

To Ann, Abby, and Dutchie,
for all your love and patience

Contents

Foreword: Win with Integrity

It was late November 1944 when Coach Bobby Dodd telephoned and let me know he would soon become the head coach at Georgia Tech. I was a senior at Highlands High School in Fort Thomas, Kentucky, and as captain and quarterback had just been part of a state championship football team. Bill Alexander was stepping down after a quarter-century as the Yellow Jackets' coach, Dodd told me, and Dodd was interested in me as a player for the next squad. He sent assistant coach Ray Ellis to visit me.

Several colleges near my home, located in the tri-state area near the Ohio-Kentucky-Indiana borders, were recruiting me, but I was excited about Dodd's call—it was from Georgia Tech! I had heard the school's fight song, "Ramblin' Wreck from Georgia Tech," on the radio, and even with my limited knowledge of the institution itself, the prospect of playing football at a school with a strong tradition got my attention.

Coach Ellis followed up Dodd's call and scheduled a meeting with me in Louisville, about 70 miles west of my home. World War II was on, and gas rationing made it difficult to travel long distances by car. So Ellis used a central location to visit players in Kentucky. I boarded a Greyhound bus and made the trip to meet with Ellis. He had brought along a record of the school song and played it during our meeting at a hotel. The visit was simple but memorable. I was impressed and signed a letter of intent to attend Georgia Tech in the fall of 1945.

The war intervened, however. Returning home from the meeting with Ellis, I found a letter from the U.S. Navy. I'd joined the Navy earlier that year with the understanding I would be able to finish my senior year of high school. But the letter ordered me to report immediately to the Great Lakes Naval Station. My Georgia Tech playing days were over before they began, and I headed off to Great Lakes. Our ship sailed for the Philippines before my 18th birthday, and our unit soon entered the Pacific Theater operations fighting the Japanese.

Thirty-six years passed before I received my next telephone call from Coach Dodd. I'd just stepped down as head coach of the NFL's Cincinnati Bengals in order to take a front-office position within the organization, and as I prepared to assume my new role, Georgia Tech president Joseph Pettit called. He wanted me to serve as director of athletics. I turned down his offer. He called twice more, and twice more I said no.

Then Coach Dodd called, and he found a way to change my mind. He convinced me to come to Georgia Tech and accept a challenge that made me step out of my career in professional football. In 1980 I became Georgia Tech's fourth director of athletics.

In the decades that separated the two telephone calls between Coach Dodd and me, Georgia Tech's football program saw many changes and achievements. The Yellow Jackets won the national championship in 1952, left the Southeastern Conference in 1964, and joined the Atlantic Coast Conference in 1979. Coach Dodd retired from coaching in 1966, although he continued on as athletics director until 1976.

Upon arriving on campus, I met with Coach Dodd and invited him to become an advisor to the athletics department. One of the highlights of my career at Georgia Tech came in 1988, just prior to Coach Dodd's death. I invited him to my office and shared some good news: the board of regents had approved renaming the football stadium in his honor. He was thrilled, as were all the Tech fans, who knew that the honor further ensured his legacy.

As director of athletics, I learned more and more about the positive tradition of Georgia Tech football and the role of the program in the lives of so many alumni and friends of this unique institution. I felt the presence of that tradition as I traveled, representing the school.

Although I have served several universities in my career, I found that Georgia Tech people are the best anywhere in the country. They insisted on one important issue: win with integrity. As I look back on Georgia Tech's football history, from John Heisman to current coach Paul Johnson, I see how the supporters have rallied around the Yellow Jackets, for better or for worse, and have never lost hope in achieving success—the right way.

Heisman's insistence on excellence is reflected in the Heisman Trophy, which recognizes the most outstanding college football player in America. During his own years at Georgia Tech, Coach Heisman's team was declared national champion in 1917, becoming the first school in the South to claim that high award. Coach Alexander followed with another national championship team in 1928. Georgia Tech's 8–7 victory over the University of California in the Rose Bowl will always be remembered for the wrong-way run of an opposing player. (Cal's Roy Riegels picked up a fumble and ran toward Georgia Tech's goal line.) Coach Dodd was the winningest football coach in Georgia Tech history, and he added a national title in 1952.

Despite all the tradition, Georgia Tech seriously considered giving up on major college football in 1980. There was talk of converting the program into a non-scholarship team or dropping football altogether. But then Bill Curry entered the scene with a plan to prevent that move. As I came on board, we set out to reestablish a successful program at Georgia Tech. We succeeded, and Georgia Tech has maintained a level of excellence since. The Yellow Jackets won a national title in 1990 with Bobby Ross at the helm and conference championships in 1990, 1998, and 2009—the league titles coming under three different coaches.

Adam Van Brimmer brings out the details of the achievements and transitions of Georgia Tech football in the pages that follow.

His narrative charts the school's history of wins and losses, championship years and droughts, innovations and traditions. The character of Georgia Tech football cannot be separated from the resilience and loyalty of the school's coaches, players, administrators, and loyal fans. With the values of scholarship, leadership, and integrity guiding Georgia Tech football, the school will always rank at the top of its class.

—Homer Rice
January 2011

Introduction

He had me at "toe."

Before I first saw Georgia Tech play football in person, I heard the late Al Ciraldo's famous kickoff call, "Toe meets leather." Ciraldo was gone by then, but just the excitement and anticipation in his voice uttering those three words captivated me. Not long after, I attended my first game: I saw the Ramblin' Wreck roll onto the field and the fans bob to the Budweiser song; I heard the whistle cheer a touchdown and the band salute a hell of an engineer; I tasted a frosted orange and the Nutty Bavarian's salty-sweet treats.

Then I started to learn something about one of the most underappreciated franchises in sports. The Yankees, the Celtics, the Fighting Irish—all steeped in history. Georgia Tech, I discovered, is as storied as the rest.

A friend, upon hearing that I was writing a 100-chapter book about Georgia Tech football, joked that it must have been hard to come up with more than 10. The difficult part, I replied, wasn't figuring out what I could put in, but what I had to leave out. There are glaring omissions, such as Ken Swilling and Rock Perdoni; the 1981 upset of Alabama; the 1892 losses to Mercer, Vanderbilt, and Auburn; the Notre Dame fish fling; and the pizza brawl.

I'm saving those, and others, for the movie version.

Yellow Jackets fans have known more moments than a clock, more colorful characters than a Hollywood studio, and more highs and lows than a roller-coaster enthusiast.

The challenge of writing this book was to strike a balance between the glory and the anguish, the heroes and the villains—the stuff that makes Techies hold their heads up high and incidents that leave them hiding their faces in their hands. This book is more comedy than tragedy, but only through acknowledging failures can one appreciate success.

Georgia Tech fans are lucky. Your program's history, and those who contributed to it, inspire and amuse. Thank you for sharing with the rest of us. With that, as Al Ciraldo would say, "Toe meets leather…"

1 John Heisman

Football, as we know it, began at Georgia Tech.

John Heisman refined the game during his 16 years coaching on the Flats. He successfully lobbied for the legalization of the forward pass. He introduced pre-snap offensive shifts, the power sweep, and the hidden-ball trick. His preference for skilled, athletic players over bulky bruisers made the game safer and more entertaining and led to the creation of the Heisman Trophy in his name.

Heisman also set the standard for a winning coach. Just as John Wooden was the Wizard of Westwood, Heisman was the Magician of Midtown. Four times his Georgia Tech teams went undefeated. The 1917 Golden Tornados won the national championship.

With a 102–29–7 record, Heisman remains the winningest coach in school history.

Georgia Tech, and all football fans, can thank the bright lights of the original Madison Square Garden for football's Heisman revolution. Heisman was months away from earning his law degree from the University of Pennsylvania when he and the Quakers played a game in the world's most famous arena. Back then, the Garden featured galvanic lights, which could cause eye trauma in much the same way the sun can if stared at.

Heisman hurt his eyes looking into those lights. Two year's worth of rest was the only treatment. Reading law journals and writing legal briefs could cause further damage, so Heisman turned to coaching. He never would use his law degree.

Heisman's first opportunity came in 1893 at Ohio's Oberlin College. Football was still a developing game at the time, and

John Heisman became Georgia Tech's first football coach in 1904. He still owns the best winning percentage (.779) in program history.

coaches bounced from job to job. Heisman did stints at several other schools before coming to Georgia Tech. He innovated at every stop. At Akron, he invented the shotgun snap and made obsolete the roll-and-kick-back snaps of the day. At Auburn, he introduced the hidden-ball trick, using the play to score a touchdown against Vanderbilt. He also can claim credit for the yardage marker, uniform numbers, and the inclusion of down and distance on the scoreboard before every play.

Heisman remained at the forefront of the game's great minds during his Tech tenure. He gradually incorporated the forward pass into his offensive schemes. He also conceived of the "Heisman shift," where players would line up in one formation and shift positions just prior to the snap, confusing the defense; and the pulling-guard play, the precursor of the power sweep.

For all of Heisman's forward thinking, he could be conservative, too. One of his coaching tenets was, "When in doubt, punt!" And the greatest sin a player could commit, in Heisman's eyes, was to fumble. The coach so despised turnovers he opened preseason practice with the same speech every year.

"What is this?" Heisman rhetorically asked his players while holding a ball in his hands. "It is a prolate spheroid, an elongated sphere in which the outer leather casing is drawn tightly over a somewhat smaller rubber tubing. Better to have died as a small boy than to fumble this football."

Heisman demanded more from his players than ball security. His players abided by his dietary rules, which prohibited fresh bread—unless it was toasted—and cabbage. Heisman also limited water consumption during practice and hot showers afterward.

The one person who refused to live the Heisman way cut short his coaching career on the Flats. His wife, Evelyn, left him during the 1919 season, and Heisman left Atlanta soon thereafter. "Wherever Mrs. Heisman wishes to live, I will live in another place. This will prevent any social embarrassment," Heisman told reporters. Evelyn Heisman stayed in Atlanta, and John took the coaching job at Penn, his alma mater.

John Heisman's Georgia Tech Record

102–29–7 (.779), 16 years
3 Southern Intercollegiate Athletic Association titles
National champions, 1917
33-game unbeaten streak (1914–1918)

ADAM VAN BRIMMER

Heisman's longtime top assistant, William Alexander, succeeded him as Georgia Tech's coach—and continued Heisman's run of success.

2 The Georgia Rivalry

Nothing sparks rivalry like mockery, jealousy, and flying clods of dirt. Throw in a dose of territoriality, and you have what's known as "clean, old-fashioned hate."

The rivalry between Georgia Tech and Georgia begins at the beginning: the inaugural game, played in 1893 in Athens. Georgia Tech showed up wearing the gold color Georgia's coach, Dr. Charles Herty, had removed from his team's uniforms two years earlier because it looked "too cowardly." Also wearing gold that day were 200 students from Athens' Lucy Cobb Institute, invited by Tech to make the one-mile trek from their campus to the playing field to cheer them on.

Georgia Tech proceeded to rout Georgia. Doing so wearing Georgia colors with local girls rooting them on led to an ugly scene. A Georgia player pulled a knife and threatened Tech players at one point, while Georgia's fans began hurling dirt clods at Georgia Tech's players in the game's closing minutes.

One dirt chunk contained a stone and hit Tech's player/coach Leonard Wood in the forehead, drawing blood. "We were greeted by a shower of rocks, sticks, and missiles," Georgia Tech halfback Will Hunter told a news reporter. The pelting continued even as the Tech train—the *Seaboard Football Special*—pulled out of the station for the return trip to Atlanta. The departure so rattled the train's engineer, he rear-ended a freight train on the trip back to campus.

4

Georgia acknowledges the incident, albeit with spin that would enrage Bill O'Reilly. "School colors, stolen girlfriends, and Yellow Jacket treachery," reads the headline above an account of the incident in the Bulldogs' 2004 media guide.

The rivalry lost its barbarism in the century that followed. The passion, however, has only intensified. Four times, one team has spoiled the other's national title hopes. Georgia Tech upset arguably the greatest Bulldogs team of all-time—so good it was nicknamed the "dream and wonder" team—in 1927. And Georgia ruined legendary coach Bobby Dodd's farewell run at a national title in 1966, defeating the Yellow Jackets 23–14 to deny them a perfect regular season.

Georgia Tech and Georgia tied five times in rivalry history. As of the start of the 2011 season, 42 of the meetings were decided by seven points or less; 16 of those by three points or less; six of those by a single point.

Wrote Furman Bisher of the *Atlanta Journal-Constitution*: "Basically, the issue is clear. Tech dislikes Georgia and Georgia dislikes Tech, in a perfectly bloodthirsty manner, of course."

Memorable moments—gut-wrenching to fans—have deepened the bloodlust:

- The 1904 game swung on a punt blocked by the goal post (stationed on the goal line in those days and not in the back of the end zone). A Tech player recovered the miscue for a score.
- The 1937 game ended in a draw because Georgia's kicker doubled as a kick returner and was too tired to boot the extra point after a 93-yard touchdown return.
- The 1960 game went to Georgia, 7–6, thanks to the Bulldogs' Pat Dye, who blocked an extra point and a field goal in the win.
- The 1978 game saw Georgia rally from a 20–0 deficit and win 29–28 on a penalty-aided two-point conversion. Georgia

Tech's defense stopped the Bulldogs on the two-pointer, but a pass-interference penalty gave Georgia a second chance.

• The 1999 game turned on a fumble in the closing minutes by Georgia's Jasper Sanks. Replays showed Sanks was down prior to losing the ball to Georgia Tech's Chris Young, but replay review had yet to be implemented in the college game. Georgia Tech won on a field goal in overtime.

• The 2008 game was highlighted by Georgia Tech's 26-point third quarter that erased a 28–12 halftime deficit and spoiled quarterback Matthew Stafford's home finale. The win snapped a seven-year losing streak by Tech.

Off-the-field maneuvers have only added to the rivalry's mystique. A pro-Bulldogs Georgia Board of Regents moved the state's business school from Georgia Tech to Georgia during the 1930s, a big blow to Tech's recruiting. Tech would later add an industrial management major.

The Bulldogs coaches have always used the academic differences between the two schools to their advantage. Georgia's legendary coach, Wally Butts, would leave Georgia Tech's calculus text with recruits as if to ask, "Can you pass this?" Butts' Tech nemesis, Bobby Dodd, would often spot the book when he would visit a prospective player at the recruit's home.

The rivalry presented a make-or-break situation for many coaches, dating back to the days of Butts and Dodd. Georgia's Vince Dooley won his first six games against the Yellow Jackets and went on to a storied career. Georgia Tech's Bill Lewis lost two straight to the Dogs in the mid-1990s and was fired.

Georgia's Jim Donnan and Georgia Tech's Chan Gailey were dismissed in large part because of struggles against the rival. Georgia Tech's current coach, Paul Johnson, won in his debut in the rivalry and has already been canonized.

Georgia Tech's Biggest Wins in the Rivalry

1927—Georgia Tech 12, Georgia 0
Georgia Tech coach William Alexander used "the Plan" to score one of the biggest upsets in college football history. Alexander split his team in two four weeks before the Georgia game and held his starters out of the three games prior to the showdown with the "Dream and Wonder" Bulldogs. The shutout spoiled Georgia's unbeaten season.

1949—Georgia Tech 7, Georgia 6
The victory that sparked "the Drought"—Georgia's eight-year losing streak in the series—came courtesy of a stroke of coaching genius by the Yellow Jackets' Bobby Dodd. With his team trailing 6–0 early in the fourth quarter, Dodd quick-kicked on a third-down play that pinned the unsuspecting Bulldogs inside their 5-yard line. Georgia Tech got the ball back a few minutes later on Georgia's 39-yard line and went on to score the winning touchdown.

1969—Georgia Tech 6, Georgia 0
Georgia Tech's Bubba Hoats and Jeff Ford prove the Bulldogs' upstart coach, Vince Dooley, is not invincible after all. Hoats tied a school record with three interceptions, and Ford intercepted a pass in the end zone in the victory that snapped the Yellow Jackets' five-year losing streak to Dooley and the Dogs.

1974—Georgia Tech 34, Georgia 14
Georgia's Dooley called this loss one of the most humiliating of his career. Georgia Tech, running first-year coach Pepper Rodgers' wishbone offense, rolled up yards on a wet and messy day in Athens. A Georgia booster told Dooley afterward, "We'll never beat Tech again." Dooley would lose to Rodgers just once more in Rodgers' six-year tenure at Georgia Tech.

1985—Georgia Tech 20, Georgia 16
Georgia Tech's Gary Lee put away a stubborn Bulldogs team with a 95-yard kickoff return for a touchdown. Georgia had come from behind to take the lead twice in the game before Lee's score put the Yellow Jackets ahead for good.

1999—Georgia Tech 51, Georgia 48 (OT)
Georgia coach Jim Donnan chose to go for a touchdown rather than take a knee, run down the clock, and kick the winning field goal in the closing seconds of this game. Tailback Jasper Sanks fumbled, and Georgia Tech's Chris Young recovered to send the game to overtime. The Yellow Jackets won on a Luke

continues

Manget field goal, although the kick came after one attempt was blocked. The kick came on third down and was recovered by the holder, and the rules at the time allowed Georgia Tech to retain possession and kick again on fourth down.

2008—Georgia Tech 45, Georgia 42
The Yellow Jackets snap an eight-game losing streak to coach Mark Richt and his Bulldogs by rushing for 409 yards and surviving a five-touchdown performance by Georgia quarterback Matthew Stafford. The Jackets' trailed 28–12 at halftime only to score 26 unanswered points in the third quarter and hang on to win in coach Paul Johnson's debut in the series.

Dodd best described what beating Georgia means to the Yellow Jackets fan base in his autobiography, *Dodd's Luck*: "Any time you beat Georgia and win a bowl game, you had a great season. Don't make a difference what you did against Florida or Kentucky or Duke, they forget those things. They remember that Georgia game and that bowl game. That was big stuff."

Just watch out for the dirt clods.

3 Grant Field

Another author once dubbed Georgia Tech's football stadium a "room with a view." Jack Wilkinson's reference in his introduction to the book *Kim King's Tales from the Georgia Tech Sideline* was meant literally. Those sitting in the compact venue have a panoramic view of Atlanta's midtown and downtown skylines.

Grant Field provides another kind of view, too. A long one. Georgia Tech has been playing football on the site since 1905. The first permanent structure went up in 1913, making the stadium the third-oldest in college football behind only the University of Pennsylvania's Franklin Field and Harvard Stadium. Grant Field has been expanded, renovated, or rebuilt nine times since students constructed wooden bleachers on the site in John Heisman's second year as coach.

The historical view from Grant Field is as breathtaking as the one from the grandstands. The Yellow Jackets' four national title teams all played in Grant Field. The program's greatest players—from Joe Guyon, Clint Castleberry, George Morris, Billy Lothridge, and Randy Rhino to Pat Swilling, Marco Coleman, Joe Hamilton, and Calvin Johnson—all performed on the same soil. Heisman, Bobby Dodd, and Bobby Ross all stalked the same sideline.

True appreciation for Georgia Tech football starts with Grant Field. The site represents the school's initial commitment to football—Heisman, hired as the program's first paid coach in 1904, insisted that the administration provide an on-campus facility and quit forcing the team to play in one of Atlanta's many parks. The school leased a parcel of land shortly after Heisman came on board. Known as "the Flats," the land was anything but. The rocky tract was home to snakes and rabbits, and Georgia Tech played Heisman's first season at Piedmont Park.

The original Grant Field began to take shape in early 1905. Heisman convinced the City of Atlanta to clear the Flats of rocks and tree stumps using prison laborers. The student body put its burgeoning engineering knowledge to practical use, constructing a set of wooden grandstands on an embankment bordering the site. Heisman's 1905, 1906, and 1907 teams played in the makeshift stadium before moving to the newly built—and much more comfortable—Ponce de Leon Park for five years.

Tech came home in 1913 after prominent Atlanta banker John W. Grant donated $15,000 for the construction of concrete grandstands on the western edge of the Flats. The school named the field in honor of Grant's deceased son in 1915.

The west stands, like the wooden bleachers built by students, sat 5,600 fans, and those who could get a ticket saw Georgia Tech's

Grant Field has been Tech's home since 1905. The first incarnation featured wooden grandstands (above); in 1947 it was expanded to accommodate 40,000 fans (top right); and other improvements were added in 1992 (below right).

rise to prominence. Heisman's 1917 squad went undefeated and became the first team from a southern school to claim a national championship. Georgia Tech won conference titles in four of the next five seasons, and the school decided to expand Grant Field for the first time. The east stands opened prior to the 1924 season, followed by the south stands a year later. Grant Field seated 30,000 by the time the 1928 team won the school's second national title.

The stadium fell into an every-20-years renovation cycle from then on. The original grandstands, those built by the students in 1913, were torn down and replaced in 1947. Dodd turned the Flats into a mecca soon after, winning a national championship in 1952 and averaging eight victories a season. There were never enough seats. As *Atlanta Journal-Constitution* columnist Furman Bisher once wrote, "To hold a ticket to watch the Yellow Jackets play was better than holding an inside straight…. Tickets to the Masters were easier to come by." Tech responded by adding erector-set bleachers behind the north end zone in the late 1950s, then topped the stadium with a second deck in the mid-1960s.

Right on cue, another renovation took place 20 years later—
and this time it was overdue. Georgia Tech football slumped
following Dodd's retirement in 1966, and as fans neglected the
program, the school neglected stadium maintenance. Homer Rice
had the facility evaluated soon after taking the athletics director's
job in 1980. The engineer's report included a disturbing assessment
of the south stands: "unsafe, condemned—must be repaired or
destroyed." The assessment also noted problems with the east

11

stands, the press box, and the locker rooms, which reeked of mold and mildew.

The facility was so substandard that Coach Bill Curry and his assistants joked that recruits should be brought to campus late at night and leave early in the morning. "The less they see, the better our chances," was the mantra. And if a recruit wanted to see the locker room, the coaches had a "lost-key" policy (the dressing rooms were locked and the student assistant with the key couldn't be found).

"It was one of the oldest stadiums in the country, and it looked it," Rice said. "And it smelled, too. The facility stunk in every sense of the word."

Grant Field was reborn—and renamed as Bobby Dodd Stadium at Historic Grant Field—with the completion of the south stands renovation in 1988. The school renamed the stadium in honor of Dodd just a few months before his death. Two years later, Georgia Tech won its most recent national championship.

The pace of stadium facelifts accelerated from there. The concourses, press box, and luxury suites were redone in 1992, and another expansion took place a decade later. The lower deck of the east stands was renovated, and a permanent structure was built in the north end zone to replace the steel bleachers installed in the 1950s.

The 2003 project resulted in the room enjoyed today. And man, what a view.

Oldest College Football Stadiums

1. Franklin Field (Penn) 1895
2. Harvard Stadium (Harvard) 1903
3. Bobby Dodd Stadium at Historic Grant Field (Georgia Tech) 1913
4. Yale Bowl (Yale) 1914
5. Scott Field (Mississippi State) 1915
6. Nippert Stadium (Cincinnati) 1916
7. Camp Randall Stadium (Wisconsin) 1917
8. Husky Stadium (Washington) 1920

4 Bobby Dodd

Bobby Dodd never interviewed for a coaching job at Georgia Tech. Georgia Tech assistant coach Mack Tharpe had no interest in Dodd or his future when he met with him one October evening in 1931. Tharpe needed a scouting report on North Carolina and couldn't prepare one himself because his car had broken down en route to Knoxville, Tennessee, to watch the Tar Heels play Tennessee. He had missed the game.

Tharpe approached Volunteers coach Robert Neyland and asked about North Carolina's stunting defensive line. Neyland pointed Tharpe toward his senior quarterback, Dodd. Dodd's description of the tactics and advice on how to counter them helped Georgia Tech play the Tar Heels to a 19–19 tie the following week.

Dodd's report was all the proof Georgia Tech head coach William Alexander needed of Dodd's coaching abilities. Alexander enlisted the program's biggest booster, Chip Robert, to summon Dodd to Atlanta and convince him to join the Yellow Jackets staff instead of Neyland's at Tennessee or Wallace Wade's at Duke.

Robert made Dodd an offer he couldn't refuse—$300 a month, a small fortune during the Great Depression. The investment turned out to be one of the best Robert and Georgia Tech ever made.

Dodd won 235 games as an assistant or head coach in 36 seasons at Georgia Tech. As a head coach, his teams won nine or more games in eight of his 22 years, played in 13 bowl games, claimed the 1952 national title, and enjoyed one of the more successful six-year runs in college football history. Dodd's heyday on the Flats is known as the Golden Era of Georgia Tech football.

Bobby Dodd (center, in sport coat) guided his team to a national title, two SEC championships, and 13 bowl games in 22 seasons as head coach.

Dodd's intelligence, first realized through that North Carolina scouting report, would key countless wins during his tenure. Alabama's legendary coach Paul "Bear" Bryant called Dodd the best game coach he'd ever known. Dodd would invent plays on the fly or quick-kick unsuspecting opponents into bad field position.

He would even take intentional safeties in tight spots: leading Southern Methodist 6–0 but losing a field-position battle in a 1953 game, Dodd twice ordered quarterback Pepper Rodgers to take safeties. The Yellow Jackets won 6–4.

"He was the kind of coach who you trusted whatever he told you," one of Dodd's greatest players, linebacker George Morris, said. "With him, you knew he'd find a way to win."

Or as Dodd's nemesis, Georgia coach Wally Butts, once put it: "If Bobby Dodd were trapped at the center of an H-bomb explosion, he'd walk away with his pockets full of marketable uranium."

Bobby Dodd's Coaching Record

165–64–8 (.713), 22 years
9–4 in bowl games
2 Southeastern Conference titles
National champions, 1952
31-game unbeaten streak (1950–1953)

Like most legendary coaches, Dodd had his idiosyncrasies. He coached practice in silence from a folding chair atop a wooden observation tower. He coached his assistants, and his assistants coached the players. Dodd so infrequently engaged in practice that when players heard his whistle—its pitch shriller than those of his assistants—it disoriented them.

"He was the big whistle," said Don Ellis, an end on the 1954, 1955, and 1956 teams. "That whistle didn't blow up there from the tower often. When it did, it always got our attention."

Dodd's practices were unconventional in other ways as well. His teams rarely hit in practice during the season. Touch football, not tackle, was the norm. And Friday practices revolved around a volleyball game.

Dodd football really became odd on game day. The Georgia Tech sideline was as ordered as a military unit answering a reverie call: Dodd, decked out in a three-piece suit, sat on a folding chair on the 50-yard line; his offensive substitutes lined up shoulder-to-shoulder on one side, his defenders on the other. Dodd's meticulous planning and chess-master-like ability to adjust showed on game day, too. His Yellow Jackets won or tied 62 percent of games decided by a touchdown or less. Georgia Tech's prowess in the clutch was so renowned, the media gave it a nickname: Dodd's Luck.

Dodd's rivals knew better, though. Alabama's Bryant dispelled the notion in his autobiography, *Bear: My Hard Life and Good Times as Alabama's Head Coach*. "Dodd's luck," Bryant said, "was really Dodd smart."

5 Homer Rice

For someone who played quarterback and focused most of his coaching energy on reinventing offensive schemes, Homer Rice sure liked to tackle. His targets didn't wear pads or head gear, though. Rice liked to tackle challenges.

A few weeks into the biggest challenge of his professional life, Rice wondered if he'd finally taken on one he shouldn't have. He'd turned down Georgia Tech's athletics director job three times before finally relenting in 1980. And only then after Bobby Dodd called and made clear to Rice that, if he didn't take the position, one of college football's most storied programs might soon cease to exist.

Rice had been recruited by Dodd as a high school senior and had even signed a scholarship offer with the Yellow Jackets. But World War II intervened, and Rice reported to the Great Lakes Naval Station instead of Rose Bowl Field, the football team's practice facility. Thirty-five years later, Dodd successfully recruited Rice again.

Dodd wasn't exaggerating the direness of Tech's situation. The 1970s had seen the decline of the football program and the athletic department as a whole. The facilities were substandard, the graduation rates stunk, there were no women's programs, and the Alexander-Tharpe Fund was more of a loose booster club than a fund-raising arm. Simply put, there was no evidence of athletic pride, be it among the alumni, students, faculty and staff, or the community.

"It was unbelievable," Rice said. "I didn't start from scratch. I started from below that point."

Athletics was sinking before Rice's eyes. Two meetings were held his first week on campus: one debated the future of Georgia

Tech's football program and was attended by school president Joseph Pettit; the other featured a "state of the union" with Dodd himself scheduled to speak. The Pettit meeting included a serious discussion about disbanding the football program, or at least making it a non-scholarship team that would compete at a lower level. Dodd's forum featured the coach telling the room, "Georgia Tech athletics is at its lowest mark in history."

"Funny, I don't remember them telling me those things were coming before I took the job," Rice said. "But that's where we were: everybody said you couldn't do it at Georgia Tech. Challenges are what I like."

Rice moved to meet the challenge quickly. Implementing the Total Person Program, an initiative aimed at developing life skills in student-athletes, was the foundation of Rice's plan to revive athletics. The Georgia Tech community bought into the notion immediately, and the Total Person Program concept earned Rice the notice and respect necessary to put the rest of the infrastructure in place.

In other words, Rice's approach opened checkbooks again.

Rice raised more than $100 million between 1980 and 1985. He used that money to refurbish nearly every athletic facility on campus and build the Edge Center, the home of the Georgia Tech Athletic Association attached to the football stadium; start seven women's programs; fund every program to a point where it could compete for Atlantic Coast Conference titles; and hire the best coaches and staff, including fund-raisers, available.

Five years into his tenure, Tech's facilities were on par with those of other ACC schools, the basketball and baseball teams had won league titles, and the football program had played in a bowl game. Five years after that, the Yellow Jackets football team won a national championship, and the men's basketball team reached the Final Four. Six years after that, Georgia Tech served as an Olympics host, with the boxing, swimming, and diving competitions held on campus.

Rice retired in 1997, having conquered the Georgia Tech challenge. John Heisman established Georgia Tech athletics. Bobby Dodd perfected it. Homer Rice resuscitated it. Rice's successor, Dave Braine, summarized Rice's influence this way: "I think when you talk about great names in Georgia Tech history, you always hear Heisman, Alexander, and Dodd. I always put Homer Rice in there because he did so much for the program."

6 1990 National Champions

Cinderella has nothing on Georgia Tech's 1990 national championship team. The Yellow Jackets got about as much respect coming in as the Colonial Army in the 1770s, pulled out more victories—and a tie—in the clutch than the Bad News Bears, and gave a closing argument to their case for a national title even Perry Mason could appreciate.

Yet, somehow, the players saw the improbable coming. Safety Ken Swilling predicted an unbeaten season prior to the opening of fall practice. That prognostication came months after offensive lineman Jim Lavin said the team acquired its "missing ingredient"—confidence. In between, the players talked championships, both conference and national, among themselves.

"We didn't talk to other people about it," offensive lineman Mike Mooney said in a 2005 interview. "They would have laughed at us."

The jeers would have been justified. The Yellow Jackets were two years removed from a 3–8 season, which included two wins against Division I-AA teams, and three years distant from a 2–9 season in which both wins came versus Division I-AA programs. Kicker Scott Sisson remembers visiting campus as a high school

Quarterback Shawn Jones throws downfield in a victory during Georgia Tech's 1990 national championship run. Jones was just a sophomore when he led the Yellow Jackets to a 11–0–1 season.

senior for a 1988 game. "They were horrible," Sisson said. "And the game I went to, they won."

Hints of what was to come dropped during the 1989 season. A freshman named Shawn Jones took over at quarterback. The defense held five opponents to 14 points or less. Coach Bobby Ross received a much-needed pep talk and vote of confidence from three influential alumni. Georgia Tech ended a 16-game Atlantic Coast Conference losing streak with a come-from-behind victory against Maryland, igniting a run of seven wins in its last eight games.

"That," Jones said of the Maryland win, "turned everything around." And it set up the miracle run the next year.

The 1990 season had more switchbacks than an alpine road. Georgia Tech trailed by 10 points in the opener only to rally for 14 points in the fourth quarter and the win. The Yellow Jackets held Clemson's potent option offense to one touchdown in a 21–19 victory. They survived the unavoidable hiccup by salvaging a tie in the closing minute against North Carolina. Tech rallied to upset top-ranked Virginia on the road and eke out a field goal victory over Virginia Tech the following week. The Jackets recovered from an early deficit to hammer rival Georgia.

"Every game was like a soap opera," outside linebacker Marco Coleman said.

The Yellow Jackets hooked followers like a daytime drama along the way. Following a 31–3 win against Maryland in Week 4, at which point the defense had yet to surrender a touchdown all season, *Atlanta Journal-Constitution* columnist Furman Bisher penned a prophetic evaluation of the Jackets. "Prepare yourself, folks, and practice constraint at the same time," Bisher wrote. "This may be the football team Georgia Tech has longed for, dreamed of, and fantasized about since the days of Robert Lee Dodd. The latter-day Bobby may have constructed a juggernaut. A powerhouse. A team of killer bees."

The Yellow Jackets certainly showed the killer instinct. Snubbed by the pollsters, who ranked them No. 2 behind once-beaten Colorado in the final regular season rankings, and an underdog in a Citrus Bowl matchup against 19th-ranked Nebraska, Georgia Tech routed the Cornhuskers.

The performance impressed the coaches voting in the United Press International poll—they named Tech their national champion. The AP pollsters stuck by Colorado despite the Buffaloes' unconvincing win against Notre Dame in the Orange Bowl. The Irish had a potential game-winning touchdown wiped out by a controversial clipping penalty.

Being known as co-champions instead of undisputed champs didn't spoil the Cinderella season for Georgia Tech's players and coaches.

"Georgia Tech is in an elite group," Ross said in the lead-up to the 20th anniversary celebration in 2010. "Not many teams win a national championship."

The Tie

The lone blemish on Georgia Tech's 1990 title season—a 13–13 tie with North Carolina—should include another mark: an asterisk. Three Yellow Jackets starters missed the game with injuries, including stars Ken Swilling and Mike Mooney, and Mooney's backup, Russell Freeman, who broke his wrist on the game's first series. Two other offensive linemen played with injuries.

"I would have fought with them to go had I known Russell was going to get hurt right off the bat," Mooney said in a 2005 interview. "I listened to the game on the radio. It was probably the longest day of my life."

It was worse in person. The Yellow Jackets outgained the Tar Heels 435–151 but had three would-be touchdown drives stall inside the 10-yard line. Kicker Scott Sisson booted the game-tying and season-saving field goal with 61 seconds left. The tie was so demoralizing players wept in the locker room afterward.

"It felt like a loss to me," offensive lineman Jim Lavin said. "We didn't get the job done. That was on us. It was the lowlight of the year."

7 Joe Hamilton

The dirt patch in front of Joe Hamilton's grandfather's house in Alvin, South Carolina, is fertile ground. For generations, the soil has yielded some of the town's finest sweet potatoes. And in the 1980s and 1990s, the patch's sweetness took root in something other than a vegetable.

The yard doubled as Hamilton's boyhood football training ground. He and the other kids his age in the tiny town played with the pigskin there almost every day, breaking only for a brief period at harvest time. Hamilton eventually traded the patch for a high school field and then college stadiums. By then, Hamilton was one of the sweetest players in the country.

"I'm not sure I've ever seen in college football an athlete like Joe Hamilton," Maryland coach Ron Vanderlinden said after Hamilton accounted for 474 yards total offense in a 1999 game versus the Terrapins. "I've never seen a quarterback like Joe Hamilton, ever."

Nobody had. Hamilton was an option quarterback who ran a pro-style passing offense flawlessly in his final three seasons at Georgia Tech. One Virginia writer called him a cross between Tommie Frazier, Nebraska's great option quarterback, and Peyton Manning, who starred at Tennessee and is in the midst of a Hall of Fame career in the NFL. Others mentioned Randall Cunningham, Andre Ware, and Charlie Ward.

With more than 10,000 yards total offense and 83 touchdowns in his four years as a starter, Hamilton belongs in a class by himself. The fact that he posted those numbers despite standing just 5'10"—with his cleats on—made him a marvel. Appropriately enough, the quarterback Hamilton most admired was another mighty mite, Boston College's Doug Flutie. "He was a guy who made something possible for me," Hamilton said. "Given his height, his ability to win and do whatever it took to help his team win paved the way for me."

Hamilton nearly followed Flutie's lead when it came to the Heisman Trophy. Flutie won the award presented to college football's most outstanding player in 1984. Hamilton was the runner-up 15 years later, and the outcry over his losing the trophy to Wisconsin's Ron Dayne still reverberates. Hamilton accounted for 3,794 yards and 35 touchdowns in his senior season and posted two of the greatest individual performances in Georgia Tech history that year. His 474 yards total offense against Maryland—in a

Joe Hamilton runs the option during Georgia Tech's 35–30 win against West Virginia in the 1997 Carquest Bowl. Hamilton set several Georgia Tech and Atlantic Coast Conference records in his career.

Thursday night game televised nationally on ESPN—came on the heels of a brilliant showing on the road against top-ranked Florida State: Hamilton completed 22 of 25 passes, including 14 of 14 in the second half, for 387 yards and five touchdowns, one rushing.

Said Florida State's Bobby Bowden afterward, "It's been a long time since our defense has been that helpless." Bowden expounded on Hamilton's talents two weeks later in a teleconference: "I haven't seen anybody do more for his football team than he's done. And he does it in a lot of different manners—running the ball, throwing the ball, leading. That's pretty doggone impressive to me."

Credit Georgia Tech offensive coordinator Ralph Friedgen as well as grandpa's yam field for Hamilton's sweet play. Just as Friedgen turned a player no other college thought could play quarterback into the leader of a national championship team, he helped "Little Joe" stand tall. Friedgen employed many of the same schemes and concepts with Hamilton as he had a decade earlier with Shawn Jones, the quarterback of Tech's 1990 title team, and got similar results. Like Jones, Hamilton helped rescue a downtrodden Yellow Jackets program. Like Jones, Hamilton led Tech to an Atlantic Coast Conference championship. Like Jones, Hamilton rewrote the Georgia Tech and ACC record books. Like Jones, Hamilton was known for his clutch play.

"In the fourth quarter, I don't think there's anybody better with the ball in his hands," Hamilton's head coach at Georgia Tech, George O'Leary, said.

Hamilton was quite a character, too. Known for his easy smile and impeccable manners—legend has it he once apologized, mid-audible, for a misspoken call change at the line of scrimmage, as in "Blue-22…no, excuse me, that should be Red-22"—Hamilton knew no strangers. Those who spent time with him usually react the same way at the mere mention of his name: a smile, a roll of the eyes, and a pause in order to decide which story to tell first. Said Allison George, who worked in Georgia Tech's sports media relations department throughout Hamilton's career, "He has a very charismatic personality. He is just fun to be around, period."

The Rhinos

Randy Rhino welcomes a visitor into his office at Georgia Tech, and it doesn't take long for one wall to attract the guest's attention. The façade is an oversized history book of 50 years worth of Georgia Tech football, covered with photographs of four blood relatives in Yellow Jackets gear and memorabilia from their careers.

Most know the ties between the Rhino family and Georgia Tech football. For those who don't, for those who study the wall and give the man behind the desk an inquisitive look, Rhino leans back in his chair and delivers his line: "Yes, my whole family bleeds gold."

Three generations of Rhinos left their mark on the Yellow Jackets. Randy's father, Chappell, played halfback for Bobby Dodd's Golden Era teams of the early 1950s and became known as "One Play" Rhino for a touchdown pass in the 1952 win against Georgia. Randy started as a defensive back and kick returner for the Yellow Jackets between 1972 and 1974 and is the only three-time All-American in program history. Randy's brother, Danny, played in Tech's secondary from 1974 to 1976. And Randy's son, Kelley, was a record-breaking punt returner for the Jackets between 1999 and 2002.

"We're real proud of the boys and what they accomplished at Tech," Chappell Rhino said. "The school, Coach Dodd, football— it's really meant a lot to us."

Chappell Rhino came to Georgia Tech to play baseball. A hard-throwing pitcher, he was an all-conference player on the diamond

Randy Rhino returns a punt for a touchdown. Rhino was a three-time All-American and set all of Georgia Tech's punt return records during his career. His son, Kelley, would eclipse his father's marks 25 years later.

who would later be inducted into the Georgia Tech Hall of Fame. Baseball wasn't a year-round sport back then as it is today, so Rhino, like many other Yellow Jackets athletes at the time, played multiple sports.

Chappell Rhino was largely a practice player on the football team. Georgia Tech's backfield featured more talent than an Oscars ceremony. Rhino backed up the likes of Leon Hardeman, Bill Teas, John Hicks, Bob McCoy, Buster Humphreys, and James Patton.

Rhino was a part of the program's turnaround. Georgia Tech finished 5–6 in Rhino's first year only to go 23–0–1 in his last two and win the 1952 national title.

For all his love for the Yellow Jackets, Chappell Rhino never forced Georgia Tech on his sons. Randy remembers vividly the Christmas when Santa left two football jerseys under the tree: one in Tech colors, the other in Georgia red and black. Randy, older than his brother by 11 months, picked the Bulldogs uniform. His maternal grandfather was a Georgia grad, and he rooted for the Dogs.

Chappell Rhino subtly brought his son around. The wake-up alarm in the Rhino household sounded exactly like the "Ramblin' Wreck" fight song, and Chappell shared his Georgia Tech experiences with Randy and Danny as they grew older. "My allegiance to the dark side was very short," Randy said.

Even so, Randy nearly took his talents to North Carolina rather than Georgia Tech. Undersized at 5'9" and living in Charlotte, Rhino wasn't on the Yellow Jackets' recruiting radar despite his family connection. The Tar Heels did recruit him, however, and featured the player he'd come to idolize in high school, tailback Don McCauley, in their backfield.

Randy starred in the North Carolina high school Shrine Game, and a Tech alum in the area began recruiting him, a normal practice at the time. Randy soon received an invitation to visit the Flats. He responded by telling his parents he was going to North Carolina. That's where he wanted to go, and he didn't want to extend the process. His father supported the decision, but his mother encouraged him to go to Atlanta "and see what they have to say."

Randy went on the trip, and his player-host, Bruce Southall, showed him a good time. Randy had just celebrated his 17th birthday, and a weekend on a college campus, including a date with an attractive Tech coed, impressed him. A meeting with Dodd sealed his change of heart. Randy had heard so many stories about Dodd from his father, he was awestruck. Dodd welcomed Randy to his office, sat him down, and said, "Son, I think you can be the next Brent Cunningham," Tech's star tailback at the time.

"That was all it took," Randy said. "I walked out of his office and signed a scholarship offer right then. He was the closer. Just hearing him talk about my dad was enough."

But Randy didn't turn out to be the next Brent Cunningham. His talents were better suited to the defensive backfield and kick returns. His first year of eligibility, he intercepted eight passes and averaged 18 yards per punt return, earning first-team All-America honors. He intercepted six more passes and recovered three fumbles the next year. His punt and kick return numbers went down because opponents kicked away from him. He moved from safety to cornerback his senior year—to make room for his brother Danny in the secondary—and opposing quarterbacks followed the punters' leads and avoided testing him. Randy still set several school records, and his storied career ultimately landed him in the College Football Hall of Fame.

Kelley's path to Georgia Tech paralleled his father's. Even smaller than Randy—5'7"—Kelley seemed destined for the Division I-AA or Division II ranks. He starred for one of Atlanta's better high school programs, Marist, and received plenty of recruiting letters but little serious interest. The letters quickly became a nuisance, and Kelley quit opening them. Randy and Kelley's mother kept up with the notes instead.

During the spring of Kelley's junior year, a letter came from Tech coach George O'Leary. Randy opened it, and the note started out like most of the others, "Hey, Kelley, how you doing? We're going into spring practice...." Randy almost stopped reading after the first paragraph but decided to read on. Good thing he did, as the second graph included a scholarship offer. "I reread it five or six times to make sure I wasn't reading something into it that wasn't there, then I gave it to my wife," Randy said. She read it and began screaming for Kelley. Kelley read it and called O'Leary to accept the offer on the spot. "Georgia Tech was the only place I wanted to go," Kelley Rhino admits.

Kelley had impressed O'Leary a few months earlier during the state high school semifinal games. Marist faced Thomas County Central in the game, and Thomas County featured a highly sought-after tailback named Joe Burns. NCAA recruiting rules prohibited O'Leary from attending the game, but because it was the state semifinals, the showdown was televised by Georgia Public Broadcasting. Kelley played well, and O'Leary would later tell him he liked the heart he showed in that game.

Kelley impressed O'Leary again once he got on campus. His effort and work ethic in practice earned him a spot on the kick coverage team as a true freshman. Kelley also spent time before, during, and after practice, volunteering to catch balls for Georgia Tech's punters. During Kelley's sophomore year, one of the punt returners got hurt, and O'Leary lacked confidence in the others on the depth chart. O'Leary found Kelley in the lunch line in the dining hall that week and invited the player to eat with him. "I've been watching you for a while, and you've been doing a good job," O'Leary told Rhino. "I'm going to give you a shot this week to return punts."

"I think I took every return from that point," Kelley Rhino said. "I got the opportunity and didn't let it go." Rhino would go on to break the Tech punt return records—his father's punt return records.

"That was very special," Randy Rhino said. "How many fathers can say their career records were broken by their own son?"

The Rhino legacy at Georgia Tech may not be over. Kelley has a young son named Austin born in 2006. "Kelley won't let me near him to start working on him yet," Randy said. "It's too early to tell if we'll be looking at a fourth-generation Yellow Jacket."

The Ramblin' Wreck

A white-and-gold Ford Model A zooms from under Bobby Dodd Stadium, rolls under a canopy of balloons, punches through a paper banner, and honks crazily while circling the grass. Cheerleaders hang from its sides, shaking pom-poms at a stadium full of screaming fans excited for a four-wheeled mascot: the Ramblin' Wreck.

The Wreck's arrival, trailed by the Yellow Jackets football team, caps a long day for the traveling pep rally. Sports' most-recognizable vehicle spends game-day mornings zipping around campus, its horn blaring a raspy litany of "Ta-Tooot. Ta-Ta-Tooooots."

The mechanical mascot's story spins back to the early 1900s. For many years, Floyd Field, dean of men, drove his 1914 Ford Model T to and from class. His Tin Lizzie was so popular, it acquired the nickname "Ramblin' Wreck" in 1926, a reference that dates back to Georgia Tech's infancy. Georgia Tech engineers working in South America at the turn of the 20th century often were called "Ramblin' Wrecks from Georgia Tech" because they designed elaborate contraptions to navigate the jungles.

The Ramblin' Wreck has led the Yellow Jackets onto the field before every home game since 1961.

Color Change

The Ramblin' Wreck originally sported a paint color best described as "cheddar cheese" gold. Coach Bobby Dodd changed the color soon after its purchase by the school, tasking Pete George, a Tech alumnus and manager of the Ford assembly plant in nearby Hapeville, Georgia, with restoring and painting it "Lincoln" gold.

Field enlisted Ramblin' Wrecks from the campus machine shop to help overhaul his Ford. But when the car struggled to endure his work commutes, he disposed of it to the student body's dismay. Many had their own beat-up wrecks by then, though, and in the 1940s and 1950s campus was littered with them. James Dull, president and dean of students, sensed the passion for that classic car and started searching for a pre–World War II Ford that could represent Georgia Tech's engineering acumen.

One nearly fell in his lap. In the fall of 1960 he spied the perfect match right outside his Towers Dormitory apartment—a 1930 Ford Model A Sport Coupe. The car's owner, Capt. Ted Johnson, chief pilot for Delta Airlines in Atlanta, had parked it there to attend a track meet. He had restored it with his son, Craig. Dull bought it for $1,000 the following May. Johnson later returned the purchase price to the school.

A few months later, on September 30, 1961, with Tech playing Rice University at home, one of college football's most enduring traditions was born. Dekle Rountree, the Student Council Ramblin' Reck chairman, had the car crank started, took the wheel, and accelerated onto the field. Don Gentry, Ramblin' Reck Club president, explained the car's acquisition to 43,501 fans.

Tech won 24–0. The Ramblin' Wreck has escorted the team onto the field before each home game ever since.

The Wreck sometimes travels to away games—such as the 2006 ACC Championship Game in Jacksonville, Florida—and has appeared at other sporting events, including basketball's 2004 Final Four in San Antonio, Texas.

The Ramblin' Reck Club is responsible for the car's physical, financial, and mechanical care. The club, founded in 1930, is comprised of students who promote Tech's spirit, history, and tradition. Each year, one club member is elected Wreck Driver and primary caretaker, and is the only person with the car keys. Because Georgia Tech does not fund the car, driver, or club, the Ramblin' Wreck is almost entirely preserved and supported by fees from unofficial appearances. It may be spotted throughout Georgia at weddings, parties, and other functions.

10 Learn the Fight Song

Tech's marching band plays its fight song fast.

I'm a Ramblin' Wreck from Georgia Tech and a hell of an
engineer,
A helluva, helluva, helluva, helluva, hell of an engineer.
Like all the jolly good fellows, I drink my whiskey clear,
I'm a Ramblin' Wreck from Georgia Tech and a hell of an
engineer.

Quick musical strokes make singers struggle to keep up.

Oh, if I had a daughter, sir, I'd dress her in White and Gold,
And put her on the campus, to cheer the brave and bold.
But if I had a son, sir, I'll tell you what he'd do.
He would yell, "To Hell with Georgia," like his daddy used to do.

Whether one has any Tech connections, the beat's energy makes most everyone nod in tune.

Oh, I wish I had a barrel of rum and sugar 3,000 pounds,
A college bell to put it in and a clapper to stir it around.
I'd drink to all good fellows who come from far and near.
I'm a ramblin', gamblin', hell of an engineer.

The old folk ballad "Son of a Gambolier," written by Charles Ives in the late 1800s, is most noted as the musical inspiration for "(I'm a) Ramblin' Wreck from Georgia Tech." Some reports cite the marching tune "The Bonnie Blue Flag," published in 1861 by Harry McCarthy.

The fight song's history includes:

- 1920—Tech student Arthur Murray, a dance instructor, organized a "radio dance." A band on campus played such songs as "Ramblin' Wreck," which were broadcast to a group of dancers—mostly Tech students—on the Capital City Club rooftop in downtown Atlanta.
- 1925—The Columbia Gramophone Company distributed a recording of Tech songs, including the fight song, making Tech one of the first southern colleges to have its songs recorded. Extensive play made it known nationally.
- 1944—Commanding officers in Higgins boats on D-Day morning are said to have led their men in the song to calm their nerves.
- 1953—Tech's glee club sang "Ramblin' Wreck" on Ed Sullivan's *Toast of the Town*, later known as *The Ed Sullivan Show*. An estimated 30 million viewers tuned in, although they heard a censored version. Sullivan reportedly made the club sing "heck" and "heckuva" in lieu of "hell" and "helluva."
- 1954—John Wayne whistled the tune in the film, *The High and the Mighty*.
- 1959—"Ramblin' Wreck" connected Vice President Richard Nixon and Soviet Premier Nikita Khrushchev in Moscow.

ADAM VAN BRIMMER

The two leaders sang the song together reportedly to reduce tension between them while conducting impromptu exchanges at the American National Exhibition at Sokolniki Park. Nixon apparently didn't know any Russian songs, but Khrushchev knew an American one because of Ed Sullivan's show—"Ramblin' Wreck from Georgia Tech."

* 1983—Tech's fight song awoke space mission astronauts. It was chosen to represent Commander Richard Truly's alma mater.

Tech's fight song likely was born a couple of years after the school opened its doors in 1888. Composed by a student en route to Athens to watch Tech's baseball team defeat rival Georgia, it became the school's official fight song in 1905.

Over the years, several people penned adaptations, including Michael A. Greenblatt, Tech's first professional bandleader, in 1912, and Frank Roman, Greenblatt's successor, in 1919. Roman's version contained trumpet flourishes and continues to be popular today.

11 Shawn Jones

"When do you want me?" With those five words, Georgia Tech's football fortunes changed in the late 1980s. Shawn Jones would play football for Bobby Ross' Yellow Jackets, and in the following half-decade he would rewrite the Atlantic Coast Conference record book, lead Tech to the pinnacle of college football, and make all those coaches who unwittingly convinced him to go to Georgia Tech because they wanted him to play defensive back instead of quarterback hang their heads in shame.

Shawn Jones scrambles for yardage during a 1991 game. Jones was the epitome of a dual-threat player, with the ability to make big plays as both a passer and a runner.

If the Georgia Tech football program had an all-time most valu able player, it would be Jones. Yes, Calvin Johnson was a superior athlete. Sure, Pat Swilling's play ensured the program continued to compete at the major college level. And of course Joe Hamilton would best Jones' records and wrest the "greatest quarterback in program history" label away. But Jones was the right player in the right place at the right time, and while he had plenty of help, he made football important again at Georgia Tech.

The Yellow Jackets program had risen from the ashes in the early 1980s behind Coach Bill Curry. Yet the day Jones committed to Ross with his "When do you want me?" question, Tech was on a six-game losing streak and hadn't won a game against a major college program under Ross. Curry had left for Alabama following the 1986 season, and Ross brought a different approach and culture to the Flats. The program slid as a result.

Tech's plight mattered little to Jones. He'd grown accustomed to flying under the radar. A native of Thomasville, Georgia, a small town near the Georgia-Florida border, his best friend growing up turned into his nemesis on the football field and basketball court during high school. Charlie Ward played quarterback and point guard for the rival school, Thomas County Central, and dominated the headlines if not the head-to-head match-ups.

Jones never wavered in his decision to attend Georgia Tech, even when his redshirt season, 1988, saw the Yellow Jackets finish 3–8 and post their second straight winless Atlantic Coast Conference record. Ross had contemplated quitting in the middle of that sorry season, and many of Jones' classmates considered transferring in the weeks following the finale. Jones thought about leaving, too, but dismissed the notion immediately. His take was, "We've got a chance. We can take over the program."

Jones took over the quarterback job the following fall—and promptly flopped. He completed just 4 of 29 passes in his debut, a 38–28 loss to North Carolina State. "I guess you could say it was a nightmare," Jones would later say when asked about his debut. Yet in some ways, Jones' early stumble should not have come as a surprise. A wishbone quarterback at Thomasville High School, Jones would need time to adjust to offensive coordinator Ralph Friedgen's complex passing offense.

Jones lost his first three games as a starter before Friedgen incorporated the option into the scheme more and Jones found some confidence. Jones threw four touchdown passes in Georgia Tech's fourth game of the season, a victory over Maryland, and the "Jones era" began. He would finish with more than 2,000 yards total offense and 15 touchdowns that season and earn the ACC Rookie of the Year Award.

More importantly, Jones showed the poise and clutch play that would define his Georgia Tech career. He ran for a 30-yard touchdown and the winning score in the final minute of a game against North Carolina and also rallied the Jackets to a one-point victory over Boston College. He turned in several more heroic efforts during Georgia Tech's improbable run to the 1990 national championship. His best games that season were Tech's biggest: the showdown with top-ranked Virginia; the season-saving games against Virginia Tech and North Carolina; the rivalry match-up with Georgia; and the Citrus Bowl versus Nebraska. His 318-yard performance against the Cornhuskers no doubt convinced a coach or two to vote for Georgia Tech in their poll and give the Jackets a share of the national title.

"The bigger the game, the better I play," Jones said in the Citrus Bowl press conference. "I put a lot of pressure on myself because I expect to make the big play when we need it. I love challenges. The tougher the better."

Jones posted an even more impressive season the following year, at least statistically. He'd mastered Friedgen's ever-evolving scheme by then and tallied 2,649 total yards. His Heisman candidacy fizzled as Georgia Tech started the season 3–4 and fell out of the national polls. Yet he led a late-season run that saw the Jackets win five of their last six games, capped off by an 18–17 victory over Stanford in the Aloha Bowl. Jones orchestrated the game-winning drive in the final minute. "I can always count on that son of a gun to rise to the occasion," Ross said of Jones.

Jones' senior season was disappointingly forgettable. Friedgen had followed Ross to the NFL following the Aloha Bowl victory, and new coach Bill Lewis' offense was a more traditional scheme. Jones had his best season as a passer but inexplicably finished with negative rushing yards. The yards he lost in being sacked outnumbered those he gained scrambling and on designed runs.

Still, he went more than 9,000 yards total offense for his career in that season, setting a new ACC record. Ross summed up Jones' play best: "I don't think there could be a more skilled athlete at his position in college football than Shawn."

222–0

Nobody held a grudge like John Heisman did. The legendary Georgia Tech football and baseball coach believed in fairness above all things. So when a professional baseball team masquerading as the Cumberland College nine embarrassed Heisman's team 22–0 in the spring of 1916, the coach vowed payback.

He got plenty the following football season. Georgia Tech's 222–0 victory on October 7, 1916, stands as the most lopsided score in football history. Heisman's team scored touchdowns on all 32 of its possessions despite never attempting a pass and without notching a first down—Georgia Tech scored within the first few plays on every drive.

Heisman made a point with the victory, and not the one he publicly claimed led him to run up the score—to shame the pollsters, who paid closer attention to point differential than strength of schedule in awarding national titles at the time. Heisman's statement was to Cumberland, or more precisely to its student manager, George Allen, who orchestrated the baseball debacle: cheaters always get what's coming to them.

But if anyone deserved a shred of understanding, it was Allen. He took no joy in the Cumberland baseball team's rout of Georgia Tech. Allen recruited 22 professionals from Nashville for the game as a matter of survival for Cumberland athletics. The school's newly hired president had decided to disband all the college athletics programs following the 1915–1916 academic year, and Allen naïvely believed a resounding win against a quality program like Georgia Tech might convince the president to reconsider.

The ploy failed. The president folded all the school's programs and canceled all games scheduled for the following fall. One of those games was against Georgia Tech's football program.

Heisman received the letter from Cumberland explaining the situation that summer. The coach sent a pointed reply: show up or face a $3,000 lawsuit for lost gate receipts. Heisman offered some honey to go with the vinegar, though—he agreed to pay for the Cumberland team's travel and pay a $500 guarantee so the players could enjoy the weekend in Atlanta.

The letter eventually found Allen, who had continued to try and quietly build support for the reinstatement of athletics at Cumberland. He saw the $3,000 demand as just one more reason for the president to be prejudiced against football and other sports programs.

Allen decided to form his own team to play in the game. Only this time, he didn't seek out professional athletes. He recruited a group of his fellow law-school students to play, luring them with shares of the $500 guarantee and the free train ride to Atlanta.

Some of the recruits evidently sensed what was awaiting them—three of them jumped the train in Nashville. Those who continued on no doubt realized their error when Georgia Tech scored 126 points in the first half.

Most of those points were scored by halfback Everett Strupper. To underscore just how lopsided the game was from the opening kickoff, Strupper stopped a yard short of the end zone on a run starting from inside the 10-yard line in the first quarter to give one of the offensive linemen, J.C. Alexander, a chance to score the first touchdown of his career. Strupper and the rest of the offense made

Alexander work for the score, though: they refused to block for him, leaving him to catch the snap and attempt to run it in by himself. Alexander succeeded—on fourth down, much to his teammates' chagrin.

Heisman refused to acknowledge the game's absurdity. He actually chastised his team at halftime. "You're doing all right," he said, "but you just can't tell what those Cumberland players have up their sleeves."

Heisman's players didn't need the pep talk. Heisman had offered them another incentive before the game, dividing them into two squads and promising the group that scored the most points a steak dinner.

Georgia Tech added 54 points in the third quarter, during which Cumberland gave up offensively. The sacrificial law students elected to punt on the first play of every possession in hopes of eliciting pity. And Heisman showed some mercy, shortening the final two quarters from 15 minutes to 12 minutes, 30 seconds. But when he discovered two Cumberland players hiding under a blanket on his team's bench, Heisman sent them back to Allen. One jumped the fence surrounding the field and fled rather than go back in the game.

Atlanta Journal reporter Morgan Blake offered the following insights in his game account: "With all due regard to the Tech team, it must be admitted that the tremendous score was due more to the pitifully weak opposition than to any unnatural strength on the part of the victors. In fact, as a general rule, the only thing necessary for a touchdown was to give a Tech back the ball and holler, 'Here he comes' and 'There he goes.'"

Cumberland's players survived, however, and proceeded to enjoy their weekend in Atlanta. And with the lawsuit averted, the college reinstated the football program four years later for the 1920 season.

13 Spring of 1951

Spring practices, Bobby Dodd–style, usually resembled spring break. Dodd's regular season practices, which featured little contact and the traditional Friday volleyball showdown, were grueling by comparison to those the coach ran in the spring. Stretching and conditioning took up a good portion of the spring workouts, which were conducted on a rather fluid schedule. Dodd would use any excuse, like a spring shower, to cancel them. Veterans didn't even participate. The risk of injury was not worth the reward of marginal improvement, Dodd believed.

The spring of 1951 marked a crossroads for Dodd's program, however. Georgia Tech was coming off a rare losing season (5–6), featuring a four-game losing streak, which would prove to be the longest of the Dodd era. The losses included a five-touchdown rout at the hands of unranked Alabama.

The season so troubled Dodd that he considered leaving Georgia Tech. He couldn't take the losing and neither could the school. He told his brother, John, he "was either going to have to quit or go to another school."

By moving to another school, Dodd could recruit better athletes—Tech's academic standards were an issue even back then—and Georgia Tech could hire a coach more suited to the grinding preparation required to get the most out of the material.

Dodd often acknowledged his shortcomings when it came to practice. He once told George Morris, one of his star players, that if he could hire Bear Bryant or Johnny Vaught to coach his team during the week and hand over the team to him on game day, Georgia Tech would never lose. "Those guys can prepare teams better than anybody, and I figure out the guys on the other side-line," Dodd told Morris.

But Dodd decided to evolve rather than quit. He fired longtime assistants Ray Ellis and Dwight Keith, who were coordinators before the invention of the term, and moved young assistants into those positions. He charged line coach Ray Graves with overhauling the defense and hired one of his former quarterbacks, Frank Broyles, to implement an early version of the option offense.

With new schemes to install and a hard-nosed attitude to ingrain, football's spring break became boot camp. Dodd held practice every afternoon for six weeks at the Rose Bowl practice field. The workouts were brief but intense, featuring full-contact drills and scrimmages. Dodd abandoned the iron-man style of play that was the norm of the time—in which the same 11 starters played both offense and defense—in favor of the two-platoon system we know today. More players lowered the impact of injuries.

Morris compared the spring to the more renowned practice sessions held by Bear Bryant and Arizona State's Frank Kush. Recounts of Bryant's first camp at Texas A&M spurred the bestselling book *The Junction Boys*. Kush's three-a-day workouts on a mountaintop were known as "Camp Tontozona."

"Bryant took his team to the desert, and Frank Kush took his to the mountains. We went to Rose Bowl Field," Morris said.

The spring of 1951 would have a similar effect to Bryant's and Kush's tactics. The approach inspired veterans like Morris, Ray Beck, Hal Miller, and Lamar Wheat—players "hungry" for success, according to Morris. Reflecting on the spring in his autobiography, Dodd said, "I could finally see some daylight after the gloom of the previous year. The sun came out. Boy, it came out from behind a dark cloud."

Georgia Tech didn't lose another game until October of 1953. The run of 29 games included victories over six ranked teams, appearances in two bowl games, and the 1952 national championship. Georgia Tech moved into the top 10 of the national polls four games into that span and stayed there for 30 straight weeks, an unheard-of run at the time. All due to the spring of 1951.

"By the end, we knew who looked good in a uniform but couldn't play," Morris said. "What was left was pretty good."

356 Yards

As Eddie Lee Ivery stretched, he wondered if it was a prelude to anything other than a long wait. *No way Georgia Tech and Air Force will play in these conditions*, Ivery thought. Snow fell like water from a showerhead, as did the mercury in the thermometer. The temperature stood at 20 degrees by kickoff. The wind blew across Falcon Field as if driven by a nuclear reactor.

And the notion that the game would be postponed, if not canceled, angered Georgia Tech's senior tailback. "I wanted to play because I'd never played in conditions like that," Ivery said. "It was snowing heavily. It was cold, but it wasn't like any other cold weather I would play in again."

Play Ivery would. The conditions seemed extreme to a native of Thomson, Georgia, who'd never seen enough snow to pack a snowball, let alone build a snowman, in his life. But it was just another mid-November day in Colorado Springs. Stadium officials commandeered a streetsweeper to clear the field of snow, and the game kicked off on schedule.

Conditions failed to improve during the game. Yet Ivery had no trouble finding his footing. And in the three hours following kickoff, he would melt college football's rushing record.

Ivery rushed for 356 yards on 26 carries in the Yellow Jackets' 42–21 victory over Air Force late in that 1978 season. He eclipsed the single-game rushing record of 350 yards held by Michigan State's Eric Allen with six minutes left in the game.

Ivery finished with 356 yards. Those who witnessed the performance firsthand say Ivery would have rushed for 100 more if he had skipped his traditional game-day egg breakfast.

Ivery spent as much time retching as running that afternoon. The eggs sat in his stomach. His uncertainty about the weather conditions stressed him out. The altitude difference between Colorado Springs and Atlanta—almost 6,000 feet—left him short of breath. Nausea hit Ivery like waves strike the beach. He'd break a long run and head for the sideline instead of the huddle. He'd vomit in a trash can and come back in a play later. The cycle would repeat.

The Yellow Jackets rushed for 510 yards as a team that afternoon. Ivery's backup, Ray Friday, ran for 115 yards on five carries. The third-string back, Darish Davis, added 73 yards on six carries.

Ivery would have easily tallied 400 yards if not for his sour stomach. Give Ivery Friday's and Davis' carries at his per-carry average that afternoon and he rushes for 506 yards. "I kind of internally said to myself, *Man, you could have gotten 400*," Ivery said. "The most important thing, obviously, was to win the game."

A Georgia Tech victory was in doubt well into the fourth quarter that afternoon. Just as Air Force's defenders couldn't tackle Ivery, Georgia Tech's secondary couldn't cover Air Force wide receiver Cormac Carney. He caught 11 passes for 204 yards. The Yellow Jackets led by just a touchdown at the start of the fourth quarter.

"We had to gain as many yards as we did to win the football game," Ivery said. "Every time we scored, they'd come right back and score."

Ivery's replacement, Friday, iced the game midway through the final quarter with a 66-yard touchdown run. Fittingly, the run came on the play after Ivery's churning stomach sent him to the sideline. Had Ivery carried on that play and not Friday, he would have not only broken the single-game rushing record on the run but also passed the 400-yard mark.

Ivery broke the record on his next carry, a 21-yarder that ended with him losing a fumble. The giveaway panicked the coaching staff: did the fumble nullify the yards on the run? No, the yards still counted. And when Georgia Tech got the ball back with four minutes to go, head coach Pepper Rodgers approached Ivery about going for 400.

Ivery's teammate, safety Don Bessillieu, overheard the conversation and urged caution.

"Don't do it," Bessillieu told Ivery. "You never know, you might lose some yards."

Ivery took that advice and stayed on the sideline. Friday proceeded to break a 40-yard run on the first play of the next possession.

Even so, Ivery's performance stands as one of the best individual efforts in college football history. Washington State's Reuben Mayes broke Ivery's rushing mark in 1984, and TCU's LaDainian Tomlinson followed with a 406-yard effort in a 1999 game. But given that Ivery did it "on a day when ice skates would have been more appropriate footwear than cleated shoes and when an agitated stomach threatened his very presence in Georgia Tech's lineup," the performance stands out from the rest.

15 The Droughtmakers

The surest way to legend status at Georgia Tech is to play memorably against rival Georgia. For eight glorious years, between 1949 and 1956, the Golden Tornado cranked out legends like Lay's does potato chips.

The winning streak is the longest by Georgia Tech in the 100-plus years of the rivalry. Tech's dominance during the period so riled Georgia fans that they gave the streak a nickname: the Drought.

"What a hideous and horrendous streak that was for Georgia," said Loran Smith, the longtime sideline reporter for the Georgia Bulldogs radio network. "Eight years. It seemed like forever."

Several Georgia Tech players helped draw out the torture session. Some rank among the program's all-time stars—Lamar Wheat, Pepper Rodgers, Wade Mitchell. And a few were destined to be little more than footnotes in the program's annals—Chappell Rhino, George Maloof. They are the Droughtmakers.

Coach Bobby Dodd was the original. His call for a quick kick on a third-down play in the fourth quarter of the 1949 game led to the winning score. Georgia Tech trailed 6–0 at the time and was pinned on its side of the field. Quick-kicking on third down meant no return by the unsuspecting Bulldogs, and a friendly bounce and roll resulted in Georgia taking over on its own 5-yard line.

Georgia Tech's defense held and forced Georgia to punt from its own end zone. The Yellow Jackets took over at the Dogs' 39-yard line and scored the winning touchdown six plays later.

"That's a big game," Dodd wrote in *Dodd's Luck*. "The two teams were pretty evenly matched, and it was the first of my eight years that I dominated Georgia. I needed those eight years because a lot of times, I couldn't dominate Georgia. They were tough, boy, let me tell you."

Wheat made sure Dodd beat Georgia in back-to-back years for the first time in his coaching career by recovering a crucial fumble in the 1950 game. The Bulldogs were driving for what would have been the go-ahead score when quarterback Mal Cook fumbled on a keeper play. Wheat, a lineman, recovered, and Georgia Tech's offense responded with a 74-yard touchdown drive. The Jackets won 7–0.

Back-to-back wins became a winning streak thanks to Maloof in the 1951 game. The fullback scored four touchdowns in the most lopsided Georgia Tech win in series history, 48–6. His scores all came on dive plays at the goal line. He still shares the Georgia Tech record for most touchdowns in a single game.

Georgia fans sensed something amiss in the series after the 1952 game. Georgia Tech's hero this time was well known for his baseball prowess but was little more than a practice player on the football team. His name was Chappell Rhino, or as he became better known following Georgia Tech's 23–9 win, "One Play" Rhino.

The Yellow Jackets faced a fourth down at the Georgia 10-yard line early in the second half. Trailing 7–3, Dodd decided to go for it, and he called a running pass that Tech used regularly in games. Oddly enough, though, at least to his offensive coordinator, Frank Broyles, Dodd called for Rhino to enter the game and throw the pass. A pitcher on the baseball team, Rhino had the arm, but he'd never been in on the play before, even in practice. "I always thought Coach Dodd called me up to get him popcorn or peanuts," Rhino said. He threw a touchdown pass to Buck Martin instead. Georgia Tech tacked on two more scores later.

The 1953 game featured a dominant performance from Rodgers. He scored four touchdowns in the 28–12 win. Mitchell, another quarterback, was the biggest Droughtmaker of all. He guided Georgia Tech to victories in 1954, 1955, and 1956—but only after he almost brought the Drought to a premature end in the 1953 game. Mitchell, a freshman, fumbled early on in the fifth win in the run. Georgia converted the turnover into a touchdown to take over the game's momentum. Rodgers eventually wrested it back. Mitchell's brush with becoming a goat inspired him the next three years. He threw the game-winning touchdown in 1954, made a game-saving tackle a year later, and keyed a second-half rout in the Drought's finale in 1956.

The Drought would be snapped the next year by an unlikely hero who to this day is known as—appropriately enough—"the Droughtbreaker." Georgia Tech fans will never forget the Drought, although one of the Droughtmakers said the streak has been blown out of proportion over the years. "I thought we had better players than they did in those years," Rodgers said. "And we had a strategic-wise coach in Coach Dodd. We were supposed to beat those guys."

16 The Droughtbreaker

Georgia's Theron Sapp stepped into the huddle and immediately knew he would get the ball even before quarterback Charlie Britt called the play.

"Give it to Sapp," said one of his offensive linemen.

"Give it to Sapp," echoed another.

"Yeah, give it to me," Sapp growled. "Give it to me."

Britt gave it to Sapp on fourth down on the goal line, and Sapp scored the only touchdown of the 1957 Georgia–Georgia Tech game. With that one-yard dive, Georgia Tech's eight-game winning streak against the rivals—dubbed "the Drought" by Bulldogs fans but known by that moniker to followers of both teams—ended.

Because Sapp's heroics led to ending the Bulldogs' longest losing streak in the century-old series, Georgia retired his jersey— forever acknowledging the Yellow Jackets' run of dominance in the series. Sapp is one of four players in Georgia's proud history to have his jersey retired, and he's by far the most innocuous. The other three are legendary running backs Herschel Walker, Frank Sinkwich, and Charley Trippi.

"I never thought I should have gotten my jersey retired, but I think I could have run for governor and won," Sapp said in remembering the game 50 years later. "If we had lost that game, there's no way my jersey would have been retired."

Some might argue Sapp's jersey retirement was justified just for his work in that one game. He not only scored the winning touchdown but recovered the fumble that set up the winning drive. Back on offense, the fullback carried seven straight times, culminating in the one-yard, game-deciding dive. "There was no way I could have not scored on fourth down and walked back to the sideline to face my teammates," Sapp said. "If I hadn't stumbled on the touchdown run, I would have probably run right out the back of the end zone."

A quarter-and-a-half later, Georgia fans stormed Georgia Tech's Grant Field to celebrate the Drought's end. A day after that, Bulldogs fan Harold M. Walker penned an epic poem named "The Man Who Broke the Drought" in Sapp's honor. Two years later, Sapp's No. 40 was taken out of circulation.

"[Herschel] Walker won the national championship for Georgia and was awarded the Heisman Trophy, but to older Bulldogs who suffered through the 1950s, Sapp's breaking the Drought was greater," reflected former Tech coach Bobby Dodd. "He silenced eight years of bragging from Georgia Tech students and alumni. Breaking the Drought was a remarkable achievement."

Georgia coach Wally Butts offered Sapp a scholarship in 1955, six years into the Drought. Butts' decision was controversial at the time—Sapp had broken his neck in a high school all-star game, and his doctor had recommended he give up football. "If you were my son, you'd never play football again," the doctor told Sapp. "One wrong hit and you could be paralyzed for the rest of your life."

"Good thing I'm not your son, then, because I'm playing," Sapp replied.

Sapp spent much of his freshman year in a cast that covered most of his torso. The following fall, he convinced Butts to let him play on the junior varsity team. He moved up to the varsity in 1957, just in time to break the Drought.

"I don't think anybody wanted to play for Georgia more than Theron Sapp," longtime Georgia radio announcer Loran Smith said. "The guy breaks his neck and still he comes in and plays? How can you top that?"

17 Pat Swilling

Imagine Georgia Tech's in-state rival being Georgia Southern and not hated Georgia. Thank Pat Swilling for ensuring the Yellow Jackets continued competing at college football's top level.

Swilling resurrected Georgia Tech during his career in the early 1980s and interrupted a push by some in the school's administration, faculty, and staff to deemphasize football. The Yellow Jackets competed as an independent—they'd left the Southeastern Conference after the 1963 season—and some talked openly of shunning the big leagues for the bush leagues.

Prominent alumni and legendary coach Bobby Dodd worked to dissuade the cynics, but it wasn't until the uber-talented Swilling arrived in 1982 and the program began a climb that landed it back in the polls in 1984 and into a bowl game in 1985 that the program's future stabilized.

"Without Pat Swilling, it would have been much, much harder for Georgia Tech football to survive," then coach Bill Curry said. "We didn't have anybody else who could do what Pat did. We would have tried, and maybe we would have done it collectively, but fortunately we didn't have to."

The hard-nosed Swilling gave Georgia Tech's defense a persona. By his junior season, the defense was known as the "Black Watch." The unit ended a six-year losing streak to the rival Bulldogs, holding the Dogs' offense to three field goals in a 35–18 Yellow Jackets win.

Pat Swilling records one of the 23 sacks in his storied Tech career. Swilling is widely credited for helping resuscitate the Yellow Jackets in the 1980s.

Then it was Swilling who set a school record—and a tone for a breakout season—with seven sacks in the 1985 opener against North Carolina State. Georgia Tech went on to win nine games that season, finish 18th in the coaches' poll, and defeat Michigan State in the All-American Bowl.

Swilling finished the 1985 season with 15 sacks and 23 for his career. And when he hit the quarterback, turnovers typically resulted—he caused nine fumbles in his career. Swilling would go on to a decorated NFL career that included a 17-sack season.

Swilling's legacy at Georgia Tech goes beyond sack records and a nine-win season. Swilling and his peers changed the culture on the Flats, and five years after he re-legitimized the program at the major college level, the Yellow Jackets won a national championship.

For all Swilling's contributions to Georgia Tech football, none of them would have happened if not for Swilling's father's insistence that he attend a college, not a football factory. The Swilling family lived in Toccoa, Georgia, located in the northeast corner of the state and in the backyards of two of the nation's premier football programs at the time. Georgia, led by Herschel Walker, won the national title in 1980, when Swilling was establishing himself as a high school phenom. Clemson, located just over the Georgia–South Carolina border, won the 1981 national championship.

Georgia Tech, meanwhile, went 1–9–1 in 1980 and 1–10 in 1981. Needless to say, Curry didn't like his chances when he headed up Interstate-85 to recruit Swilling. But Curry, who played at Georgia Tech for Bobby Dodd and then for the Super Bowl–champion Green Bay Packers in the NFL, kept his recruiting pitch simple: Do you want to be just another great player in a great program, or do you want to be the player that establishes a great program?

"He'd already made up his mind to go somewhere else, I believe," Curry said. "But his father intervened." The senior Swilling recognized the players-as-campus-celebrities atmosphere in Athens and Clemson. And he wanted his son to excel in the classroom as well as on the football field. "I'm not going to tell you you're going to get Pat Swilling, but you will get a chance," the father told Curry.

Maybe Swilling bent to his father's will, and maybe he just liked what Curry was selling, but he ended up at Georgia Tech. And he never regretted the decision. "The whole experience—the academics, the poor records—it was all great for me," Swilling said. "I learned to persevere through."

18 The "Greatest Victory"

Georgia Tech upset top-ranked Alabama well before kickoff of what Bobby Dodd would classify as the "greatest victory" of his career.

The Crimson Tide's legendary coach, Bear Bryant, sensed his team's national title hopes were in danger shortly after awakening on the morning of November 17, 1962. He walked to the window of his Georgian Terrace Hotel suite to find it raining, just as it had been when he went to bed the night before. Bryant spent the rest of the morning sulking, smoking, and grumbling.

"This is Dodd's weather," Bryant told all visitors, including a prized recruit from the Atlanta area named Kim King. "This is Dodd's kind of weather."

King would go on to a storied playing and broadcasting career at Georgia Tech. Yet that encounter with Bryant, and what transpired that afternoon at Grant Field, would stick with King and become one of his most oft-told stories. He, his girlfriend, and his parents entered Bryant's suite that morning to find the Bear sitting in an armchair staring at the rain out of the window, with a pack of cigarettes at each elbow. Bryant's mood was so dour that Kim's father tried to cheer Bryant up by reminding the coach he had the veteran, national championship–contender on a 26-game unbeaten streak. The opponent, Georgia Tech, was the unranked, under-achieving team that had tied Florida State—pre–Bobby Bowden Florida State—the week before.

Bryant responded with a shake of his head. "It's raining. It's a sloppy field. This is Dodd's weather. This is Dodd's weather. He'll figure out how to play in this weather. He knows how to win in this kind of weather," Bryant told the Kings.

Truth be told, Bryant would have been wary of going against a Dodd-coached team in a climate-controlled domed stadium. Bryant and Dodd were as friendly as two rivals could be, a relationship born of mutual respect. Even with a 5–1 coaching record against Dodd going into the 1962 game, Bryant predicted Georgia Tech would be the biggest obstacle to Alabama repeating as national champion that season.

"Georgia Tech," Bryant told a *Sports Illustrated* reporter for the magazine's college football preview issue, "will be the No. 1 team in the nation." The Yellow Jackets fell short of Bryant's expectations. They climbed to fifth in the rankings in early October only to lose

Bobby Dodd and the 1962 team celebrated the "greatest victory," a 7–6 upset of a top-ranked Alabama team coached by Paul "Bear" Bryant and quarterbacked by Joe Namath.

twice in a three-week span. Georgia Tech had an All-American at quarterback in Billy Lothridge and one of the most underrated players in Tech history in the offensive and defensive backfields in Mike McNames. But the famous "Dodd's Luck" failed the coach and his team that season: the Jackets lost to LSU on a kick return for a touchdown in the third game of the season; Auburn upset Georgia Tech two weeks later by building a wind-aided 17–0 lead and holding off a Tech rally.

Yet Bryant feared the Yellow Jackets as if they were the Green Bay Packers that rainy November afternoon at Grant Field. Bryant showed his paranoia early, calling a pass play from a shotgun formation on the game's first play. The decision prompted a telling remark form a pro scout watching the game in the press box. "Who is he trying to kid? Bear's teams don't pass on the first play from scrimmage. They don't pass from the 23-yard line, and they haven't run from the shotgun once this year," the scout said, according to a pair of *Sports Illustrated* reporters sitting nearby.

Bryant continued to coach out of character. He responded to Georgia Tech's first sustained drive of the game—one that ended in an interception—by going for it on fourth down deep in his own territory on the ensuing possession.

The play failed, at least officially. Georgia Tech's Buck Martin, who was in on the tackle, would later admit from his vantage point on the ground that the official's foot—used to mark the spot of the ball—was beyond the first down. Martin gave the foot a forearm shiver as he got to his feet, knocking the official off balance and altering the spot.

Martin's quick thinking aside, Bryant's decision to go for it would haunt the coach afterward. The Jackets failed to convert the turnover on downs into points, but the miscue would give Georgia Tech a field position advantage and prompt Bryant to make additional desperate moves.

Alabama struggled to run the ball early, so Bryant opened up his offense in the second quarter. He called on quarterback Joe Namath to pass, and the man who would go on to be known as "Broadway Joe" in the pros played like Subway Joe. He threw an interception on his own 28-yard line, a mistake that led to the eventual winning touchdown.

The second half was a case study in coaches outsmarting themselves. Georgia Tech's Dodd quick-kicked on his team's first possession, content to pin Alabama's hapless offense deep in its territory and try to win the game 7–0.

The sound plan went wrong when Namath found his rhythm. The quarterback moved Alabama to midfield before the drive stalled, at which point Bryant elected to follow Dodd's lead and play a field-position game. The Tide punter pinned Georgia Tech back on its own goal line.

The Yellow Jackets got a reprieve a few punt exchanges later, with McNames intercepting Namath and returning the ball to midfield. Dodd played it conservative again, running two low-risk plays and quick-kicking on third down. But again Alabama moved the ball and executed its own quick kick.

Pinned on its 15-yard line with less than eight minutes left in the game, Georgia Tech made a critical mistake on special teams. A low snap forced the punter, Lothridge, to bend down and scoop up the football to kick it away. He touched his knee on the ground in the process, giving Alabama the ball at the 9-yard line.

The Tide scored a touchdown four plays later. The score now 7–6, Bryant faced another conundrum—kick the extra point, tie the game, and hope for another scoring chance or go for two points and the lead?

Fearing that a tie would cost his team a national title, Bryant elected to go for two. The quarterback sneak failed. Tech still led 7–6. "There was no question; we had to go for the two points," Bryant told reporters after the game. "It was my call, and I'll take the blame, but when you're No. 1 in the country, you don't play for the tie."

Remarkably, Alabama would get two more chances to score, only to see both drives end in interceptions. The last came on a play in the closing minutes from the 13-yard line, well inside field-goal range.

"If I had it to do over again, I would run two quarterback sneaks and kick [a field goal]," said Bryant, who had his quarterbacks throw a season-high 38 passes in the loss.

The win touched off a week-long celebration around Atlanta. Dodd dubbed it the "greatest victory I've ever been associated with"—if not the most well-played—for a Georgia Tech football team given the opponent and the circumstances. The Yellow Jackets would go on to finish 7–3–1 and play in the Bluebonnet Bowl.

Calvin Johnson

No less an authority than *Sports Illustrated* dubbed Calvin Johnson a "legend by the end of his second game." Not true. Johnson achieved such lofty status long before he led the rally against Clemson.

Georgia Tech head coach Chan Gailey thought so much of Johnson as a high school player, he took his entire coaching staff on a recruiting visit. After securing a verbal commitment from Johnson on that trip, Gailey bought all his assistants a steak dinner. Teammates thought so much of Johnson, they deemed him the team's best player before his first official practice. He'd wowed them during summer workouts.

Fans thought so much of Johnson, the first orders for No. 21 jerseys came hours after Johnson made a spectacular touchdown catch during his first scrimmage. Johnson launched himself backward to catch the wayward throw.

"That guy is all skill...there's not enough adjectives to describe him," fellow wide receiver Demarius Bilbo said of Johnson just one week into his first week of practice with the Yellow Jackets.

Most who follow Georgia Tech knew Johnson to be the best football player to ever don a Yellow Jackets jersey prior to that second game of his career, at Clemson on September 11, 2004. Johnson's performance in the win merely affirmed that belief. He caught eight passes for 127 yards and three touchdowns in the victory. His two circus catches for scores in the final two minutes rallied the Jackets from a 10-point deficit.

Such showings would become the norm for Johnson. He posted 13 100-yard performances in 38 career games at Georgia Tech. He set career records in almost every receiving category despite playing only three seasons at Tech and facing double- and triple-teams in every game. He won the Fred Biletnikoff Award, given to the nation's top wide receiver, in 2006 and was twice a first-team All-American.

Then there were the catches: the third touchdown grab in the Clemson comeback, a jump ball with a Clemson defender literally hanging from his arms with 11 seconds left; the "Spider-Man" grab of a pass thrown well behind him as he ran a crossing pattern against North Carolina State in 2004; a diving touchdown catch in the 2004 Champs Sports Bowl; the 48-yard catch-and-run in what would be his career finale, the 2007 Gator Bowl.

Calvin Johnson won the 2006 Fred Biletnikoff Award, presented to college football's best receiver. Johnson finished 10th in the Heisman Trophy voting that year and was the No. 2 pick in the 2007 NFL Draft.

Gailey calls Johnson the best wide receiver he's ever coached, a shocking statement considering Gailey once designed routes for Hall of Famer Michael Irvin. Johnson's position coach at Georgia Tech, Buddy Geis, summed up the receiver's abilities in a 2006 *Sports Illustrated* story: "I've worked with Joe Horn, Marvin Harrison, and Sterling Sharpe. Calvin's got everything they have, but he has more of it."

Johnson's talents remained hidden for much of his childhood. His football talents did, anyway. He was a baseball prodigy, equally adept at fielding shortstop and tracking down drives in the power alleys as an outfielder. He was good enough that major league scouts encouraged him to enter the baseball draft out of high school rather than attend college.

Johnson played other sports growing up with his sister and ultra-competitive neighbors. Kickball, basketball, Ping-Pong, and, yes, football all were hotly contested in the Johnson household. "She's the one who made me want to compete," Johnson said of his sister, Erica, who is four years his senior. "That's where a lot of my athleticism comes from."

Yet Johnson never played Pop Warner or organized football of any kind until middle school. He didn't attend elite summer camps for promising young players. He played for a run-first high school team.

His physical attributes made him a highly sought-after recruit, however. He was 6'4" and more than 200 pounds by his junior year of high school. He ran the 40-yard dash in less than 4.5 seconds. His vertical leap was literally beyond measure—the machine topped out at 45 inches, and Johnson cleared that mark by at least two inches. But what made Johnson a legend with Gailey and his coaching staff was his work ethic, one that ultimately led him to become the second pick in the 2007 NFL Draft and put him on the path toward a Hall of Fame career.

"There are a lot of great athletes who stop improving because they think they've arrived," Gailey said. "Calvin knows he hasn't."

20 Wrong Way Riegels

Roy Riegels broke perhaps the biggest run in Georgia Tech football history. That Riegels played for Cal and not the Yellow Jackets only made his 69-yard dash more memorable.

Riegels is better known as "Wrong Way" Riegels. He perpetrated the greatest gaffe in college football history in the 1929 Rose Bowl game between his Bears and Georgia Tech. Anybody who's ever seen footage of the play in question knows what happened: Riegels recovered a fumble, became confused during the scramble, and ran toward Georgia Tech's end zone instead of his own. The film, perhaps the most recognized homemade movie clip this side of the Zapruder film, tells only part of the story, however.

Riegels did not score a touchdown for Georgia Tech, a common misperception. Riegels' wrong way run didn't even set one up—the blunder ultimately led to a safety, worth two points, not six. And he wasn't tackled by one of his own teammates; a fellow Bear actually convinced him of his error and turned him around short of the goal line, where he was buried by Georgia Tech tacklers.

The historical confusion is somewhat ironic given the circumstances. At the time, the Rose Bowl was the only bowl and the biggest football game in existence, college or pro. Every media outlet in the country covered the game. Writers devoted an estimated 450,000 column inches to the game.

And every person who listened to the game on national radio never forgot broadcaster Graham McNamee's call of the wrong way run: "What am I seeing? What's wrong with me? Am I crazy? Am I crazy? Am I crazy?"

Cal's Roy Riegels runs the wrong way with a fumble he recovered during the 1929 Rose Bowl. His gaffe led to the deciding score in the game—a safety—and Georgia Tech's second national title.

Riegels wasn't crazy, just discombobulated. The linebacker was one of several Cal players fooled on a misdirection run by Georgia Tech halfback Stumpy Thomason. Riegels chased the play anyway, and when Thomason lost the ball at the end of his long run, the pigskin was batted around and ended up in Riegels' arms.

Riegels knew something about playing offense. This was the era of limited substitutions and two-way players—iron-man football. But the only time Riegels, a center, touched the ball on offense was at the snap. The unfamiliarity showed. Riegels' first move with the ball in his arms was away from the sideline and toward the middle of the field, not toward an end zone. A teammate immediately yelled "wrong way" in an attempt to get Riegels running up the wide-open sideline toward the Cal goal.

Riegels misinterpreted the instructions, however. He turned upfield all right, just the wrong way. Had Riegels looked to Georgia Tech's sideline he might have realized his error right away. The players jumped from the bench and cheered him on until coach Bill Alexander quieted them by saying, "He's just running the wrong way. Every step he takes is to our advantage. Let's see how far he goes."

Riegels' Cal teammate Benny Lom kept him from going all the way for a score. He caught up with Riegels halfway through his return and signaled for him to turn around. But Riegels thought the fleet-footed Lom wanted Riegels to lateral him the football. "Get outta here, Benny. This is my ball!" Riegels screamed at Lom.

Lom eventually got Riegels to turn around, but Georgia Tech's speedy backs had caught up by then. They tackled him at the 1-yard line.

Cal, like most teams of the day, ran a three-yards-and-a-cloud-of-dust offense and decided to punt on first down rather than risk a safety by running the ball off the goal line. Georgia Tech blocked the kick for a safety and a 2–0 lead. The Golden Tornado would go on to win the game 8–7. The safety set up by Riegels was the difference.

Riegels became a Georgia Tech hero, albeit an unwitting one. He is even a member of the Georgia Tech letterman's club, inducted in an honorary capacity in 1971. "Believe me," Riegels told the club during the ceremony, "I feel like I've earned this."

Wrong Way Lessons

Roy Riegels wasn't the only football player to mistakenly run the wrong way in a football game. And over the years, he reached out to those who suffered the same indignity. Riegels sent a letter to a high school defensive lineman who returned an interception the wrong way in 1957. The end of the letter, published by the Associated Press, read: "For many years I've had to go along and laugh whenever my wrong-way run was brought up, even though I've grown tired of listening and reading about it. But it certainly wasn't the most serious thing in the world. I regretted doing it, even as you do, but you'll get over it."

21 1928 National Champions

Georgia Tech's run to the second national championship in school history will forever be remembered for the wrong-way run of California's Roy Riegels in the Rose Bowl. But Riegels' gaffe was far from the defining moment in the Yellow Jackets' season. The miscue doesn't even rank among the top three in a season in which Georgia Tech football became a campus religion.

"Georgia Tech's football team of 1928 inspired such a frantic enthusiasm on the part of us as underclassmen that we felt like this was the only thing in life," Tech grad Dana H. Johnson said. "When we yelled during those games, it was as much like games where gladiators did their things with real swords and shields."

Georgia Tech coasted to a 5–0 start behind the play of stars Stumpy Thomason, Warner Mizell, Ronald Durant, Peter Pund, and Frank Speer and a trio of newcomers off the Tech freshman team—Tom Jones, Roy "Father" Lumpkin, and Vance Maree.

The Jackets finally faced a challenge from their sixth opponent, Vanderbilt. The Commodores of the 1920s in no way resembled the program most associate with Vandy today. Vanderbilt was a power-house coached by one of the game's legends, Dan McGugin. The Commodores came to Atlanta on November 10 with a perfect 6–0 record. Their stout defense was the first to shut down Georgia Tech's bruising rushing game, and frustration turned to desperation late.

Durant called the offensive plays for the Jackets, with coach William Alexander offering minimal guidance. One of the few instructions the coach gave Durant was never to call a deep pass against what was then known as a deep diamond defense, which positioned a safety more than 20 yards off the line of scrimmage.

"An interception and long runback were too likely," Alexander told his biographer, Edwin Camp.

Durant called not just for a bomb, but a bomb on a triple reverse. Alexander had dreamt up the play as a way to prank the Georgia Tech defense in practice. The quarterback was the intended receiver on the play, with a wide receiver throwing the long pass. Durant's idea was the handoffs and misdirection would convince the defense the play was a run and leave the quarterback wide open. But could the wide receiver throw a good enough pass?

The throw found its target for a touchdown, although Alexander acknowledged the Vanderbilt safety was in position to intercept the pass at around the 10-yard line. Georgia Tech went on to a 19–7 victory.

Alexander asked Durant afterward why he disobeyed the coach's orders and called the play. "Coach, I had tried everything else, and nothing would go," Durant told him. "There wasn't anything else to do."

The escape against Vanderbilt led to something else the next week against Alabama: a letdown. The Crimson Tide scored two early touchdowns, only the fourth and fifth scores allowed by the Georgia Tech defense all season, and went into halftime tied with the Yellow Jackets. The poor play enraged the notoriously stoic Alexander. The coach compared his team to "false alarms loafing in the limelight." Alexander did more than berate his players during the break. He also adjusted his defense to stop Alabama. Georgia Tech shut out the Tide in the second half and won 33–13.

Alexander's team would wrap up the regular season with easy wins against Auburn and Georgia. The 9–0 record was impressive but not enough to guarantee the Rose Bowl bid. Southern Conference rivals Tennessee and Florida had the inside track to Pasadena. Both were more highly regarded than Georgia Tech and either would likely have earned the berth with an undefeated record. But Tennessee stumbled to a scoreless tie against Kentucky. The game featured a controversial call by the officials, who ruled that a Volunteers running back had stepped out of bounds on a touchdown run. The play was called back, and the game ended in a tie. The outcome motivated the Vols for their season finale a week later—against undefeated Florida. Tennessee pulled out a 13–12 victory, leaving Georgia Tech as the conference's only undefeated team.

Only after all that did Riegels get a chance to run the wrong way and hand Georgia Tech the national title.

22 "The Brawl for It All"

The saboteurs failed, but not for lack of trying. They set a fire. They spit and threw ice. They messed with the phones. They stalled the game prior to a crucial field goal.

Their identities are unknown. And in the end, who they were didn't matter, anyway. Georgia Tech upset top-ranked Virginia on November 3, 1990. And the victory, shown on national TV, would earn the Yellow Jackets enough respect to eventually win a share of the national championship.

A Virginia newspaper dubbed the game "The Brawl for It All." The Cavaliers were No. 1 for the first time in school history, and Georgia Tech came in unbeaten if not unscathed. The Yellow Jackets had tied a mediocre North Carolina team two weeks earlier, an outcome that prevented the showdown from being between two top-10 teams.

Somebody didn't want the game to be played regardless of rankings. A vandal or vandals snuck into the University of Virginia's Scott Stadium the night before the game and built a fire near midfield. The playing surface was artificial turf, so the flames didn't spread beyond a small area. Still, there was talk of postponing the

Scott Sisson celebrates after connecting on the game-winning field goal in the 1990 showdown with top-ranked Virginia, a game known as the "brawl for it all."

game until the grounds crew proposed cutting out the burnt section and replacing it with spare turf from the baseball diamond's infield.

The game back on, the Yellow Jackets were welcomed outside the stadium by an unruly crowd. It was homecoming weekend, and the celebration had started early. The Virginia fans spit at the Yellow Jackets, threw ice at them, and called them names. Georgia Tech's players actually enjoyed the reception.

"That's when I knew that Tech was getting some kind of notoriety," fullback William Bell told author Jack Wilkinson for his book *Focused on the Top*. "Fans don't just hate you because you're not a good team. They hate you because you're going to cause problems with their team."

Except Georgia Tech didn't trouble No. 1 Virginia, at least not initially. The Cavaliers scored on the second play of the game, with quarterback Shawn Moore hooking up with wide receiver Herman Moore on a bomb. The Cavs added field goals on their next two possessions and led 28–14 at halftime.

"That was one game where, if the defense was on the field, you stood up and watched," Bell said. "Other games, you come to the sideline, you sit down on the bench and rest. But their offense was so good you caught your breath as quick as you could and then stood up and watched. But we didn't get rattled."

The players didn't, but offensive coordinator Ralph Friedgen did. His radio in the press box coaches booth malfunctioned throughout the first half. Virginia's fix-it men—not the same ones who repaired the turf—solved the connection issues before half-time. By that time, Friedgen's frustration with the situation had amused the reporters sitting next door in the press area.

Friedgen's mood brightened in the second half along with Georgia Tech's chances at victory. Linebacker Calvin Tiggle came up with two takeaways on Virginia's first two possessions, and the Yellow Jackets seized the momentum. They tied the game late in the third quarter to set up a back-and-forth fourth quarter.

Virginia retook the lead on another Moore-to-Moore bomb; Georgia Tech answered with a touchdown followed by a Scott Sisson field goal for a 38–35 lead. The Cavaliers countered, scoring an apparent touchdown on the following possession. A penalty wiped out the score, though, and forced a tying field goal.

Georgia Tech took possession with 2:34 left. Quarterback Shawn Jones and Bell methodically moved the Jackets down the field, reaching the Virginia 20-yard line with seven seconds left to bring on Sisson again.

"I don't know if Scott understood that even before he kicked it, we knew we had won the game," Bell said. "When we got into field goal range, we just assumed. We just assumed it was automatic."

The saboteurs had one more trick, however. Virginia coach George Welsh called timeout to freeze Sisson, and the break inexplicably lasted longer than normal. Georgia Tech offensive line coach Pat Watson kept Sisson loose on the sideline, telling a joke minus the punchline—he couldn't remember it—during the break. Once the players returned to the field, Georgia Tech's holder, veteran Scott Aldredge, worked on Sisson. He huddled the kicking team up and asked his teammates to describe their vision for the Atlantic Coast Conference championship ring they would all soon don.

Sisson finally got to kick and prove Bell correct. The kicker knew the boot was good as soon as it came off his foot—he started celebrating before the ball split the uprights. "There was no question about it, no leaning or looking or anything," Sisson told a Rivals.com writer for a 2006 story. "I hit the ball, turned, and started running."

23 Clint Castleberry

Georgia college football teams boasted three Heisman Trophy– caliber players going into the 1942 season: the Yellow Jackets' Clint Castleberry and the Bulldogs' Charley Trippi and Frank Sinkwich. Sinkwich won the award that season, and Trippi would be the runner-up in 1946. But the player dubbed the "most dangerous runner in America," Tech's Castleberry, never claimed college football's top honor—mainly because he never got the chance. Castleberry, an Atlanta native, was a freshman in 1942. He turned in a spectacular season nonetheless and finished third in the Heisman voting behind Sinkwich and Columbia's Paul Governali. But Castleberry's show-down with Sinkwich in the season finale, No. 2 Georgia Tech vs. No. 5 Georgia, would be one of the last games Castleberry would play.

Castleberry enlisted in the Army Air Corps following that season. The United States, drawn into World War II with the Japanese attack on Pearl Harbor a year earlier, needed every able-bodied male. Castleberry ended up in flight school and drew bomber-pilot duty.

Clint Castleberry finished third in the Heisman Trophy balloting during his freshman year. Castleberry joined the Army Air Corps to fight in World War II following that season and was killed in action in 1944 off the west African coast.

Castleberry and his crew disappeared off the West African coast while flying a mission on November 7, 1944. Search-and-rescue crews spent six days investigating what happened to the bomber. They found only a few pieces of unidentifiable wreckage on the ocean.

The tragedy ended what many Georgia Tech followers maintain was one of the most promising careers in college football history. The legendary Bobby Dodd claimed Castleberry would "have probably been an All-American for three years and been the great-est back in Georgia Tech history. He was a great football player. He might have been the best of them all, had he lived."

Said Castleberry's teammate, Jim Luck, "He was here, he made good things happen, and then he was gone."

Castleberry attracted plenty of acclaim in his short career. Notre Dame scout Wayne Millner was the one who labeled Castleberry the "most dangerous runner in America" in his report to Notre Dame coach Frank Leahy. An *Atlanta Journal* reporter, Ed Miles, called Castleberry "a crazed jackrabbit." Football historians would simply classify Castleberry as a "lost legend."

Castleberry was far from a prototypical football star. He attracted little recruiting interest outside the state because of his size: he stood 5'9" and weighed 155 pounds, which negated his straight-A grades and undefeated high school career in the eyes of Notre Dame, Navy, and the other powers of the day. Castleberry possessed unrivaled speed and quickness, however. He embarrassed opponents with his skills as an open field runner and kept defenses guessing in his role as halfback in a single-wing offense.

The *Journal*'s Miles summed up Castleberry's debut in the 1942 season opener against Auburn by noting, "Tech's Old Guard on the shelves of the West Stands hailed the freshman Castleberry as the fanciest runner to hit the Flats since they have forgotten well." Wrote Miles' contemporary, the *Atlanta Constitution*'s Jack Troy, "Castleberry darted, stopped, changed direction, darted some more, and often galloped when given shirt-tail distance on scrim-mage plays."

Castleberry earned national attention later that season in Georgia Tech road upsets of Notre Dame and Navy. Against Notre Dame in South Bend, Indiana, Castleberry recovered a fumble, threw a touchdown pass, and set up the game-winning touchdown with a long punt return. Versus Navy, Castleberry scored on a 95-yard interception return, led two other scoring drives, and batted down three would-be scoring passes by the Navy quarterback. A *New York Herald* reporter wrote that Castleberry possessed the "best features of a wraith and an antelope."

A late-season knee injury slowed Castleberry and led to the Yellow Jackets losing its final two games, to Georgia in the finale and to Texas in the Cotton Bowl. But the disappointing finish failed to soil Castleberry's legend: his No. 19 jersey stands as the only uniform ever retired by Georgia Tech.

24 William Alexander

An axiom of the coaching profession is, "Those who can't play, coach." Fortunately for Georgia Tech, William Alexander wasn't much of a player.

Alexander arrived on the Flats in 1906 at the age of 16 and walked on to John Heisman's team. Alexander's playing career topped out two years later, when Heisman named him a captain—of the "scrubs," or scout team. Alexander would impress Heisman enough with his work ethic and football knowledge to stay on as an assistant coach following graduation. Then Heisman would pick Alexander as his successor as head coach.

Alexander would end up spending the last 44 years of his life, save for a military stint during World War I, at Georgia Tech. His death in 1950 left the school with a job vacancy: Alexander was the school's athletics director at the time.

Alexander's head coaching career spanned 25 seasons. His success falls short of the men who preceded and succeeded him—Heisman and Bobby Dodd—but the stability and character he provided solidified Georgia Tech's reputation as a football power during the golden era of the game.

Alexander employed the same mojo as a coach as he did as a player: he offset a lack of talent with strong heart and brains. Legendary Notre Dame coach Knute Rockne summed up Alexander's coaching career best when he said, "Bill Alexander gets more out of less than any coach of America."

Not that the Yellow Jackets lacked for glory years under Alexander. He won a national championship in 1928 and eight conference titles during his tenure. His teams played in five bowls at a time when playing in those games was a privilege, not a right, for major college programs. He coached several Georgia Tech greats, including Red Barron, Father Lumpkin, Peter Pund, Clint Castleberry, and Phil Tinsley.

But Alexander also posted nine losing seasons. His greatest season, 1928, was followed by eight straight years of .500 or worse finishes. Dodd came to Georgia Tech as an assistant during that span and once commented that the third-stringers at Tennessee, where Dodd had played, were better than Georgia Tech's starters.

Alexander finally fielded a championship team again in 1939. Georgia Tech finished 8–2, went undefeated in Southeastern Conference play, and won the Orange Bowl. Yet even that team lacked material.

Edwin Camp, Alexander's biographer, wrote of the 1939 team, "If ever there was a coaching masterpiece, it was the Old Man's leadership and planning with a squad that offered only speed, intelligence, and determination as substitutes for power and individual prowess."

Alexander often subtly poked fun at his team's plight in the way he diagrammed plays: Tech's players were always marked by small Xs while the opponents appeared on the chalkboard as giant Os. "Bill Alexander's life was an eloquent illustration of the phrase, 'It matters not whether you win or lose, but how you play the game,'" wrote *Atlanta Journal* sports editor Ralph McGill.

Indeed, Alexander faced little criticism. Health issues, not team performance, prompted his move from the head football coach's office to the athletics director's suite following the 1944 season. The school and fan base thought enough of Alexander to elevate his hand-picked successor, Dodd, to head coach. "No one else could have commanded the support of school, public, and players as did Coach Aleck while losing so many games," Dodd said.

Alexander's approach and dedication won over many would-be critics. Colorful coaches were as much the norm then as they are now. Alexander's mentor, Heisman, was a celebrity coach, and one would think Heisman's persona would rub off on his successor. Yet Alexander was more stoic than fiery. His first locker room speech as a head coach set a record for brevity. "It would be good to start off with a win," he said. He reacted to the wrong-way run by Cal's Roy Riegels during the 1929 Rose Bowl by telling the excited players on his bench to sit down.

Alexander's cook once inadvertently served him leftover dog food for breakfast. When his wife told him of the mix-up, his response was, "It was a little flat, but not bad."

Still, Alexander could conjure some fire in certain situations, especially those that involved criticism of his players. Alexander once exiled an assistant coach from the locker room for berating the team following a narrow loss. Alexander may best be remembered for bridging the gap between two legends. But in doing so, he was a legend himself.

25 General Leonard Wood

Leonard Wood enrolled at Georgia Tech not for the education but to play football. Wood already held a doctorate of medicine the day he rode his horse onto campus for the first time in the fall of 1893. A 33-year-old Army officer stationed at nearby Fort McPherson,

Wood needed a football fix. Georgia Tech and its fledgling program, started the previous year by a group of students, needed a coach.

Wood registered as an undergraduate and signed up for a wood shop course. Whether he ever attended a class or not is still a matter of debate, but Wood definitely represented the school on the football field. An accomplished football star—not to mention a national hero—before heading the Georgia Tech "Blacksmiths," Wood took up the game the previous year while living in California. He'd been posted to the San Francisco area after leading the U.S. Army's campaign against the Apache Indians and capturing the tribe's chief, Geronimo. Wood joined San Francisco's Olympic Club and agreed to captain the club's football team in a series of games against college teams, including the University of California Bears. Wood was to lead the Olympia team again in 1893 only to receive orders to relocate to Fort McPherson to serve as the base's surgeon general. Wood arrived in Atlanta that August and quickly discovered the South had a passion for the game, even in its infancy.

Wood and another non-traditional Georgia Tech student, Frank Spain, headed the team in 1893. Wood played left guard, halfback, and kicker, and his toughness quickly earned the respect of his teammates. In one of the team's first practices, Wood cut his brow. Rather than bow out of the workout, he bandaged the wound, finished practice, and then stitched himself up.

Wood would cement his reputation with his play in Georgia Tech's four-game season. He scored three touchdowns in the season-opening win against Georgia—the first meeting in the storied rivalry—and starred in a 10–6 win against Mercer, a 6–0 loss to St. Albans, and a scoreless tie with Auburn. The Blacksmiths' 2–1–1 mark made them the first winning team in school history.

Wood seemed an appropriate coach for a misfit team. The football program attracted a medical student, Park Howell, to enroll at Georgia Tech as well as an Atlanta attorney named John Kimball. Another player was a local insurance agent. Wood's

General Leonard Wood (right) was Georgia Tech's first star player. He led the 1894 team to a 2–1–1 record and its first victory over rival Georgia.

tenure at Georgia Tech lasted only one season. He organized a base team at Fort McPherson for the 1894 season. Georgia Tech was among Fort McPherson's opponents. Wood's team won 34–0, and Wood was not well-received by his former teammates—one Georgia Tech defender bit Wood on the leg at the end of a run during the game.

Still, Wood will be remembered as Georgia Tech's first gridiron star. He's also one of the greatest heroes to ever attend the school: he would go on to command the U.S. Army Rough Riders in the Spanish-American War—Teddy Roosevelt was his second-in-command—and serve as Governor-General of Cuba and later the Philippines. He rose to the rank of Army Chief of Staff and ran for president in 1920. He lost the Republican nomination to Warren Harding.

26 Option Football

The refrain started the day Georgia Tech hired Paul Johnson as its football coach. "The triple-option won't work at Georgia Tech and on the major college level." Yellow Jackets fans should have known better. The offense, or at least variations of it, had been employed on the Flats before. And with great success.

Bobby Dodd built a power and won a national championship running the "belly series." Pepper Rodgers brought respectability back to Georgia Tech—and upset a ranked Notre Dame team without attempting a pass—using the wishbone. Ralph Friedgen mixed the option into his scheme and turned Shawn Jones and Joe Hamilton into two of college football's more accomplished quarterbacks. Johnson's capturing an Atlantic Coast Conference title in his second season as coach of the Yellow Jackets employing the "double slot" should not have come as a surprise.

"If you execute the offense efficiently, you are going to be good," Johnson said. "The defense might stop it once or twice or a dozen times, but one breakdown and it goes for a touchdown. That's why coaches have been running the option forever." Or since the 1940s, anyway. University of the Pacific coach Larry Siemering pioneered the option's forerunner, the belly series. He came up with the scheme in 1947 while watching Pacific's quarterback, Eddie LeBaron, experiment with some trick ball-handling during a practice.

Siemering implemented the scheme a play at a time starting with the 1947 season. By 1949, LeBaron's senior year, Siemering had refined the offense. Pacific went unbeaten that season, scored 75 points or more in three games, and averaged 503 yards and 50 points.

Bobby Dodd's 3 *Musts* for Running the Option

1. Do not slow the play by allowing the quarterback to stay with the fullback too long.
2. Do not let the quarterback arrive at the faking area ahead of the fullback.
3. The fullback must continue his faking after the quarterback pulls the ball back.

LeBaron's play that season earned him a spot in the East-West Shrine Game. Coaching at the all-star event was Georgia Tech's Dodd. Taken by how LeBaron, a 5'8", 165-pound player, could take over games, Dodd asked LeBaron to show him the basic belly plays.

One year later, after only the second losing season of his coaching career, Dodd decided to adopt the belly series at Georgia Tech. He hired Frank Broyles to implement it. The Yellow Jackets proceeded to go the next two seasons without a loss. Writing about the offense following the 1953 season, Dodd called the belly series "the most successful part of our offense" and estimated the Yellow Jackets were running the option 70 percent of the time.

One of Dodd's belly series quarterbacks brought the option back to the Flats in 1974. Pepper Rodgers' version, the wishbone, had evolved from the belly series over the previous two decades. Texas coach Darrell Royal and his offensive coordinator, Emory Bellard, perfected the scheme in the late 1960s, winning the 1969 and 1970 national championships.

Royal was notoriously generous with his peers, and he would conduct wishbone clinics for coaches during spring practice. Rodgers visited Austin in the spring of 1972. Rodgers' first UCLA team had gone 2–7–1 in 1971, but with the wishbone in place, the Bruins went 8–3 in 1972 and 9–2 in 1973. Rodgers became such a wishbone disciple, he wrote a book about the scheme, *Installing Football's Wishbone T Attack*, published in 1974—much to Royal and Bellard's chagrin.

"That jackass went back out and put the wishbone in at UCLA and had a book published before Christmas," Bellard told a writer for the OU Insider website. "Boy, that takes a lot of gall there, now."

Rodgers failed to achieve Dodd- or Royal-like success with the wishbone at Georgia Tech. The Yellow Jackets' best season running the scheme was 1975, when they finished 7–4.

Johnson would recapture the Dodd option magic upon his arrival in 2008. Johnson's double-slot scheme is a variation on the wishbone, with the halfbacks lined up outside the tackles—in the slots—rather than in the backfield. These slotbacks go in motion pre-snap to be in position to catch option pitches. The alignment also allows them to be a bigger threat in the passing game and be more effective blockers.

Johnson's first Georgia Tech team won nine games and defeated Georgia to snap a seven-game losing streak to the rival. A year later, the Yellow Jackets won 11 games, the Atlantic Coast Conference championship, and played in a major bowl for the first time since the 1966 season.

Johnson picked up the option by default. He was a 26-year-old coaching the defensive line at Georgia Southern in the early 1980s when Gardner-Webb offered him a defensive coordinator's job. Georgia Southern's coach, Erk Russell, didn't want to lose Johnson,

Another Georgia Tech Option Connection

The triple-option offense borrows concepts from several schemes, including the belly series and the wishbone. Another source, and the approach that most closely resembles today's triple-option, was the Veer. Naturally, one of that offense's pioneers has a Tech connection. Homer Rice, Georgia Tech's athletics director from 1980 to 1997, developed the scheme originated by University of Houston coach Bill Yeoman during his 25-year coaching career. He wrote two books on the subject, *Homer Rice on Triple Option Football* (1973) and *Winning Football with the Air Option Passing Game* (1985).

so he offered him the Eagles' offensive coordinator job. Ironically, Russell tasked Johnson with abandoning the double-slot option in favor of the I formation. Three games into his first season as an offensive coordinator, Johnson went to Russell and asked his boss to go back to the option. Russell agreed.

Georgia Southern won national titles in Johnson's second and third seasons as offensive coordinator before he left for Hawaii. He won two more championships with the Eagles as a head coach in 1999 and 2000. "From having coached defense, I knew it was tough to play against," Johnson said. "We started having a lot of success. That's where we got our identity at Georgia Southern. That's where I got my identity. That was kind of my calling card, my ticket."

It still is. And he's silenced Georgia Tech's anti-option crowd in the process.

27 Kim King

Kim King always heeded the advice of Bobby Dodd—never try to do too much. As a player, King managed the game like a good quarterback should, handing off to Lenny Snow and taking cues from center Jim Breland. He's best remembered for a game the Yellow Jackets won without scoring a touchdown. And as a color analyst on Tech's radio broadcasts, he let Al Ciraldo and then Wes Durham do the talking. King expressed more in two syllables—"woo-hoo"—than most analysts do in two hours.

King, with all due respect to Dean George Griffin, was Mr. Georgia Tech football. He spent four decades around the program playing, broadcasting, fund-raising, and promoting, and as a native Atlantan followed the Yellow Jackets all his life. An aggressive form of cancer cut short King's life, killing him at age 59. But even with less than two weeks to live, he attended a football game, riding around Grant Field in the jump seat of the Ramblin' Wreck.

"That was so special to him because of all the things he'd been involved with at Tech, he'd never ridden in the car," Durham said. "He was really weak at the time—it was touch and go whether he'd make it to that game to ride around Grant Field. So it was a great moment."

King developed an affinity for Georgia Tech as a small boy. His father would take him to Yellow Jackets games as well as the old Scottish Rite Classic, the Thanksgiving Day game played between Georgia Tech's and Georgia's freshman teams at Grant Field.

King realized a dream of moving from the stands to the field after his accomplished prep career at Brown High School. He broke most of the Atlanta city school offensive records while at Brown, then set 13 Georgia Tech passing records as a three-year starter. And while the numbers don't look that impressive now—2,763 passing yards is one season's work for quarterbacks these days—King led Georgia Tech to two bowl games and a No. 8 final ranking in the 1966 season.

That season and that team is perhaps the most underrated in Georgia Tech history. The tailback, Snow, plowed for yardage week after week, and the defense, stocked with converted fullbacks at linebacker and end, held six of 11 opponents to a touchdown or less. The kicker, Bunky Henry, was a world-class golfer who played in the Masters.

Then there was King, a junior at the time who had evolved into a dual-threat quarterback. "Kim King is a thin, handsome blond-haired young man, extremely personable, who looks and acts more like the quarterback's best friend than the quarterback," wrote *Sports Illustrated*'s Dan Jenkins of King.

The Yellow Jackets started that season 9–0 despite playing three of those games without King due to a broken hand. Dodd called the 1966 team his "favorite of all teams" because of its big-play ability.

Oddly, the game that would make King an instant legend lacked big plays, at least offensively. Georgia Tech and Tennessee both came into the 1966 game with 3–0 records and top-10 rankings. The nationally televised showdown turned on three interceptions thrown by Tennessee's quarterback and two Henry field goals, including a 41-yarder for the win. Tech's first home win against a ranked opponent since 1962's "greatest victory ever" against Alabama, the Tennessee victory led to the students storming the field. A gaggle of spectacle-wearing freshmen, decked out in their RAT caps and sportcoats, hoisted King on their shoulders and carried him off the field.

King would be privy to many more memorable moments after his playing career. Dodd made him the radio color analyst in 1974, ordering him to "keep your mouth shut. Don't you say a lot. You understand?" King didn't, but he had plenty of chemistry with Ciraldo, who took to calling him the "young left-hander" during broadcasts. King approached the job tentatively—he had no formal training—but quickly embraced it.

"It's been a great way to be part of the Tech program and get to know coaches and players, and continue the interest I've had since I was a player myself," King told a writer for the Georgia Tech alumni magazine in 1996.

King always wore his Tech allegiance on his sleeve in the broadcast booth, and his analytical skills helped fans understand the game. "He knew what he was watching and he loved the program; he loved what it stood for," Durham said. "He wanted to make the game easy for the fan to follow, but he also wanted them to know how much he was invested in it emotionally."

King's radio work made him one of the public faces of Georgia Tech football, but he did just as much behind the scenes. He served as a trustee for the institute and a fund-raiser for the athletics department. He regularly served on search committees to fill high-profile positions at the school, including president. King's efforts in

Students carry quarterback Kim King off Grant Field following the 1966 victory over Tennessee. King would be a part of Georgia Tech football for all of his adult life, working as the team's radio color analyst following his playing days.

the early 1980s, in conjunction with then–athletics director Homer Rice, to raise support to modernize the athletics department changed the course of Georgia Tech athletics.

Yet King summed up his contributions by referring to Georgia Tech as simply a "hobby of mine."

"He had the storybook life: he grew up here, came to play for the college in his hometown, had a really good playing career, and went on to be a tremendously successful businessman here," Durham said. "He loved this place."

Georgia Tech is better for it.

28 George Morris

Georgia Tech's 1952 national championship team featured so much talent, six players made All-America. One of those Yellow Jackets stood out from the rest, though, at least in Coach Bobby Dodd's opinion: George Morris.

Dodd called Morris the greatest player he coached in 36 years in the profession. Morris was certainly the most influential. He was the linchpin in Georgia Tech's rise from good program to powerhouse in the early 1950s. In Morris' junior and senior seasons, the Yellow Jackets posted a 23–0–1 record, won two Southeastern Conference titles, and claimed one national championship. Georgia Tech's defense allowed just 4.9 points a game in 1952, with Morris, a linebacker offenses schemed to avoid, recording 114 solo tackles.

Morris was known for his toughness, a reputation he protected zealously. He played at a time when face masks were optional equipment but never hesitated to stick his nose into a pile or challenge blockers head on. He suffered a head injury late in his senior season and was encouraged to wear a face mask for the final few games. He agreed on condition he could remove it for the rivalry game with Georgia. He feared the mask would negate his psychological edge against the rivals—he never lost to the Bulldogs—and lead Georgia's players to deem him "a chicken."

Morris idolized Dodd, who stole Morris out from under Mississippi's young head coach, Johnny Vaught, in 1948. Morris, born and raised in Vicksburg, Mississippi, recalled during a 2005 interview the instant connection he made with Dodd. The coach wanted smart players who loved the game. Morris wanted a smart coach who made the game fun. "[Dodd] didn't have a lot of rules," said Morris, who died in 2007, "and he cared about his players."

Morris thrived under Dodd's tutelage. A large player for that era at 6'2" and 210 pounds, Morris could control the line of scrimmage as both a center and linebacker. He was athletic enough to intercept 11 passes in his college career. He is a member of four halls of fame, including the College Football Hall of Fame.

Morris made contributions to Georgia Tech and college football beyond his playing days. Military service delayed his professional career, and he played only one year in the NFL. He returned to Atlanta and started a business. He also became a respected game official with the Southeastern Conference, calling some of college football's biggest games for three decades.

Morris was the head linesman for the 1984 Orange Bowl, the de facto national championship game between Nebraska and Miami. One of Morris' favorite anecdotes is from that game, which Miami won 31–30 when Nebraska failed on two-point conversion

Linebacker George Morris is a member of four halls of fame, including the College Football Hall of Fame, and the player the legendary Bobby Dodd called the greatest he ever coached.

with less than a minute left. Nebraska called a timeout to set up the two-point conversion play, and Morris called over the referee, Jimmy Harper. "Jimmy, I got something bothering me," Morris said. "Did we ice down that beer in the locker room for after the game?" After Harper laughed, Morris told Harper, "You looked a little tense. I thought I'd pull you over and loosen you up."

Morris had a similar effect on most who knew him. He stayed involved with Georgia Tech athletics and the football program until the day he died and for years led the Bobby Dodd Foundation, which promotes scholarship, leadership, and integrity within the coaching profession. He partnered with the Atlanta Sports Council on a successful bid to relocate the College Football Hall of Fame to Atlanta.

Morris was so affable, even his rivals liked him. "It is doubtful that any former player had more admirers from one-time adversarial camps," longtime University of Georgia sideline reporter Loran Smith wrote of Morris at the time of his death.

29. The $125,000 Tackle

Jake Rudolph never could remember the play that made him famous. Nicknamed "Mouse" by Georgia Tech teammate Lum Snyder, the 5'7", 155-pound Rudolph upended Alabama's Bobby Marlow on a fourth-down play on the goal line late in the Yellow Jackets' 1952 win against the Crimson Tide.

Rudolph, who died of a stroke in 2008, couldn't recall the tackle because the collision knocked him unconscious. Marlow weighed 195 pounds, huge for a tailback at that time. As the headline in the *Atlanta Journal* read, "A little man charged an elephant and saved a football game for Tech."

The play is remembered as the "$125,000 tackle." Georgia Tech trailed 3–0 at the time of Rudolph's stop, and the tackle ensured the Yellow Jackets would win the game with a touchdown drive. They did, and the victory would send the Jackets to the Sugar Bowl and earn the school the bowl's $125,000 payout.

The victory epitomized Georgia Tech's program under Dodd. The Yellow Jackets were smart and hard-working and could do the improbable in clutch spots. Rudolph's son, Steven, summed up his father's approach: "Be humble, play with class, persevere, play smart, make the fewest mistakes."

One of Rudolph's Georgia Tech teammates, quarterback Darrell Crawford, said that Mouse embodied Dodd's type of player. "Jakie was what Coach Dodd called a safe player, very few errors," Crawford told the *Atlanta Journal-Constitution* for Rudolph's obituary. "[Dodd] would play a person who had those attributes over a person who was a better athlete because Coach Dodd believed you won games by making fewer mistakes."

Rudolph correctly filled the hole on the fateful showdown with Marlow. A safety, Rudolph's assignment in goal-line situations was to anticipate soft spots in the defense in front of him. Alabama blocked the play well, and Rudolph moved to plug the gaping opening. Marlow made no attempt to avoid Rudolph. With 40 pounds on the Georgia Tech safety and the goal line a little more than a body length away, he lowered his shoulder to run over Mouse.

Marlow was one of the greats of his era, widely considered the best running back in the South at the time. Tech's Dodd certainly thought so—following Marlow's 180-yard performance against Georgia Tech in the 1950 game between the two teams, Dodd said, "Bobby Marlow is the best back that I have ever coached against."

Said Harry Lee, a Marlow teammate, "You can talk before or after, but Bobby Marlow is the best running back to ever play at the University of Alabama. Bobby would have been a great running

Georgia Tech safety Jake Rudolph upends Alabama's Bobby Marlow on the goal line to preserve the Yellow Jackets' 1952 victory over the Crimson Tide. The play is known as the "$125,000 tackle" because it ensured Georgia Tech a Sugar Bowl bid, which paid out $125,000 to participating schools at the time.

back in any era. He was such a powerful runner. Bobby was tremendously strong, and that was way before any strength training programs."

But like most big and strong football players, Marlow had a high center of gravity. So as he lowered his shoulder to take on Rudolph, Mouse dropped to his knees and powered his upper body upward into Marlow's midsection. The blow knocked Marlow head over heels. He landed on the 3-yard line, giving Georgia Tech the ball on downs and setting up the Yellow Jackets' comeback.

The Mouse has been roaring with Tech fans ever since.

30 1952 National Champions

Georgia Tech claims four national championships. Like boxing title belts, however, championships come from several different organizations. Today, titles come from just two sources: the Bowl Championship Series and the Associated Press. Strip away the formal titles, and you have the coaches (BCS) and the media (AP).

Not so long ago, there were many more. Every company that ran a wire service put out rankings and crowned a national champion. And back before cable television made it possible to watch teams from Miami to Honolulu all in the same day, those wire services often awarded titles to different teams. The consensus national champion was rare.

Georgia Tech's 1952 title team was no exception. The Yellow Jackets claimed the International News Service (INS) national championship, while Michigan State was awarded the AP and the United Press (UP) titles. The Hearst family operated the INS, and the service would later merge its poll with the UP to form the UPI (which would eventually become the coaches' poll and later a part of the BCS).

To Coach Bobby Dodd, there was no dispute in 1952. He called his Yellow Jackets "the best football team that I coached." They went 12–0, outscored opponents 325–59, and played just two close games all year. The Yellow Jackets were led by the "Rambling Rookies" backfield and a defense that featured two linebackers named to Tech's all-time team—George Morris and Larry Morris—plus defensive back Bobby Moorhead. Six players on the 1952 team made first-team All-America.

Highlights from That Championship Season

The 1952 national championship season included several jaw-dropping performances:

- Georgia Tech so dominated the opener against The Citadel that Dodd called a freshman practice squad player who hadn't dressed for the game out of the stands and played him in the second half.
- Halfbacks Leon Hardeman and Bill Teas—"the Two Horsemen"— combined to rush for 246 yards in a win against Southern Methodist, prompting an SMU fan to tell a reporter, "I never did see two young halfbacks make such a mess out of a football game in my whole life."
- The Yellow Jackets rushed for 405 yards against Tulane.
- Defensive back Bobby Moorhead returned two interceptions for touchdowns in a victory over Auburn.
- Punter Dave Davis booted an 80-yard punt against Army.
- Seldom-used halfback Chappell Rhino became "One Play" Rhino by tossing a touchdown pass to Buck Martin in the regular season finale against rival Georgia.

"Tech is the greatest team in the country," Duke coach Bill Murray told a *Life* magazine reporter following a 28–7 loss to the Yellow Jackets. The Blue Devils were ranked sixth at the time of the game. Yet Georgia Tech never had a chance at a consensus national title. Michigan State started the season No. 1 in both the AP and UP polls, two spots ahead of the Yellow Jackets. The Spartans finished 9–0 and beat three ranked teams, including No. 6 Notre Dame 21–3. Tech beat two ranked teams during the regular season. The Yellow Jackets also defeated a fellow unbeaten team, Mississippi, in the Sugar Bowl. But they could climb no higher than second in the AP and UP polls. There was no BCS national title game.

What's more—and what irked many members of Tech's 1952 team—Michigan State was prohibited from going to a bowl and putting its perfect record on the line against a top-tier opponent.

Michigan State was in its three-year probationary period with the Big Ten in 1952. The school joined the league in 1950, replacing the University of Chicago, which had left the conference in 1946. The Spartans would not be eligible to represent the Big Ten in a bowl game until 1953.

So despite winning the league title and holding onto the No. 1 spot all season, Michigan State missed the Rose Bowl and a match-up with No. 5 USC. Big Ten runner-up Wisconsin went instead. The Spartans and Badgers had not met during the regular season, but Wisconsin had lost two games and tied another.

The Badgers lost their third game of the season to the Trojans in Pasadena. Had Michigan State played USC in what essentially was a home game for the Los Angeles school, Georgia Tech might have ended up as undisputed national champion. Consensus national titlist or not, the 1952 Yellow Jackets are considered one of the best teams in school history.

Georgia Tech's 1952 national championship team included first-team All-Americans (left to right) halfback Leon Hardeman, linebacker George Morris, end Buck Martin, defensive back Bobby Moorhead, center Pete Brown and tackle Hal Miller.

31 Al Ciraldo

Al Ciraldo's trademark bark, "Toe meets leather," was like a call to prayer for Georgia Tech fans. The Yellow Jackets' longtime play-by-play announcer uttered those words at every opening kickoff for four decades. If fans weren't in their seats—be it in Grant Field or on the living room couch—at game time, those three words captured their attention immediately.

Ciraldo joined the Georgia Tech broadcast team in 1954 and left the airwaves in 1996. He retired at age 75 after calling more than 1,000 football games and another 400 basketball games. With all apologies to his modern-day successor, Wes Durham, Ciraldo will always be known as "the Voice of the Yellow Jackets."

"What you admired most about Al was his longevity," Durham said. "He did games there for a generation-and-a-half. The fact that here we are, more than a dozen years after his death, and Tech fans still remember him and talk about him really demonstrates what he meant to the fans."

Ciraldo's zeal for Georgia Tech's football and basketball teams was reflected in his dramatic calls. He was as animated in the broadcast booth as the fans were in the stands. He stomped his feet, waved his arms, and let the excitement and tension come through in his voice.

"Once the game starts, I want those folks out there involved," Ciraldo told the *Georgia Bulletin*, a Catholic newspaper, in 1979. "High school or college, small game or big game, I want them with me."

Ciraldo never struggled to attract an audience, even when just starting out in broadcasting. But then, a 15-year-old calling minor league baseball games is hard to miss. He covered the Akron Yankees in a one-man booth, doing play-by-play and color. Serendipitously, one of the Akron players would one day bring Ciraldo to Georgia Tech. John Hyder played outfield for the 1937 and 1938 Yankees. The man better known as "Whack" spent just the second half of those seasons in Akron but formed a bond with the teenager in the broadcast booth.

World War II postponed Ciraldo's broadcasting career. He served in the Pacific theater under General Douglas MacArthur for the duration of the conflict. Upon arriving home, he fell in love with a south Georgia "belle." He moved south, married the girl, and enrolled at the University of Florida to study broadcasting.

Three years later, his degree in hand, Ciraldo relocated to Atlanta. He landed a job calling high school sports at a Decatur radio station. He excelled at the gig and was hired away by the biggest radio station in town to cover high schools and University of Georgia basketball.

About the time Ciraldo started calling Georgia hoops, Georgia Tech hired Ciraldo's old friend, Hyder, to coach its basketball team. Hyder immediately set out to accomplish two goals: 1) build Georgia Tech basketball into a respectable program, and 2) lure Ciraldo to the Flats.

Ciraldo joined Hyder in 1954. He sold radio advertisements, called basketball games, and worked as the football color analyst. Twenty years later, he switched seats to do play-by-play at the behest of the football coach, Bobby Dodd, who wanted one of his recently graduated players, quarterback Kim King, to do the color.

King knew nothing about broadcasting at the time, but Ciraldo's versatility allowed King to grow into the position. The two would partner for close to 30 years, until Ciraldo gave up the play-by-play duties following the 1993 basketball season. Ciraldo spent his last three years on Georgia Tech's broadcast team doing pregame, postgame, and halftime shows.

Al Ciraldo called Georgia Tech football and basketball games for 42 years and will forever be known as the "Voice of the Yellow Jackets."

"The nerves, the tension, the sweat: Al put all of that into a broadcast, which is why I thought he was such a great broadcaster," King said in his book, *Tales from the Georgia Tech Sideline.*

Ciraldo called many of Yellow Jackets' most memorable games, including the 1962 showdown with Alabama and Joe Namath dubbed "the Greatest Victory Ever," the pass-less upset of Notre Dame in 1976, and the 1990 national title run. He shared the radio booth with a sitting president in 1977, when Jimmy Carter joined him for seven minutes of the Georgia Tech–Navy game. Carter is an alumnus of both schools.

Ciraldo was, in Durham's words, "old school to the bone" but was also known for several trademark phrases, including "Toe meets leather" and "Goottt!" to signify made baskets during hoops games. He addressed Georgia Tech fans during broadcasts as "brothers and sisters" and coined the basketball phrase "bunny shot," the origins of which go back to his childhood. He hunted rabbits with his father, and bunnies were so plentiful, he didn't have to aim to hit one.

Ciraldo died in 1997. Georgia Tech's then athletics director, Homer Rice, eulogized Ciraldo succinctly: "His deep-seated love for Georgia Tech was matched only by the affection of Georgia Tech and its fans, friends, and alumni toward him."

32 A Streak Unlike Any Other

Every streak, winning or losing, is made from the same recipe: equal parts talent, execution, coaching, and luck. The last two ingredients played a major role in Georgia Tech's 31-game unbeaten streak stretching from late 1950 into the 1953 season. Bobby Dodd was Georgia Tech's head coach, with Frank Broyles running his offense and Ray Graves his defense. And luck was so much a theme of Dodd's coaching career, he folded it into the title of his autobiography, *Dodd's Luck.*

Looked at as a whole, the Yellow Jackets' 31-game unbeaten streak was surreal. Every streaking team benefits from a bounce here and there, a wise coaching move from its sideline or a gaffe from the other, and a few things fit for a *Twilight Zone* episode. But Georgia Tech's run is littered with more odd twists and turns than a mountain road.

The first came in the second game of the streak, the 1950 season finale against rival Georgia. The Yellow Jackets defense dominated the Bulldogs due in large part to good scouting: Georgia tipped the play call pre-snap with the right tackle's hand position and the halfback's alignment.

The next spring marked the watershed moment of Dodd's tenure at Georgia Tech: the hiring of Broyles, the grueling spring practice of 1951, and the move to two-platoon football. The Yellow Jackets opened the 1951 season with a convincing 21–7 win against highly regarded SMU followed by a 27–0 shutout of Florida.

For Week 3, cue the *Twilight Zone* theme song. Georgia Tech trailed Paul "Bear" Bryant's Kentucky team 7–6 late when the Bear elected to go for it on fourth down deep in his own territory. Bryant initially sent his punt team on the field before changing his mind. The decision proved unwise. The ball carrier slipped and fell down in the backfield, and Georgia Tech took over on downs. Quarterback Darrell Crawford threw the game-winning touchdown pass on the next play—Tech 13, Kentucky 7.

After a 25–7 victory over LSU in Week 4, Tech was off to a 4–0 start, extending the unbeaten streak to six games. After the win, Dodd proclaimed, "We might have a better football team than I thought we had." One week later, a coaching move again helped extend the streak. The Yellow Jackets scored four touchdowns on the same play, a play-action bootleg pass Dodd first ran as a high school quarterback in Kingsport, Tennessee. The "Kingsport play" took advantage of Auburn's overly aggressive defense. Tech would set up the play with off-tackle runs, then call the play, with wide receiver Buck Martin dropping to his knees to block at the snap before hopping up and sprinting down the sideline. Georgia Tech won 27–7 to run the streak to seven games.

The streak was endangered the next two weeks. Georgia Tech beat Vanderbilt 8–7 on a late safety, with the Yellow Jackets' Ray Beck tackling Vandy's punter when he slipped on a muddy field. The Jackets' tied Duke 14–14 the next week thanks to another special teams play by Beck. A blocked punt fell into his arms, and he returned it 60 yards for the tying touchdown.

Those narrow victories (and a tie) got Georgia Tech rolling. The Jackets posted convincing wins in the final four regular season games of 1951 and won the Orange Bowl on a Pepper Rodgers' field goal to finish 11–0–1. They carried the momentum over to the 1952

Unbeaten Streaks
The longest unbeaten streaks in major college football history:

63—Washington, coached by Gil Dobie and Claude Hunt (1907–1917)
56—Michigan, coached by Fielding Yost (1901–1905)
47—Oklahoma, coached by Bud Wilkinson (1953–1957)*
34—USC, coached by Pete Carroll (2003–2005)*
34—Miami, coached by Butch Davis and Larry Coker (2000–2002)*
33—Georgia Tech, coached by John Heisman (1914–1918)
32—Pittsburgh, coached by Pop Warner (1914–1918)*
31—Georgia Tech, coached by Bobby Dodd (1950–1953)
31—Oklahoma, coached by Bud Wilkinson (1948–1950)*
30—Texas, coached by Darrell Royal (1968–1970)*

All victories, no ties

season, needing little luck or wise coaching in starting the national championship season 8–0 and extending the run to 22 games.

Alabama threatened the streak in the ninth week of the 1952 season. Georgia Tech trailed 3–0 late in the fourth quarter and needed a goal-line stand to set up the game-winning drive. On the deciding fourth-down play, Alabama handed to star running back Bobby Marlow, who found a hole in the middle of the line. Georgia Tech's 155-pound safety, Jake Rudolph, stepped up into the gap and stopped Marlow short.

The Yellow Jackets would cruise to victories over Florida State and Georgia, and trounce sixth-ranked Ole Miss 24–7 in the Sugar Bowl to close out the championship season and extend the streak to 26 games.

Luck and coaching assumed a role in the streak during the 1953 season. Georgia Tech's 0–0 tie with Florida on September 26, 1953, came in the midst of Hurricane Florence. Both the field and the ball were slippery, and a fumble by Gators quarterback Doug Dickey helped extend the unbeaten streak to 28 games.

Dodd can be credited with the Yellow Jackets' 6–4 victory over SMU the next week. Tech led 6–0 in the fourth quarter but was losing the field-position game. SMU twice pinned the Yellow Jackets offense inside their own 5-yard line. But rather than risk a turnover or punting gaffe, Dodd told quarterback Rodgers to take intentional safeties.

The Yellow Jackets easily won the next two games to extend the unbeaten streak to 31 games. The run would end on October 24, 1953, with a loss to top-ranked Notre Dame in South Bend, Indiana. Over the course of two full seasons and parts of two others from 1950 to 1953, Coach Bobby Dodd's Yellow Jackets had amassed a record of 29–0–2.

33 Eat at The Varsity

Georgia Tech students might slip a red pointed paper hat into their college scrapbooks to remind them of The Varsity, Atlanta's famous drive-in fast-food restaurant just across the freeway where cashiers demand, "What'll ya have?"

They might also add a menu to remember lingo picked up while ordering.

"A naked dog" equals a plain hot dog on a bun.

"Bag of rags"? Potato chips.

"Chili steak with strings" means a hamburger with chili and a side of fries.

During a "V-Run," students aim for the red neon "V" marking the North Avenue spot where workers and diners have fun with food. Cooks make homemade chili and fried fruit pies; customers in cars roll down their windows so carhops can attach trays to their doors; and workers sport pointy paper Varsity hats.

The Varsity began at a time when Tech and Atlanta were more compact and less crowded. The late Frank Gordy, a onetime Tech student, opened his restaurant in 1928 on a 70-by-120 foot lot with a white picket fence. Today, the double-decker restaurant sits on more than two acres. It promotes itself as the world's largest drive-in with enough space for 600 cars thanks to a two-story parking garage.

What makes The Varsity truly special is its people, particularly the carhop "curb men." They sing and dance, and two are as famous as any Georgia Tech football star:

- Flossie Mae—the late John W. "Flossie Mae" Raiford started working at the downtown restaurant in October 1937 and sang the menu to customers for over 50 years while wearing eccentric hats—one with insect spray, another with ladies' slippers. In 1987, at 80 and still a carhop, he said a manager had once told him to find a gimmick to entertain customers. He decided to make hats.
- Nipsey Russell—Julius "Nipsey" Russell, the late actor/comedian and carhop No. 46, made customers laugh. The Atlanta native and World War II army medic—who reached the rank of captain—later became best known for his TV game show appearances from the 1960s to 1990s, such as *Hollywood Squares* and *To Tell the Truth*. He played a leading role in the 1978 film, *The Wiz*, the African American musical version of *The Wonderful Wizard of Oz*. Russell reportedly talked about The Varsity and his fellow employees on national television and remained Gordy's friend.

The Varsity has also seen many famous diners: Clark Gable, Elvis Presley, Muhammad Ali, investor Warren Buffett, and presidents Franklin D. Roosevelt, Jimmy Carter, George H.W. Bush, and Bill Clinton.

The restaurant holds more than 800 seats, some of which face TVs. When the Georgia Tech Yellow Jackets play home games, more than 30,000 people may eat there. The Varsity has added several other Georgia locations throughout the years, including Athens, Alpharetta, Norcross, and Kennesaw.

Gordy, the restaurant's founder, attended Reinhardt Academy in Waleska, Georgia, in the mid-1920s and enrolled at Georgia Tech, where he reportedly dropped out. He opened The Varsity in April 1928. For the 55 years he presided over his business, he personally greeted customers. Proud of his fresh ingredients, his company's motto became "No Food Over 12 Hours Old." When asked what happens with leftovers, Gordy reportedly smiled and answered, "We don't have any."

Bill Curry

Bill Curry twice came to Georgia Tech facing a hairpin learning curve, and twice he took the turn like a car on rails. Curry the player joined Bobby Dodd's program in 1960, and though it took him three years and four games to crack the starting lineup, he left as an All-American. Curry the coach took over the program in 1980, and though he had just four years' experience in coaching, all as an assistant, he left with a conference Coach of the Year award to his name.

"Things come very tough for me; I don't learn easily," Curry told *Sports Illustrated* in the middle of his seven-year coaching tenure at Georgia Tech. "That's why I was an offensive lineman."

Curry's lineman-like approach to football made him a success. His Yellow Jackets teammates named him the captain of the 1964 team. Georgia Tech started that season 7–0, and Curry was impressive enough to be named second-team All-America, earn an invitation to the Senior Bowl, and be taken in the 1965 NFL Draft,

Bill Curry was an All-America center for Georgia Tech in 1964. He returned to his alma mater as the head coach in 1980.

albeit with the second-to-last pick in a 20-round format. He then spent 10 years in the NFL, snapping the ball to Bart Starr and Johnny Unitas and playing in three Super Bowls and two Pro Bowls.

"I had a great admiration for him—for his toughness and competitiveness," said Kim King, who was a freshman quarterback at Tech when Curry was a senior. "He was an overachiever on the field and seemed to always rise to any level of competition."

Georgia Tech won seven games in each of Curry's three years as a player. Yet Curry's greatest contributions to the Yellow Jackets came as a coach. Hired to replace another former Georgia Tech player and overachiever, Pepper Rodgers, Curry inherited a program that the campus community and the fan base at large had lost interest in.

Curry likes to characterize his hiring as one made out of desperation. "They couldn't get a decent coach to come there under those conditions," he said, "so they took me." But he was picked from a strong group of candidates. The pool included Jerry Glanville and Bobby Collins, who would later win at SMU before the program was brought down by the Pony Express pay-for-play scandal.

Curry's coaching résumé was thinner than a play sheet upon his return to the Flats. He first donned a headset four years earlier as Rodgers' offensive line coach with the Yellow Jackets. He moved to the NFL ranks in 1977, joining Starr's Green Bay Packers staff as the line coach. Curry spent three years there before Tech called him home.

Curry's start at Georgia Tech matched what one would expect from such a green coach: his first two teams won one game each. Curry admittedly had much to learn, but he had help: Dodd tutored him, pointing out his many early mistakes as a play-caller; Homer Rice, the athletics director and a football coaching legend himself, mentored Curry as a leader.

The poor records were misleading, according to Rice. The schedule was brutal, with Georgia Tech facing seven opponents ranked in the top 10 in Curry's first two years, including two No. 1s. Then there was the lack of fan and institutional support in the years leading up to his arrival that limited his team's talent those first few years. "Bottom line, we were at ground zero," Rice said. "Curry restored us to national prominence."

The rise began in 1982, when Georgia Tech started to drop several Southeastern Conference teams off its schedule in preparation for joining the Atlantic Coast Conference in football the next season. The Jackets went 6–5 in 1982, and while they took a step back record-wise in 1983, going 3–8, the talent level improved. Curry was making strides in recruiting. John Dewberry took over at quarterback. Pat Swilling, Ted Roof, and Cleve Pounds started on defense. "You meet him, and the credibility is right there," Roof said of Curry's success with recruits.

Georgia Tech became nationally relevant again in 1984, breaking into the top 20 for several weeks. Curry coached the Jackets to a 9–2–1 record and a bowl berth in 1985. Curry was named ACC Coach of the Year following the 1985 season.

Curry might still be coaching at Georgia Tech had his success not attracted attention from one of college football's highest-profile programs, Alabama. The Crimson Tide lost coach Ray Perkins to the NFL's Tampa Bay Buccaneers and contacted Curry, who sought advice from his mentor, Dodd. Dodd told Curry to go for two reasons: the first was to take his message—that you could have a good football team and still graduate players—to a football factory; the other reason revolved around Alabama's ability to contend for national titles.

Interestingly, Curry won at Alabama and improved the program's classroom reputation only to be run out of Tuscaloosa following the 1989 season while Georgia Tech won a national title four years after Curry left.

The Whistle

Success has sounded the same for Georgia Tech's football team for going on a century: *waaAAOOOOOOOOOOOOOOOOOOOOOOOooo.*

The Georgia Tech steam whistle, a campus fixture since the 1890s, bellows with each Yellow Jackets touchdown and following every victory. Located just behind the west grandstands of Grant Field, the whistle joins the fans in the stands in blowing off a little steam.

"That is one sweet sound," Georgia Tech running back Tashard Choice said following a 2007 win. The whistle erupts with the volume of a jet engine. First-time visitors have been known to ask how Tech gets an old steam-driven locomotive to pass through campus at exactly the right moment.

The brass whistle, 17 inches tall and 5½ inches in diameter, is controlled via a numerical control panel in the attic of the Archibald D. Holland Building. The facility is home to the power plant that supplies steam and chilled water to 80 percent of Tech's campus.

The plant's Saturday shift operator is charged with punching in the five-digit code that cues the whistle. He follows the game via Wes Durham's call on a boom box—he can't see into the stadium from the control room and the television is not hooked up to cable or satellite.

The whistle is a familiar sound to those who live, work, or study on campus. The whistle's sounding dates back to Georgia Tech's shop days and marked the end of a shift. Nowadays, the whistle operates on a timer synchronized with an atomic clock via the Internet. It blows at five minutes to the hour on weekdays to signal the end of that hour's classes, or a 10-minute warning to the beginning of the next.

"Georgia Tech without the hourly voice of the whistle would be akin to a class roll without George P. Burdell, a less feisty Buzz, or a campus without Junior's," wrote Lea McLees of the Georgia Tech Research Institute in the faculty newspaper—named the *Whistle*—in 2004.

The current steam whistle was forged and created on campus by the Georgia Tech Research Institute's Machine Services Department in 2003. The new instrument replaced a decades-old whistle that had cracked during a 2002 football game. The power plant's superintendent used his last spare part to repair the whistle following that game, prompting the fabrication of another. The new whistle was installed in the summer of 2004.

**✳ ✳**

Georgia Tech and Georgia don't agree on much when it comes to football—not even the number of times the two programs have played each other. Georgia Tech's tally is two games greater than Georgia's, and it has nothing to do with the math skills of those in Athens. Georgia doesn't count the games played between the programs in the 1943 and 1944 seasons.

The results of those games still appear in Georgia's record books. But next to both the Bulldogs' 48–0 loss in 1943 and their 44–0 loss in 1944 stand asterisks, placed there by Georgia's long-time sports information director, Dan Magill. "The reason was the fact that those were not true Georgia Tech teams," Magill said.

The Tech faithful scoff at such a notion. Magill's reasoning is sound: during World War II, Georgia Tech was home to a naval officers training program, which brought players from other schools drafted into the military to campus. The Yellow Jackets roster included Vanderbilt star John Steber and Michigan's Mal Stamper. Alabama-bound players Phil Tinsley and Bill Chambers also ended up at Georgia Tech because of the Navy program.

Yet the core of those teams were Tech players. Frank Broyles was the quarterback. Eddie Prokop and George Mathews played running back. Bob Davis starred at tackle. Three freshmen were among the starters. "I was 17 years old and a freshman, and I played most of the Georgia game," Davis said. "We did have some [Navy program players], but we lost some midway through the season. It's been a mean rivalry at times, and this is just one example."

Mathews admits Georgia Tech had a "material advantage in players" over Georgia in those years. But the discrepancy had as much to do with what Georgia didn't have than what Tech did. The Bulldogs won a national championship in 1942 behind the backfield tandem of Heisman Trophy winner Frank Sinkwich and Charley Trippi. The duo, along with nearly all the other returning players from the title team, joined the military. And unlike Georgia Tech, Georgia was not among the schools awarded an Army or Navy training program.

Mathews remembers then–Georgia coach Wally Butts' recruiting pitch went something like, "Come to Georgia and play with 17- and 18-year-olds and those who failed the military physical."

The Bulldogs still posted respectable records in those seasons, going 6–4 in 1943 and 7–3 in 1944. Georgia Tech, meanwhile, went 8–3 and finished No. 13 in the polls in both seasons. The Yellow Jackets won the Sugar Bowl in 1943 and lost in the Orange Bowl in 1944.

The asterisks have remained in the Georgia record book, unchallenged, since Magill placed them there in 1945. Magill retired in 1979, but his successor, Claude Felton, never considered changing them out of respect for Magill.

Georgia Tech insiders consider the asterisks too silly to make an issue of. The surviving players from the 1943 and 1944 teams have an inside joke about the marks: since Georgia doesn't count those two games, Georgia Tech shouldn't count the 1942 loss to the Bulldogs. The Jackets played that game without injured star running back Clint Castleberry as well as without coach William Alexander, who suffered a heart attack prior to the game.

Magill and the Georgia faithful don't see the humor. And Magill defends the asterisks vehemently more than a half-century later. "There's no question about it, there's no way they are true Georgia–Georgia Tech games. There's no question about that," Magill said. "We had a freshman team. We still carry the scores, we just have the asterisks to explain the facts."

37 The Pass-less Upset

Most quarterbacks would object to their coach, two plays into a game, removing all passes from their game plan. Georgia Tech's Gary Lanier had a different reaction as he came to the sideline for a timeout early in a 1976 game against Notre Dame. He'd just been driven to the Grant Field turf by Irish slobber-knocker Ross Browner and witnessed an elaborate sack dance.

Yellow Jackets coach Pepper Rodgers called a timeout while Browner was in mid-gyration. He gathered his offensive assistants around him and informed them the last play was the last pass he'd call that afternoon.

"That's the last time they strut on Grant Field," Rodgers said.

Lanier overheard the end of the coaches' conversation. As Rodgers turned to let his true freshman quarterback in on the change of plans, Lanier spoke first. "Coach, I don't have a problem with that," Lanier said.

Notre Dame defenders would be the ones with the problem with Georgia Tech's unbalanced attack the rest of the afternoon. The Irish fared much worse against Lanier the pitcher than they did Lanier the passer. Two hours after Browner got jiggy with it following his sack of Lanier, the Yellow Jackets danced off Grant Field with one of the strangest wins in college football history.

Georgia Tech's offense totaled 368 yards, all on the ground, in a 23–14 upset of 11th-ranked Notre Dame. Lanier tossed the ball around all afternoon, but the ball always went backward on option pitches. Lanier never attempted a forward pass. "Maybe it was just our day," Lanier said. "Everything we did seemed to work. As for

Gary Lanier drops back to throw. The quarterback is best known for leading the Yellow Jackets to an upset of Notre Dame in which he didn't attempt a pass.

not throwing a pass, those who saw me throw a ball understood why we didn't pass."

Nobody was supposed to see Lanier do much of anything in 1976. A true freshman, he opened the season as the fourth-string quarterback. His chances of playing were so slim, he practiced with the flankers, not the quarterbacks, for much of the season. The option can thin a team's quarterback ranks quickly, however. The starter and backup went down with injuries before the end of September. The third-stringer, Mike Jolly, took over in the third game of the season and led the Jackets to a tie with Clemson. Jolly suffered a season-ending ankle injury the next week against Virginia.

Lanier became the starter. He finished up the Virginia game, leading Georgia Tech to victory. Tech split the next four games with Lanier at quarterback heading into the Notre Dame showdown, with the freshman being predictably inconsistent.

One of the losses during the stretch was a humbling 31–7 defeat at the hands of Duke. Lanier played poorly. He even made a couple of uncharacteristically bad pitches. Rodgers collared Lanier on the sideline following one of those miscues and offered a surreal pep talk: "Lanier, don't worry about it. It's not your fault, it's mine. I should never have had a quarterback of your abilities out there."

Yet the next week, with the Irish visiting Atlanta for homecoming, Lanier was back out there. He played brilliantly, too, at least after Rodgers scrapped the passing game. Notre Dame's defensive coaches focused on stopping the fullback dive and tasked the defensive ends with smacking Lanier on every play. But with David Sims and Eddie Lee Ivery at the halfback spots, Lanier had two great runners to pitch to.

"He wasn't as good as some of the other option quarterbacks I had," Rodgers said of Lanier, "but he could pitch the ball as well as anybody I've ever seen."

Rodgers mixed in some misdirection calls, too, and Georgia Tech turned an early 14–3 deficit into a 16–14 lead late in the third quarter. The running game chewed up the clock while the defense turned in a performance almost as impressive as the offense. Notre Dame managed just 178 yards and was shut out in the final three quarters. The Irish rushed for 21 yards in the second half.

"Nobody remembers or talks about it, but the defense was tremendous," Lanier said. "It seemed like we as an offense were on the field the whole game. We'd score or punt, and they'd get the ball right back."

But Lanier and the offense understandably received all the accolades after the historic win. Lanier woke up early the morning after the game specifically to read the newspaper. He was anxious to read Rodgers' public comments regarding his performance. He expected the coach to be complimentary. He got a good chuckle from Rodgers' words instead.

"Of all the quarterbacks who have beaten Notre Dame, Lanier was the worst," Rodgers' quote read.

"What a great line," Lanier said. "Memorable."

Almost as memorable as the pass-less upset.

38 "Indian" Joe Guyon

The recruitment of Joe Guyon certainly would have drawn the ire of the NCAA enforcement staff. But then, in 1916, college athletics' internal affairs division did not exist. To woo Guyon, who a sportswriter would later call "the greatest football player the South ever saw," Georgia Tech's John Heisman arranged a part-time job for him at an Atlanta Ford plant and hired Guyon's brother, Charlie, as an assistant coach.

Then Heisman arm-twisted the fledgling NCAA into classifying the college Guyon previously attended, the Carlisle Indian Industrial School of Jim Thorpe lore, as a prep school. Never mind that Carlisle won a national title or that Guyon made Walter Camp's All-America team while playing for the school. What would today potentially result in the NCAA issuing the death penalty to the Yellow Jackets football program back then led to Georgia Tech becoming one of college football's earliest powerhouses.

With Guyon in the backfield for the 1917 and 1918 seasons, Tech outscored opponents 957–49. The Golden Tornado offense

Joe Guyon was so dominant in the Yellow Jackets' backfield in the 1917 and 1918 seasons, a reporter described him as "almost a team by himself."

scored more than 100 points in three games during the stretch. The team lost just one game and won two conference titles as well as a national championship.

Heisman had a deep and talented team, with Albert Hill, Everett Strupper, and Judy Harlan in the backfield along with Guyon. But the player known as "Indian Joe" was the superstar.

Atlanta Constitution reporter Ralph McGill once wrote that Guyon was "almost a team by himself."

Guyon gained national attention by rushing for 344 yards on just 12 carries—an average of 29 yards per tote—in the sixth game of his career, an 83–0 win against Vanderbilt during the national title season of 1917.

Guyon stood 6'1" and weighed 195 pounds, big enough to play offensive tackle in that era. Heisman used him in that role as well as in the backfield, and McGill once wrote that Tech's backs "could follow that big fellow and run to glory because he cleared the way, and I mean he cleared it." Guyon made the All-America team as a tackle in 1918.

Guyon's passing talents also drew attention. New York sportswriter Sam Blake compared Guyon's accuracy to that of a trapshooter breaking a clay pigeon: "Joe is the most deadly man in this respect [passing] I ever saw."

Yet Guyon's greatest skill was his speed. He was the fastest player on Tech's team and was the first option in the running game. Asked how he developed such fleet feet, Guyon spilled his secret: "When I was a kid, I heard a man say the only good Indian was a dead Indian, and from then on I was a pretty fast Indian."

Guyon was a member of the Chippewa tribe, born in 1892 on the White Earth Indian Reservation in Minnesota. His birth name was O-Gee-Chidah, which roughly translates to "Big Brave." He joined Thorpe at Carlisle to play for Pop Warner in 1912.

He left Carlisle for Keewatin Academy, a private prep school, in 1914 with the intention of improving his academics. The government-operated primary school on the White Rock Reservation educated children through only the sixth grade, and Guyon needed to expand his learning to play football at a major university.

By 1916 Guyon was a strong enough student to receive a scholarship offer from a college in North Carolina. He arranged to visit, but his travels took him through Atlanta, where Heisman intervened with the factory job and a spot on his staff for Guyon's brother.

Guyon went on to play professional football and baseball and was enshrined in both the College Football and Pro Football Halls of Fame. Heisman summed up Guyon best when he wrote, "I rate Guyon among the three or four greatest players of all time."

39 The Georgia Tech Marching Band

Georgia Tech's marching band has long been one of the best in the land, but for almost 100 years, music was little more than a hobby for the musicians.

The Institute introduced its first music degree program, music technology, in 2006. Prior to that—and the band's origins date to 1908—students could only minor in music. Whether musicians attend the Institute for a music degree or not, they put in enough time to earn one. And those who oversee the program likely would hold degrees in choreography engineering if there were such a course.

On the field at halftime, they move in organized rows right, left, up, down, backward, forward, and diagonally. They form tight circles that bloom into loose circles that become straight lines in seconds. They shape patterns while also playing.

One impressive way to view the Marching Yellow Jackets is from high above Grant Field. From there, the forming of the giant "GT" looks fluid: band members don't run about finding their special spot to stand; rather, they play and walk in orderly lines, weaving in and out of other rows, as they magically create Georgia Tech's initials.

The Institute's music tradition dates to 1908, when 14 students started the Georgia Tech Band. One of those students, Mobile,

Notable Dates in Georgia Tech Band History

1954   Two of the nine women enrolled at Tech—trombonist Teresa Thomas and flutist Paula Stevenson—become the band's first female members. Women students were admitted into Tech in 1952.

1963   The music department is created under Tech's General College. Band participation eventually receives academic credit.

1970   Athletics director Bobby Dodd reportedly requests the band stop playing "Dixie" at basketball games. He later expanded his request to include football games. "Here Comes the King"—known as the Budweiser song—was substituted for the song played at the end of the football third quarter and during the second half of basketball games. The song was chosen because of its popularity when the band played it as part of an Atlanta Beverage Company advertisement.

1976   School leaders move the music department from the General College to the College of Sciences and Liberal Studies. They relocate it to the College of Agriculture in 1991 to provide better collaboration with artists and media groups.

1992   During halftime between Tech and rival University of Georgia, the Tech band played a prank that gained media attention. As the musicians took the field for their halftime performance, several band members brought a tarp inscribed with the GT logo onto the field and covered the midfield logo commemorating the UGA football program's centennial. The fans' boos drowned out the band's performance.

1995   A certificate in music is established.

1998   A music minor is created.

2001   The marching and symphonic bands perform in Dublin, Ireland, during the St. Patrick's Day celebration.

2006   The master of science in music technology degree is approved, giving Georgia Tech its first degree program in music.

2007   A group of Tech alumni leads an effort to endow a scholarship for a student marching band trumpeter. It was created in memory of their deceased friends. At the time, three members of the trumpet line died while either still in school or shortly after graduating, all in the span of several years.

2008   To mark its 100th birthday, the Marching Yellow Jackets march in the Macy's Thanksgiving Day parade in New York City.

Alabama, native Robert L. "Biddy" Bidez, directed the group. The musicians officially chartered the band on January 1, 1911, making it one of the school's oldest student organizations.

From those roots grew the institute's fight song, "(I'm a) Ramblin' Wreck from Georgia Tech," with various tweaks and adaptations by different people throughout the early years. Michael A. Greenblatt is credited for writing the first "Ramblin' Wreck" arrangement and score as a handwritten manuscript. Greenblatt had taken over as bandleader in the fall of 1912 because Bidez had graduated.

Billy Walthall, a member of Tech's first four-year graduating class, added the lyrics.

Georgia Tech's band has been attracting talented musicians to the school since 1908 despite the Institute not introducing a music degree program until 2006.

But Frank Roman, who became band director in 1914, is credited with adapting and copyrighting the song. His musical version remains popular today. Roman's "Up with the White and Gold," was copyrighted in 1931. Under Roman, the band possibly was the first to broadcast live dance music over the radio, playing a campus dance concert that was transmitted over wireless radio to an Atlanta club several blocks away.

And in 1925, Georgia Tech became what is believed to be the first southern college to have its songs recorded. The Columbia Gramophone company sold a recording of Tech songs by the Georgia Tech Band and Men's Glee Club.

The marching band performs at all home football games. The pep band, a delegation of marching band members, performs at all home basketball games. Some musicians also travel to most away games, as financed by the Georgia Tech Athletic Association.

40 Scott Sisson

Scott Sisson inherited his nerve from his mother. How else to explain his father's inability to handle big-game pressure? Every time Scott, Georgia Tech's kicker between 1989 and 1992, lined up for a crucial field goal, Neal Sisson made a beeline for the top row of the stadium. The elder Sisson spent plenty of time in the nosebleeds.

Scott Sisson hit seven final-minute field goals in his storied career. He made countless other pressure kicks. His ability to come through in the clutch was so well-known he was a first-team All-American as a senior despite connecting on less than 80 percent of his field goals.

"I wasn't a high-percentage kicker," said Sisson, who connected on a pedestrian 60 of 88 field goals in his career, "but I made the big ones."

Fear made for a great motivator. Sisson dreaded Coach Bobby Ross' wrath, which he often vented at the kicker. A week after Sisson hit a tying and winning field goal in the upset of top-ranked Virginia during the 1990 national championship season, Sisson shanked a long attempt early in a game against Virginia Tech on a cold and windy day. Ross met Sisson before the kicker made it to the sideline.

"Kick the ball!" Ross screamed. "You're thinking too much. You're guiding it." Naturally, Sisson nailed two clutch field goals late in that game to give Georgia Tech a 6–3 win.

Sisson never regretted playing for Ross, no matter how many times the coach verbally abused him. Ross was the only coach to take a chance on Sisson, despite the kicker's self-marketing effort. Sisson mailed letters and videotapes to major college programs around the Southeast only to be rebuffed.

By November of his senior year of high school, Sisson was resigned to a future playing soccer at Furman or Birmingham Southern. But then he tagged along with teammate Jess Simpson on a late-season recruiting visit to Georgia Tech. One of Ross' assistants asked Simpson, a blue-chip recruit, about his friend. Simpson informed the coach Sisson was the player on the front page of that day's newspaper: he'd made a game-winning kick in a high school game the night before. Ross' recruiting coordinator called a few days later and invited Sisson on a recruiting visit. Georgia Tech eventually offered Sisson a scholarship, the only school to do so.

Sisson quickly made Ross and his staff look like the smartest men at the coaches' convention. He won the starting job the following August and started every game of his career. As a senior, he was a finalist for the Lou Groza Award, given to the nation's top kicker. He finished second to Memphis State's Joe Allison.

Scott Sisson made seven game-winning field goals in his Georgia Tech career, making him the greatest clutch kicker in program history.

Yet Sisson will always be remembered for what he won, not lost. For all the heroes of the 1990 national title season, Sisson was the player to make season-saving plays. He made the tying kick with 61 seconds left at North Carolina, two kicks late against top-ranked Virginia (one to go ahead, another to win) and two more versus Virginia Tech (to tie and to win). The winners at Virginia and Virginia Tech came with less than 10 seconds remaining.

The kicks that tested Sisson's composure most were those with the Yellow Jackets trailing. Recalling the Virginia game, Sisson considers the earlier kick—made with seven minutes to go—as more pressure-packed than the game-winner with eight seconds remaining.

"As a kicker, you're always looking at the worst-case scenario," Sisson told Rivals.com for a 2006 story. "I was thinking, *If I miss this, we're still tied with the No. 1 team in the nation.*"

117

Sisson's Last-Second Field Goals

- **Georgia Tech 13, Boston College 12** (November 25, 1989), 35-yarder with 42 seconds left
- **Georgia Tech 13, North Carolina 13** (October 20, 1990), 27-yarder with 61 seconds left
- **Georgia Tech 41, Virginia 38** (November 3, 1990), 37-yarder with seven seconds left
- **Georgia Tech 6, Virginia Tech 3** (November 10, 1990), 38-yarder with eight seconds left
- **Georgia Tech 24, Virginia 21** (September 19, 1991), 33-yarder on final play
- **Georgia Tech 19, Furman 17** (November 9, 1991), 37-yarder with 21 seconds left
- **Georgia Tech 16, N.C. State 13** (October 3, 1992), 29-yarder on final play

His father, Neal, failed to rationalize the kick the same way. He'd scurried up to the top row of Scott Stadium prior to the earlier kick and had stayed there. A neighbor eventually came up and talked Sisson down to his seat for the game-winning boot. Years later, father and son made a pilgrimage back to Charlottesville. Neal led Scott up to the last row and told him the story.

"You have no idea," father told son, "how much pressure there is watching you kick."

41 Shout "To Hell with Georgia!"

Georgia Tech fans tend to be narrow-minded, at least when it comes to battle cries. No matter the opponent, the most popular chant references only the rival:

"What's the good word? To hell with Georgia!"

"What's the good word? To hell with Georgia!"

"What's the good word? To hell with Georgia!"

The battle cry harkens back more than a century. Soon after the *Blueprint*, Georgia Tech's yearbook, published the lyrics to the "Ramblin' Wreck" fight song in 1908 under the title "What Causes Whitlock to Blush," fans bastardized the words.

The line, "But if I had a son, sir, I tell you what he'd do, he'd yell like hell for Georgia Tech like his daddy used to do," became, "But if I had a son, sir, I tell you what he'd do, he'd yell, 'To hell with Georgia!' like his daddy used to do."

Some argue the latter version is the original. Legend has it Georgia Tech student Billy Walthall wrote the words to the song during the return trip from the first Georgia Tech–Georgia football game in 1893. Georgia Tech won the game easily and was literally run out of Athens by Georgia fans, who threw clumps of mud at the

Buzz, Georgia Tech's mascot, cues the crowd with Georgia Tech's most popular battle cry.

"To Hell, to Hell to Hell with Georgia" Lyrics
(to the tune of "Battle Hymn of the Republic")

Don't send my boy to M.I.T.
The dying mother said.
Don't send my boy to Emory
I'd rather see him dead.
But send my boy to Georgia Tech
'Tis better than Cornell.
But as for University of Georgia:
I'd RATHER SEE HIM IN HELL!

Chorus:
To hell, to hell to hell with Georgia,
To hell, to hell to hell with Georgia,
To hell, to hell to hell with Georgia,
The Cesspool of the South!

Mine eyes have seen the glory of the stomping of the dogs,
We will teach those poor darn farmboys they should stick to slopping hogs,
When the Jackets are triumphant we will raise a mighty cheer,
"We'll do the same next year!"

On the field between the hedges there arose a mighty stench,
In the dog machine the engineers will throw a monkey wrench,
When the Jackets are triumphant we will raise a mighty yell,
"Them dogs can go to hell!"

Mine eyes have seen the glory of the NCAA,
They're investigating Georgia players to see how much they're paid,
After counting all the cars, and the loans alumni made,
They outpaid the NBA.

visitors throughout the second half, on their way to the train station, and at the team train as it left for Atlanta. Traumatized by the experience, Walthall allegedly coined the "to hell with Georgia" line.

Today, the saltier version is the official lyric, posted on the Georgia Tech website. "It's catchier," claims one diehard Georgia Tech fan. "And it means more to us Tech fans sung that way."

The "to hell with Georgia" cry spawned its own songs. The first "Up with the Gold and White" was written by three members of Georgia Tech's Glee Club around 1915, with the lyrics first appearing in print in the 1916 *Blueprint*. The song includes references like "down with the red and black" and "drop the battle axe on Georgia's head."

An even less subtle song came later. Sung to the tune of Georgia's "Glory, Glory" fight song—itself a takeoff on "Battle Hymn of the Republic"—Georgia Tech's "To Hell, to Hell to Hell with Georgia" refers to the rival school as "the cesspool of the South."

"As is expected from major schools confined in the same state, neither wants to bow down in combat to the other. It's rivalry, it's war, it's Clean Old-Fashioned Hate. How else can you explain it?" writes Kyle Kessler in the *T-Book*, a guide distributed to Georgia Tech freshmen outlining the school's traditions.

"The Plan"

Blame it on William Alexander. The next time a team sits a player or players in order to save them for a future game and messes up your fantasy team or ruins your weekend outing, know that Georgia Tech's legendary football coach started the trend.

Alexander did more than rest a player or two for a game in the 1927 season. Six games into the 11-game schedule, Alexander split his team in two. His 11 starters plus one reserve spent the next four weeks practicing for the season finale against Georgia while the rest of the team focused on the three opponents in between. Dubbed "the Plan," the move led to arguably the biggest upset in the storied history of the in-state rivalry.

Georgia's 1927 team was the most dominant of the era. The Bulldogs, or the "Dream and Wonder" as they were known by the media, featured All-Americans Chick Shiver and Tom Nash. Georgia's defense was the equivalent of a titanium chastity belt; by the time they faced Georgia Tech a week after Thanksgiving, The "Dream and Wonder" squad had shut out six of its nine opponents and allowed just 23 points all year. Beat Georgia Tech, and the Dogs were shoo-ins for the Rose Bowl and a shot at the national title.

Georgia Tech, meanwhile, had seen a promising season sour with an ugly Halloween weekend loss at Notre Dame. The Yellow Jackets had started the season 4–0 with three shutouts but gave up 26 points to Knute Rockne's Fighting Irish. Demoralized, Georgia Tech played Vanderbilt to a scoreless tie in Nashville the next week.

Georgia Tech's final four games were at home that season, the stretch culminating in the Georgia game. Alexander was under pressure to beat the Bulldogs after losing to them by a point the year before. Tech blew a 13–0 halftime lead in the 1926 game, losing 14–13 in the second matchup between the two programs since the renewal of the rivalry, which had been on hold since the United States entered World War I in 1917.

The rivalry's interruption continued beyond the war's end due to an incident following a baseball game between the two schools in 1919. Georgia students celebrated a victory that day with a parade only the brothers of Delta Tau Chi of *Animal House* fame could appreciate. A fake tank inscribed with the words "Georgia in Argonne" was the first float, followed by a tiny car bearing students in Tech sweaters and a sign that read "1917 Tech in Atlanta"—a not-so-veiled reference to the fact Georgia Tech fielded athletic teams during World War I while Georgia did not. A mule and a female coed in a yellow outfit brought up the rear of the parade.

Georgia Tech administrators missed the humor in the prank and severed ties with Georgia for the next six years. The rivalry resumed in 1925 with a 3–0 win for the Yellow Jackets, but the 1926 loss guaranteed Tech's first losing season since 1903, and Alexander knew spoiling the Bulldogs' Rose Bowl hopes would be the best revenge.

So he enacted "the Plan." The reserves pounded LSU, Oglethorpe, and Auburn. The starters, which included backs Stumpy Thomason, Warner Mizell, and Ronald Durant and linemen Peter Pund and Frank Speer, rested and prepared. Equipment consisted of crude pads and leather helmets at the time, and four weeks away from game-day contact allowed the starters to go into the Georgia game as healthy as they'd been all season.

The extra time also allowed Alexander and the assistant coach he put in charge of the starters during the four-week break, Don Miller, to scheme for the Bulldogs' go-to play that season, a dump screen pass. Miller had been a member of Notre Dame's legendary "Four Horsemen" backfield and had an intimate understanding of the Bulldogs offense, which had been adapted from Irish coach Knute Rockne's scheme. Georgia Tech stuffed the play and stymied Georgia's attack all day to shut out the Bulldogs 12–0.

"The Plan" worked perfectly.

43 Debate the Fifth Down

For all the debate surrounding the Bowl Championship Series, the format would have settled the greatest debate in Georgia Tech football history: the true 1990 national champion.

Georgia Tech and Colorado shared the title that season. The Yellow Jackets finished 11–0–1 with wins against four ranked teams. The Buffaloes posted an 11–1–1 mark with victories over five ranked teams.

Ask anyone associated with Georgia Tech, and they'll say there is no debate. Not only were the Jackets unbeaten, they point out, but their team didn't need five downs to win any of their 11 games.

That's right, five downs.

Colorado's infamous "fifth-and-goal" victory over Missouri on October 6, 1990, kept the Buffaloes in the national title chase. The Buffs started the season in the top five by virtue of an undefeated regular season the year before. An Orange Bowl loss to Notre Dame was all that kept Colorado from the 1989 championship.

The ranking allowed the Buffaloes to withstand a season-opening tie with Tennessee and a loss two games later to Illinois. The defeat dropped them to No. 20 in the polls, but wins the next two weeks over ranked teams Texas and Washington moved Colorado back up to No. 12 in the Associated Press poll released October 2.

That same release included the poll debut of Georgia Tech at No. 23. The unheralded Yellow Jackets had gone 7–4 in 1989 but hadn't sniffed the rankings since the 1984 season. Their 3–0 start included a convincing 27–6 victory over 25th-ranked South Carolina and got the pollsters' attention.

Both Georgia Tech and Colorado played road games against unranked opponents on October 6. The Yellow Jackets went to suburban Washington, D.C., and trounced Maryland 31–3; the Buffaloes traveled to Columbia, Missouri, and downed Missouri 33–31. Only one of those victories included college football's greatest injustice.

Colorado trailed Missouri 31–27 with 2:32 left. The Tigers had just taken the lead on a 38-yard screen play that went for a touchdown. And Colorado, with backup quarterback Charles Johnson under center, needed to go 88 yards for a winning touchdown thanks to a clipping penalty on the kickoff return. The Missouri fans, rabid from witnessing a back-and-forth game on a sweltering afternoon, could sense the upset.

Colorado's Johnson quickly shook the crowd's—and the Missouri defense's—confidence. He converted a third-and-11 from the Buffaloes' 23-yard line with a 22-yard pass. The strike startled Missouri's defense. Colorado was an option team, and while the Buffs didn't disdain passing, Johnson's completion in such a crucial spot swung the momentum his team's way.

By the time the game clock ticked close to 30 seconds remaining, Johnson had guided the Buffaloes to the Missouri 9-yard line. Tigers coach Bob Stull called timeout to let his winded and shell-shocked defense regroup.

Colorado's coaches used the break to draw up what should have been the game-winning play. Tight end Jon Boman caught the play-action pass from Johnson along the sideline without a defender near him. But he slipped and fell three yards shy of the goal line. The play was good for a first down, though, and Johnson rushed his team to the line of scrimmage and spiked the ball with 28 seconds left.

Cue the confusion.

The spike rule had just been implemented. Prior to the 1990 season, college quarterbacks had to throw an incomplete pass in the direction of a receiver to stop the clock. A spike had been considered intentional grounding. For many of the officials on the field that day, Johnson's spike was the first they'd ever experienced. Some weren't even sure what happened—they thought the ball had been kicked and was being reset.

Colorado compounded the officials' confusion by running the ball on the next play and immediately calling timeout. The referee went to the Buffaloes' sideline to inform coach Bill McCartney the timeout was his last. In doing so, he neglected to signal a change of down to the head linesman and the man holding the down marker.

Meanwhile, in the grandstands beyond the Colorado sideline, a Missouri fan was suffering a heart attack. The paramedics transferred him to the track behind the Colorado bench during the timeout. The down marker guy—a diehard Missouri fan named Rich Montgomery—admittedly became distracted by the situation going on across the field.

"I'd like to say I wasn't distracted," Montgomery told ESPN's Tom Friend for a story on the 20th anniversary of the game. "But even most of the Colorado players were turned around looking."

Montgomery never changed the marker from second to third down; hence neither did the scoreboard operator. Colorado's McCartney checked the marker and the board during the timeout and waved the referee over to tell him the Buffaloes intended to run the ball on the next play, then spike the ball to stop the clock and allow for one last play—what everybody on the field thought would be fourth down but in actuality was fifth down. McCartney huddled with the referee because his concern was that the Missouri defenders would intentionally sit on the Colorado runner after the first play in order to let precious seconds tick off the clock.

The Tigers did just that. They stopped Colorado running back Eric Bieniemy at the 1-yard line and slowly unpiled. The officials halted the clock for six seconds to get everybody off the ground, then restarted it. Johnson spiked the ball with two seconds left.

The spike should have ended the game. But because of the confusion over the earlier spike, the play came on what was believed to be third down. The fans realized the error, chanting "fifth down, fifth down" but those on the field were oblivious. Colorado ran its fifth-down play, with the quarterback Johnson scoring as time expired.

The Buffaloes won 33–31. Colorado wouldn't lose another game all season, winning convincingly in all but the Orange Bowl rematch with Notre Dame. The Buffaloes won that game 10–9, albeit courtesy of a controversial penalty that wiped out a punt return for a touchdown by the Irish's Rocket Ismail.

The AP named Colorado its national champion the day after the Orange Bowl. Georgia Tech's steady climb up the polls—the

Yellow Jackets defeated No. 1 Virginia during their run—culminated in a 45–21 trouncing of No. 19 Nebraska in the Citrus Bowl. The coaches awarded Georgia Tech the United Press International (UPI) title.

The debate raged. The Yellow Jackets were the only unbeaten team. Colorado had a loss and would have had two if not for the fifth down. Jim Lavin, an offensive lineman on the 1990 team, summed up the Tech perspective best: "There are not a whole lot of absolutes in sports: four downs in football, three outs in baseball, and that's about it," Lavin said. "So to me, there's no debate."

44 1917 National Champions

College football officially became the South's sporting pastime in the fall of 1917. Georgia Tech ended three-plus decades of football dominance by Northeast colleges by capturing the 1917 national title. Ivy League schools like Yale, Harvard, Princeton, and Penn were powers as the sport migrated slowly west and south. Michigan, the University of Chicago, and Pittsburgh became contenders after the turn of the 20th century. Michigan won the first bowl game, the Rose, in 1901, by which time most southern schools at least fielded teams.

More importantly, southern high schoolers had taken up the game at the turn of the century. By the time John Heisman established the Golden Tornado as one of the South's pioneering programs in the 1910s, Georgia prep schools were producing quality players. Fifteen of the 21 players on the 1917 roster were Georgia kids. Ten of the 11 starters came from Georgia high schools. And they dominated.

Georgia Tech went 9–0 and outscored its opponents 491–17. The Golden Tornado posted seven shutouts. They defeated Penn 41–0 and hammered Auburn 68–7 one week after the Tigers had played Big Ten conference champion Ohio State to a scoreless tie.

"Tech is the best team in the land today," said Penn coach Bob Folwell, following his team's loss to the Golden Tornado. "No team will even come close to beating it, unless it lets down and takes things easy."

Heisman kept his team focused and motivated. The closest game Georgia Tech played all season was a 32–10 win against Davidson. The Golden Tornado turned down a Rose Bowl matchup against a 4–3 Oregon team because half the team had committed to joining the armed forces to fight in World War I. More than half of Georgia Tech's starters made All-America teams, including future Hall of Famers Walker Carpenter, Everett Strupper, Joe Guyon, and Bill Fincher.

"I consider the 1917 Tech team the best football team I have ever coached," Heisman said. "It's the best team I have seen in my long career as a coach. I was lucky in having under me a team whose members possessed much natural ability and who played the game intelligently. I have never seen a team that, as a whole, was so fast in the composite."

The Golden Tornado was the original greatest show on turf, albeit in the running game. Fullback Judy Harlan and quarterback Albert Hill joined halfbacks Strupper and Guyon in the backfield to run behind star tackles Fincher and Carpenter. Plus, the Heisman shift—pre-snap formation changes considered revolutionary at the time—confused defenses during an era before teams had access to scouting video.

According to the *New York Times*, "The attack of the Georgia team was largely of the shift variety, with variations from which a plunge, end run, or punt could be worked. Tech had great execution of the plays, specializing in sweeping end runs and off-tackle smashes from its 'jump shift' formation."

The *Times* wasn't the only eastern newspaper to heap praise on Georgia Tech. A *Philadelphia Ledger* reporter wrote that "the dopesters will have to look farther south than the Mason-Dixon line for All-American material." A *New York Sun* story read, "Football, once an eastern specialty, now a national sport, and in recognition of that fact we are glad to acclaim Georgia Tech the greatest 11 in the country.... Georgia Tech looms up as one of the truly great teams of all time."

Such recognition forced the media and public to accept that football had evolved into a national game. Cal became the first West Coast team to win a title in 1920, and Alabama, Notre Dame, USC, Stanford, Illinois, Minnesota, Southern Methodist, Texas Christian, and Texas A&M would build championship-caliber teams in the 1920s and 1930s.

The South would evolve into the game's base over the course of the 20th century along with the Midwest. Georgia Tech's 1917 team started that trend.

Bobby Ross

Georgia Tech's Homer Rice put Bobby Ross in an unenviable situation with a call from a pay phone at an Interstate 75 rest area in January 1987. Rice wanted to interview Ross for the Yellow Jackets' coaching vacancy. Bill Curry had resigned to take the Alabama job earlier that day, quitting via telephone because Rice was out of town. Rice and his wife were on vacation, en route to Florida's Marco Island.

Rice spent the final hours of the drive—Curry had reached him at a Gainesville, Florida, hotel where he and his wife had stopped for the night—compiling qualifications and candidates on a legal pad. Ross topped the list. He'd left Maryland, where he'd won three Atlantic Coast Conference titles in five years, a few weeks earlier. But Ross had already accepted an assistant coaching position with the NFL's Buffalo Bills. He was to start his new job in two days.

Ross contacted his new employer and was told he'd be fired if he even interviewed with Georgia Tech. Ross had already turned down head coaching opportunities at Cal and Purdue. He was genuinely excited about the prospects of coaching professionals.

Bobby Ross is carried off the field following the Yellow Jackets' 1990 Atlantic Coast Conference title–clinching victory over Wake Forest. Georgia Tech would earn a share of the national title a little over a month later.

Rice was persuasive, however. He could not guarantee Ross he would get the job if he interviewed, but he talked Ross into spurning Buffalo and coming to Atlanta, anyway. Rice picked Ross up at the airport and took him straight to the president's house. Two hours later, with the blessing of the president and the Georgia Tech Athletic Association board, Rice offered the now unemployed Ross the head coaching job.

If Ross knew what he was getting into, he might have declined. Ross' tenure mirrored that of his hiring. He faced frustrating situations and choices. He lost nine players off his first team to academic failures. Many of the remaining players bristled under his strict coaching style. He won just one game against a Division I-A opponent in his first two seasons, a period he described to a *Baltimore Sun* reporter late in the 1990 season as "pure agony." He nearly quit three times and gave his team an ultimatum—commit on the practice field and in the classroom or leave the program—another time. He stared down a rebellion on the eve of the Yellow Jackets' first New Year's Day bowl game in three decades.

Ross trusted his belief in Georgia Tech every time. And he was ultimately rewarded. Ross spent just five seasons with the Yellow Jackets, so he falls short of the legend status held by predecessors like John Heisman, William Alexander, and Bobby Dodd. But for the better part of three years—starting with a come-from-behind win against Maryland four games into the 1989 campaign, spanning the 1990 national championship season, and stretching to the 1991 Aloha Bowl victory over Stanford—Georgia Tech football reclaimed the glory it had been longing for since Dodd stepped down as coach following the 1966 Orange Bowl. The Yellow Jackets went 26–6–1 during that stretch and spent 14 weeks in the national rankings.

The success never came easy. From the start, the relationship between Ross and his team was rocky. His strict approach, molded from his playing days at Virginia Military Institute and an early coaching stop at The Citadel, alienated players recruited by the more easy-going Curry. Curry played for Dodd, after all, a coach who despised practicing and would stage volleyball games rather than scrimmage.

Ross required players to attend a team breakfast every morning to ensure they went to class. He also mandated study halls. Many players refused to buy into his system. Twelve freshmen quit the team in Ross' first year. "There's two ways to skin a cat, and they were used to skinning it the other way," a Ross assistant, George O'Leary, says in the book *Focused on the Top*.

The lack of commitment showed on the field. A 48–14 loss to Duke followed by a 33–6 defeat at the hands of Wake Forest in his first season nearly drove Ross to resign. He got in his car and drove around Atlanta's perimeter highway, Interstate 285, repeatedly, while thinking about whether to stay or go. He stopped for his favorite vice, ice cream, several times during the circumnavigation. Ross contemplated quitting again after a 1–4 start in 1988. That time, his assistants, led by Ralph Friedgen, talked him into staying. The next season, 1989, Ross began to doubt again following an 0–3 start. But a pep talk and vote of confidence from three influential alumni led to Ross giving his team an ultimatum.

The put-up-or-shut-up talk penetrated, and Georgia Tech defeated Maryland 28–24 days later to begin the run of success. It ended three years later, when Ross deplaned in San Diego on the flight home from the 1991 Aloha Bowl victory. Fed up with the challenges coaching at Georgia Tech entails—the 15 credit hours of calculus each student must earn, fickle alumni and fans—Ross had resigned to take the San Diego Chargers head coaching job. The move was inevitable given the depth of Ross' frustration.

"This is a hard place to coach," Ross said in an interview conducted a month before Georgia Tech won the 1990 national title. "All these nice things have been happening here, and I haven't been able to enjoy it one bit.... This job started out being a tough job, and it hasn't stopped."

Ross looks back fondly on his Tech tenure now. He calls winning the 1990 championship the crowning achievement of his coaching career, which included a Super Bowl run with San Diego. Still, Rice wonders if Ross, knowing what he knows now, would again eschew an NFL assistant's job to interview at Georgia Tech, as he did back in 1986. "I don't know," Rice said. "But the funny thing is now he calls it the best job he ever had."

46 Bobby Grier

Bobby Grier and Don Ellis collided, and the penalty flag flew. Pittsburgh's Grier was at fault in the opinion of the only man who mattered, the nearest official. The pass interference penalty would set up the only score in the 1956 Sugar Bowl. Georgia Tech would win 7–0, its sixth bowl win in six years and the finale of a 10–1 season.

That penalty is not what makes Grier a significant figure in Georgia Tech football history, however. That he had the opportunity to draw the flag is. Grier is black. And of all the prejudices the world has ever known, the one that existed in the Deep South in the 1950s—that white and black players shouldn't share the same athletic field—is among the most absurd.

Grier's skin color became an issue shortly after Pitt and Georgia Tech accepted Sugar Bowl invitations. Black players had competed with whites in few places in the South, most notably the Cotton Bowl in Dallas, but Sugar Bowl officials believed the free spirits of New Orleans would see past race.

The Sugar Bowl committee assured Pitt officials that would be the case—and that the school's mixed-race fan base would be welcomed, too—in inviting them to the game. Pitt officials made it clear they would not acquiesce to southern racism as Boston College had in forcing its star running back, Lou Montgomery, to sit out the 1941 Sugar Bowl.

Big Easy residents ultimately proved their color-blindness; Georgia's governor Marvin Griffin did not. On December 2, 1955, the day after a black woman named Rosa Parks was arrested for her refusal to surrender her seat on a Montgomery, Alabama, transit bus to a white passenger, Griffin sent a telegram to the Georgia board of regents. The letter urged the board to bar state university teams from events in which the races mixed on the field or in the stands. Griffin had run for governor on a segregationist platform and intended to stop Georgia Tech—the school his son attended at the time—from playing against Grier in the Sugar Bowl. "The South stands at Armageddon.… The battle is joined. We cannot make the slightest concession to the enemy in this dark and lamentable hour of struggle," Griffin's telegram read. "One break in the dike and relentless seas will push in and destroy us. We are in this fight 100 percent."

Griffin's stand was far from popular. Schools, lunch counters, and buses were one thing to the people of Atlanta; football was another. Georgia Tech's Golden Era of football was still underway. Bobby Dodd's program ranked among the best in the country, averaging 10 wins a season between 1951 and 1956. Many fans wanted the team to play. Georgia Tech students and fans picketed the governor's mansion. They marched on the state capitol. They hung and burned Griffin in effigy, an odd approach considering the racial undertones.

Griffin's letter incensed his fellow public officials, as well. Georgia Tech's president refused to pull his team out of the game. A board of regents member, David Rice, classified Griffin's stance as "ridiculous and asinine." The board chairman gave the Yellow Jackets the university system's blessing to play.

Ellis, an end on Georgia Tech's 1956 team, said the governor didn't speak for him, the team, or the school. "He was being a horse's backside," Ellis said almost 50 years later. "It was all political, and politics had no place in football."

Politics and race played no part in the game. Grier showed his skills, starring on both offense and defense. His 28-yard run was the longest of the game. As for the conspiracy theorists who wondered if the pass interference call might have been racially motivated, the official who threw the flag was from Pittsburgh. Whether racism played a role or not, the penalty was controversial. Video replays show contact, and many, including Grier, said Ellis initiated it.

Ellis disagrees. "I had him beat on the play, and he tried to catch up," Ellis said. "He ran right into me as I was going to catch the pass. And I would have caught it, too. We would have won that game."

47 South Bend Sorrow

All good things must end, but it took a confluence of surreal events to halt Georgia Tech's 31-game unbeaten streak of the early 1950s. The Yellow Jackets came into the 1953 season as the defending national champions. They hadn't lost a game since 1950 and were in the midst of the Golden Era on the Flats.

But Tech followers knew if the streak had an expiration date, it was October 24, 1953. The Jackets renewed their series with Notre Dame that afternoon. The top-ranked Fighting Irish featured a backfield that included tailback John Lattner, who would go on to win the Heisman Trophy, and future College Football Hall of Fame quarterback Ralph Guglielmi.

The Notre Dame players with the biggest impact on the game, however, were Wayne Edmonds and Dick Washington. Edmonds and Washington were black, and southern prejudice at the time discouraged whites from playing against blacks in southern stadiums, like Georgia Tech's Grant Field. Notre Dame coach Frank Leahy feared a riot if the two teams played, as agreed, in Atlanta. "See you in South Bend," Tech coach Bobby Dodd told Leahy, according to Dodd's autobiography, *Dodd's Luck*.

Looking back, the game's relocation should have been an omen. Murphy lived in the visitors' locker room of Notre Dame Stadium and laid down his law on Georgia Tech. First, quarterback Pepper Rodgers got hurt on the opening kickoff. Then his backup, Bill Brigman, suffered an injury in the second quarter. "The Irish were doing away with our quarterbacks," said Wade Mitchell, the freshman third-string quarterback.

Still, Georgia Tech trailed by just a touchdown at halftime. The game's momentum changed while the two teams were in the locker room, however. Notre Dame's Leahy suffered an apparent heart attack and was rushed to the hospital. As the two teams stood in the tunnel, waiting to take the field, Georgia Tech's players heard unusual sounds from the Irish players standing behind them: sniffling.

"I turned around, and their eyes were glassy. Some were crying," Georgia Tech player Dick Inman said in recalling the game. "They looked like a bunch of wild men."

"I thought to myself, *Oh, heck, it is going to be a tough second half*," Mitchell told Al Thomy for the book, *The Ramblin' Wreck*. "*They're going out there to win one for Leahy, if not the Gipper.*"

Notre Dame's players channeled their grief in the second half— with a little help from an error-prone Georgia Tech. The Yellow Jackets tied the game early in the third quarter, but the Fighting Irish answered with a passing touchdown, the first score allowed through the air by Tech's defense in 22 games.

Notre Dame's defense held on the ensuing possession and forced Georgia Tech to punt from its own end zone. Punter Jim

Carlen fumbled the snap, and the Irish recovered for a touchdown. "[The snap] was high," said George Morris, whose brother, Jimmy, was the long snapper on the blown punt. "I don't know that it was too high, but it was high."

Both teams would score late touchdowns. Notre Dame won 27–14.

"It was an odd feeling because we'd never been beaten," said Inman, whose Georgia Tech freshman team went undefeated as well. "There was no sense of panic during the game because we were thinking eventually we were going to break one."

The loss broke the streak instead.

48 Paul Johnson

Every Georgia Tech football coach dating back to—and including—Bobby Dodd used the same crutch whenever the Yellow Jackets failed to meet expectations: the academics are too tough. Then along came Paul Johnson.

Johnson is one of the few Tech coaches to actually come from a college with tougher academics and bigger recruiting challenges than the Institute's. So when Johnson left the Naval Academy for Tech in December 2007 and was confronted with the notion that Tech's curriculum would handcuff him as it had the coaches before him, he scoffed.

"If there were a ceiling here and we couldn't compete for championships, I wouldn't be standing here," Johnson said at his introductory press conference. "One thing that drives me is the chance to compete for championships."

National championships. Johnson owns four title rings from his days at Georgia Southern, a Division I-AA school. And Johnson needed less than a year from his hire date to convince fans similar expectations were realistic at Georgia Tech. The Yellow Jackets won nine games his first season and tied for a league division title.

The gruff, no-nonsense Johnson changed the culture at Georgia Tech in a way not seen since the days of John Heisman. And Heisman replaced a series of player/coaches, not an accomplished leader like Chan Gailey, as Johnson did. Johnson took over a program comfortable in its mediocrity, resigned to bowling in Boise or Seattle or San Jose, and established a three-letter standard: BCS. The Yellow Jackets reached that goal in Johnson's second season by winning the ACC title and playing in the Orange Bowl.

"He wills the organization he's in to succeed," one of Johnson's Georgia Southern assistant coaches, John Pate, said.

Johnson alienates folks along the way, from players to fans to media. He possesses a dry sense of humor lost on many, and he likes criticism the way others enjoy in-grown toenails. None of it matters, and Johnson doesn't care. "Where coaches make big mistakes is in wanting their people to like them. But I've never worried about that. I'm going to be me," Johnson said. "If they like me, fine. If they wouldn't piss on me if I was on fire, fine. But they're going to respect me. And that's the one thing. If you operate that way, you usually get both eventually."

Johnson's success is a product of his innovative "double slot" option offense and his ability to get the most from his talent. His early teams were loaded with NFL draft picks, but those Yellow Jackets featured piecemeal offensive lines. The starting tackles on the 2008 team were converted tight ends.

"He looks at his talent, and he maximizes it," said athletics director Dan Radakovich, the man who hired Johnson at Georgia Tech. "He flat out has figured out how to be successful."

Johnson teams, be they at Georgia Tech or Navy or Georgia Southern, are a reflection of their coach. In other words, they are overachievers who carry a big enough grudge on their shoulders to knock the opponent down. That attitude broke the carbon-fiber ceiling Johnson's predecessors placed on Georgia Tech because of academics. The season prior to this book's publishing (2010), the Yellow Jackets went 6–7. Fans still expected Georgia Tech to contend for the ACC title the next season. Such is the power of the Johnson effect.

Bowl Success

New Year's Day is often celebrated the same way by Georgians: watch the Rose Parade in the morning, eat a dish of hoppin' johns and a few pieces of cornbread at lunch, watch Georgia Tech play in a bowl game in the afternoon.

As of the end of the 2010 season, the Yellow Jackets have played in 39 bowl games in their history, 19 times in the major New Year's Day bowls. The Jackets current streak of 14 straight bowl appearances is the fourth-longest active run in the country.

Georgia Tech's bowl prowess is easily underappreciated nowadays. Any team with a full roster and a sober schedule-maker should play during a holiday season littered with as many bowl games as candy canes. But much of the Yellow Jackets' bowl success came when playing in the postseason was more privilege than right. Their first bowl season, 1928, they played in the only bowl contest: the Rose Bowl.

Georgia Tech was the first program to both play in and win each of the four traditional major bowls. Tech won the 1929 Rose Bowl, 1940 Orange Bowl, 1944 Sugar Bowl, and 1955 Cotton Bowl. The Jackets' could have claimed the "grand slam" a decade sooner if not for a 14–7 loss to Texas in the 1943 Cotton Bowl.

Head coach Bobby Dodd so established Georgia Tech's bowl supremacy, the media nicknamed him the "Bowl Master." Dodd's teams appeared in 13 bowl games and won nine. His Jackets' won six straight bowls between 1952 and 1956.

Many Georgia Tech bowls have historical significance:

- The 1929 Rose Bowl is well remembered for Cal's Roy Riegels' wrong-way run.
- The 1952 Orange Bowl was the first decided by a field goal in the closing moments. Georgia Tech's Pepper Rodgers booted the 22-yarder for a 17–14 win against Baylor.
- The 1956 Sugar Bowl was among the most controversial of the segregation era, with Georgia's governor initially banning Georgia Tech from playing in the game against Pittsburgh because the Panthers' roster included a black player, Bobby Grier.
- The 1991 Citrus Bowl victory over Nebraska earned the Yellow Jackets a share of a national championship.
- The 2004 Humanitarian Bowl featured P.J. Daniels' NCAA bowl-record rushing performance. Daniels rushed for 307 yards and four touchdowns.
- Georgia Tech legendary coaches William Alexander, Bobby Dodd, and Bobby Ross all capped their tenures on the Flats in bowl games. Alexander and Dodd lost; Ross won.

The Yellow Jackets' bowl prowess comes with an asterisk: the program went 43 years between major bowl appearances. Dodd's finale, the 1967 Orange Bowl, would be Georgia Tech's last in a top-tier bowl until Paul Johnson coached the 2009 Yellow Jackets to an Atlantic Coast Conference title and an Orange Bowl berth. (The 1991 Citrus Bowl was not considered a major bowl although it was the tie-in for the ACC champion.)

Georgia Tech's Greatest Bowl Performers

1. **Pepper Rodgers.** The kicker/quarterback led the Yellow Jackets to bowl wins in 1952, 1953, and 1954. He kicked the game-winning field goal in the 1952 Orange Bowl, threw a touchdown pass and kicked a field goal in the 1953 Sugar Bowl, and accounted for 23 points passing and kicking in the 1954 Sugar Bowl. He hit on 16 of 26 passes for 195 yards and three touchdowns in the finale.

2. **Shawn Jones.** The quarterback accounted for 318 yards total offense in the national title–clinching victory over Nebraska in the 1991 Citrus Bowl and led a come-from-behind win in the closing seconds a year later in the Aloha Bowl. Jones scored on a sneak play with 14 seconds left in the Aloha Bowl against Stanford, cutting the Yellow Jackets' deficit to 17–16. He then pitched to Jimy Lincoln on an option play for the game-winning two-point conversion.

3. **Joe Hamilton.** The 1999 Heisman runner-up accounted for 906 yards total offense in three bowl appearances in his career. He threw three touchdown passes and caught another in the 1999 Gator Bowl win against Notre Dame and accounted for 356 yards and three touchdowns in the 1997 Carquest Bowl victory over West Virginia.

4. **P.J. Daniels.** The tailback rushed for an NCAA bowl record 307 yards and four touchdowns in the 2004 Humanitarian Bowl win versus Tulsa. Daniels' performance came despite the absence of a Yellow Jackets passing game—four different quarterbacks took snaps in the game and accounted for just 19 yards passing.

5. **Frank Broyles.** The quarterback guided Georgia Tech to bowl appearances in all three of his seasons on the Flats, winning two. He passed for 304 yards in a losing effort to Tulsa in the 1945 Orange Bowl.

Among the more nondescript bowl games Georgia Tech has played in over the years are the All-American Bowl, Aloha Bowl, Bluebonnet Bowl, Carquest Bowl, Champs Sports Bowl, Emerald Bowl, Humanitarian Bowl, Liberty Bowl, Oil Bowl, Seattle Bowl, Silicon Valley Classic, and Sun Bowl.

50 Buzz

Buzz the mascot runs onto the field, aims for the giant "GT" painted at midfield, and embarks on his signature Buzz Flip. He lands on his back—intentionally. The football fans roar. That's his job: use high energy to fuel the crowd. Yet he meets their screams with silence. He is allowed to use only hand singles and body language, like a fuzzy, bug-eyed mime who has downed too many caffeinated Cokes. When the band strikes up the "Budweiser Song," for instance, Buzz makes motions to drive the conductor from his post and then takes over as bandleader.

He will jab back if an opposing mascot swats his massive compound eyes or the yellow-and-black-striped "abdomen" flapping from his behind. Buzz is never supposed to start a fight, but he may defend himself.

None of that bantering and entertaining comes naturally. Before becoming Buzz, the person behind the costume has to attend a spring clinic for several days to train and master "Buzz mannerisms": how to stand and walk, perfect the hand gestures, and perform that signature flip. Classes titled "Buzz movement" and "skit advice and coordination" are held in conjunction with cheerleading tryouts. The clinic ends with a costumed audition. The previous Buzz helps choose the successor, whose identity is supposed to remain secret until his term ends.

Buzz the mascot grew out of the Yellow Jackets nickname for Tech students, which dates back to the turn of the 20th century. The costumed mascot came much later—1972 to be exact. Tech fan Judi McNair wore a homemade yellow-jacket costume to games that year, rode on the Ramblin' Wreck, and appeared in the 1972

Buzz debuted as Georgia Tech's mascot in 1972 but didn't become a fixture on the sideline until late in the 1979 season.

Georgia Tech *Blueprint* yearbook. The idea faded following that season but was revived a few years later by student Richie Bland.

Like all truly great designs, Bland sketched his first yellow-jacket costume on a bar napkin. He and his roommate then tracked down a costume designer at Atlanta's Six Flags amusement park and asked him to make the outfit. The finished product cost Bland $1,400.

Bland and the suit made its first appearance—a surprise one— at a pep rally before the Tennessee game in fall 1979. Bland made his football game debut a few weeks later. "I remember I had to be very sneaky that first appearance," Bland said in the alumni article. "I got stopped by security before I could get onto the field. I managed to somehow get away from them and ran straight onto the field."

By spring 1980, Bland's Buzz was an official member of Tech's cheerleading squad. He passed the job to his friend, Jeff Cooper. Traditions—such as auditioning for the part and doing push-ups when Tech's football team scores—evolved throughout the decades. The costume developed also, with the addition of white wings, long white gloves, black tights, and black high-tops.

The Buzz performers tend to get too into character from time to time, and the acrobatics have led to injuries similar to those suffered by football-playing Yellow Jackets he shares the field with. One past performer hurt his knee while hurdling the press table at a basketball game. Another remembered little kids stomping his feet and hitting him in the groin. He also acknowledged he'd been dropped during overhead passes in the student section. A third man broke his heel during a 1995 football game.

Yet other unplanned stunts caused only excitement. At homecoming 1988, one female Buzz, possibly the first, rode a limousine into the stadium as part of the "Buzz for President" theme. In the alumni association article, she remembered acting on a whim, climbing out of the sunroof, and standing atop the car as it drove onto the field.

In 1996 the student playing Buzz, who also belonged to Tech's parachute club, glided into the baseball stadium. He suited up again in November 1997 and landed on the 50-yard line at Bobby Dodd Stadium during a nationally televised football game.

At least one other mascot pleased the fans in other ways: he washed the suit. "I would take the costume apart, take the foam out of the stinger and wash it in a washing machine," Kevin Manous, who portrayed Buzz from spring 2000 until May 2003, said in the alumni article. "You couldn't do that with the head. I would take that into the shower and use shampoo and conditioner on it. Then I'd hang it to dry in the shower at my fraternity house, Theta Xi. That scared some guys first thing in the morning."

Buzz Away from the Court and Field

Buzz is a busy mascot. Apart from his main job, leading the cheers at Georgia Tech, he competes and attends events. Buzz has won three national mascot titles and was the runner-up in a National Cheerleaders Association contest in 2004. Buzz is involved with charity events, sports conventions, and such official Institute functions as the annual President's Dinner. The mascot also may be hired for private social events, including weddings and birthday parties.

He has appeared in *Sports Illustrated* and *ESPN The Magazine*, and in many sports television commercials. An endowment scholarship helps pay Buzz's expenses and is given to the students who play the character.

51 Gainesville's "Jolly Giant" and "Mr. Cool"

Bobby Dodd wanted a pair of highly touted recruits out of Gainesville, Georgia, in 1960, but then so did every other coach in the South. Billy Lothridge, a quarterback, and Billy Martin, a tight end, were a dream duo: tremendous athletes with a passer-receiver relationship first honed in touch football games played in the street that passed by both their homes.

Dodd got a commitment from them the afternoon before the scholarship signing period opened. Knowing well that his rivals would make a last-gasp recruiting pitch for the pair that evening, Dodd conned them into visiting his house for a home-cooked meal and a night of pool. The trio shot billiards for hours, and just after midnight, Dodd replaced the pool cues in their hands with pens. They signed scholarship offers right there in Dodd's parlor.

Needless to say, Dodd saw potential in Lothridge and Martin, nicknamed "the Jolly Giant" and "Mr. Cool" by their high school coach. Both lived up to expectations. They started all three seasons

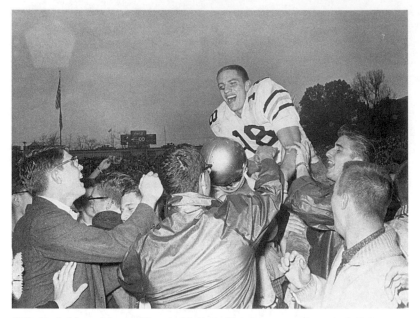

Billy Lothridge celebrates Georgia Tech's 7–6 victory over top-ranked Alabama in 1962. Lothridge was the runner-up to Navy's Roger Staubach in the 1963 Heisman Trophy balloting.

and both made first-team All-America as seniors. Lothridge finished as the Heisman Trophy runner-up that season. Navy quarterback Roger Staubach won the award.

Lothridge was a triple-threat: he could run, throw, and kick, much like a young Bobby Dodd. Lothridge averaged 41 yards a punt his senior year, kicked 12 field goals, and was widely considered the best kicker in college football. A *Time* magazine reporter described Lothridge in a 1963 issue as a "one-man gang. He runs, he passes, he punts, he kicks, he calls 80 percent of Tech's offensive plays, and, what's more, he beats Coach Bobby Dodd at his own game: pool. Small wonder that Dodd calls Lothridge 'the most valuable player in college today.'"

What made Lothridge really special, according to Martin, were his leadership skills. Lothridge played quarterback with a "linebacker mentality" and guided the Yellow Jackets to 21 wins and two bowl games in his three seasons. Teammate Taz Anderson described Lothridge as a player "who always delivered in the clutch." Tech was ranked in the top 10 at some point in all three seasons and upset top-ranked Alabama late in the 1962 season in what Dodd called "the greatest victory ever."

"Billy wasn't the best thrower around. He wasn't the best runner. He was average to good at all those things," Martin told the *Gainesville Times* for a 2009 story, "but when he got into the huddle, there was a different attitude."

If Lothridge dominated the huddle with his presence, Martin did likewise once Georgia Tech's offense lined up to run a play. Martin stood 6'6" and weighed around 225 pounds, making him the largest man on the field for most plays. That he was athletic enough to run routes and catch passes—56 in three seasons, all from his buddy Lothridge—made him all the more intimidating.

"I think he was a forerunner of what we see today in football, because he had a big frame and could block very well for the run, yet he had enough speed to get downfield, run good routes, and make receptions," the late Kim King said of Martin upon Martin's 1997 induction into the Georgia Sports Hall of Fame.

Learn the Many Nicknames

Georgia Tech is the national champion of nicknames. Known today as both the Yellow Jackets and the Ramblin' Wreck, the football team played under several other monikers dating back to its 1892 formation.

Georgia Tech started off as the Blacksmiths only to be called Engineers, Tech Boys, Techity Techs, and Techs before Coach John

Heisman announced in 1905 the team would be known as the Yellow Jackets.

During Georgia Tech's 1917 national title run, northern sportswriters referred to the team as the Golden Tornado. The Yellow Jackets averaged 55 points a game that season and featured a backfield that would later be considered on par with Notre Dame's Four Horsemen of the 1920s. Georgia Tech destroyed opponents the way a tornado would a structure in its path. The Golden Tornado nickname stuck and was commonly used through the team's 1928 title run.

Yellow Jackets is the most enduring label and has roots beyond Heisman's mandating its use in 1905. Georgia Tech's first football team adopted gold as a team color. But a dye in that shade of yellow didn't exist at the time. Fans wore yellow clothing to show their support instead, with the men donning yellow sportcoats and jackets. Heisman took over the program in 1904 and quickly recognized an identity crisis. He claimed the Yellow Jackets nickname for the program in an interview with the *Atlanta Constitution* in November 1905. A year later, Atlanta's other newspaper, the *Atlanta Journal*, printed an editorial cartoon that forever associated the nickname with the flying insect of the same name. The cartoon showed a bug tormenting a Georgia football player and a caption that read, "Somebody's going to get stung."

The yellow jacket insect would adorn the school's programs and yearbooks in the years that followed. Yet the bug didn't become the football team's mascot for another six decades. Buzz made its debut in 1972 and didn't become widely recognized as the school's symbol until 1979. Even today, Buzz is considered by many fans as a secondary mascot behind the Ramblin' Wreck car, a gold-and-white painted 1930 Ford Model A Sport coupe.

The Ramblin' Wreck became the school's mechanical mascot in 1961. The nickname dates back to the turn of the 20th century, however, a reference to the makeshift vehicles built by Georgia Tech graduates working in the jungles of South America. Those engineers scavenged parts from tractors and automobiles to construct motorized vehicles. Their peers referred to the finished products as the Ramblin' Wrecks of Georgia Tech.

53 Death Knell of Football

Georgia Tech disbanded its football program five years into its existence. Actually, football at Georgia Tech died one game into the 1897 season. The team lost to Georgia 28–0 in the opener and broke up one week later after a Georgia player suffered serious injury in a game against Virginia and died the next day.

Football was a brutal game back then, played without pads and on a field with no boundaries. The forward pass was illegal, and most teams ran variations of two plays: a run up the middle and a run around the end. Both produced jarring collisions. Paralysis and death were commonplace.

Georgia public officials considered killing football following the Georgia player's death. Georgia Tech, Georgia, and Mercer canceled the remainders of their seasons immediately following that game. The Georgia legislature passed a bill that would banish the sport and sent it to then Governor William Yates Atkinson to be signed into law.

The *Atlanta Journal* hailed the governmental action as the "Death Knell of Football" in a headline. Atkinson vetoed the bill instead—at the behest of the dead player's mother. Rosalind Gammon, whose son Richard Von Gammon played fullback for Georgia, sent a letter to Atkinson imploring him not to sign the legislation. Her son "cherished" football and would not want to be the cause of the sport's banishment. She wrote:

> It would be the greatest favor to the family of Von Gammon if your influence could prevent his death being used for an argument detrimental to the athletic cause and its advancement. His love for his college and his interest in all manly sports, without which he deemed the highest type of manhood impossible, is well known by his classmates and friends, and it would be inexpressibly sad to have the cause he held so dear injured by his sacrifice. Grant me the right to request that my boy's death should not be used to defeat the most cherished object of his life.

Atkinson championed higher education throughout his tenure as governor. He created the first state college for women, the Georgia Normal and Industrial School for Girls in Milledgeville. But he is best known for sparing college football in the state. A descendent of Atkinson, Georgia Historical Society CEO Todd Groce, noted Atkinson's claim to fame in erecting a historical marker in his honor in 2010. "All loyal [Georgia football] fans ought to thank him for his political courage," Groce said.

The governmental reprieve failed to guarantee football future's at Georgia Tech, however. The school fielded a team in 1898, with former Georgia star R.B. "Cow" Nalley serving as volunteer coach. Nalley had been a halfback on the 1897 Georgia team, lining up alongside Von Gammon.

Georgia Tech went 0–3 and scored just six points in Nalley's lone season as coach. The team would go winless again the next season and again in 1900 and 1902 before the legendary John Heisman took over as coach and turned Tech into a powerhouse and a part of the state's fabric.

54 Eddie Lee Ivery

Eddie Lee Ivery owns two of the longest runs in Georgia Tech football history. His favorite run as a Yellow Jacket, however, came 15 years after his playing career ended.

Ivery scampered to the dais to collect his diploma during the 1992 commencement ceremony. The player who rushed for 3,500 yards and helped end a six-year bowl drought with arguably the greatest individual performance in college football history remembers that last run the best. After all, it was the "longest and hardest" of his life. "When I walked down the aisle and got that diploma," he said, "my Georgia Tech career was defined."

Ivery never should have attended Georgia Tech. Or so his friends and neighbors in Thomson, Georgia, told him in the days leading up to and following his signing a scholarship offer with the Yellow Jackets. Some said he'd never graduate. Others doubted he'd stay eligible. The real cynics forecast that he'd flunk out.

Georgia Tech's top recruiter, Dick Bestwick, convinced Ivery otherwise. Bestwick visited Ivery at his high school prior to signing day. He pulled Ivery out of math class. He told the heralded recruit, who'd rushed for 1,700 yards in 10 games during his senior season, that he'd be better off at Georgia Tech than at Georgia. Bestwick wrapped up his recruiting pitch by promising that he'd see Ivery graduate.

"For the first time in my life, I saw some sincerity on a man who really cared for me as a human being," Ivery said. "He didn't just want me to come to school and play football. He cared for me as a person—a person he wanted to see graduate from Georgia Tech. That won me over."

Eddie Lee Ivery rushed for more than 3,500 yards in his career, with 1,562 of those coming in his senior year, 1978.

Getting Ivery literally changed the look of the Yellow Jackets offense. Head coach Pepper Rodgers was a wishbone disciple, and his first two Georgia Tech teams rushed for better than 3,000 yards. But by 1977, he knew the wishbone didn't give the Yellow Jackets the best chance to win. Not with Ivery in the backfield. He rushed for 900 yards that season on just 153 carries, or 14 a game. So Rodgers shelved the option in favor of the I formation for Ivery's senior year, 1978.

"Eddie was the only reason for the switch," Rodgers said. "It was strictly because of him. In the best sense of the game, the I formation is not anywhere near as good an offense as the wishbone. But Eddie Lee was special. He was good enough to make it work."

Rodgers made Ivery work. Ivery averaged 22 carries a game his senior season and was also active in the passing game. Ivery rushed for more than 100 yards in eight of Georgia Tech's 12 games in 1978. In half of those games he eclipsed 150 yards.

His 356-yard performance against Air Force shattered college football's single-game rushing record and ensured the Yellow Jackets would snap the program's longest bowl drought since the 1930s.

"I can remember so many games getting in that huddle and calling his number and looking in his eyes," said quarterback Gary Lanier, who spent the 1978 season handing off to Ivery. "He'd been beaten and beaten and beaten, and you're wondering, *Is he going to be able to make it? Can he run it one more time?* He always did."

Ivery was so reliable, he failed to make it to his scheduled graduation day, pursuing an NFL career instead. The Green Bay Packers picked him in the first round of the 1979 draft. Soon after Ivery retired from professional football, Bestwick called him. His old coach insisted he finish his education. Ivery returned to school part-time in 1990 and earned his degree in industrial management in 1992.

"Dick Bestwick lived up to his word: from 1975 to 1989, he encouraged me to get that diploma," Ivery said. "And all the critics back home who said I would never play football at Georgia Tech and graduate were answered."

55 Pepper Rodgers

The two women, clad in leotards and leggings, stood facing 95 testosterone-laced young men. "Lean...now reach...now stretch, 2, 3, 4..." came the feminine voice over the loudspeakers.

So went pre-practice stretching at Georgia Tech during the Pepper Rodgers era. The women were instructors from an Atlanta dance studio; their charges were the Yellow Jackets. The session would seem unorthodox, even at a time when disco and free love were the rage. But then Rodgers always tested the limits of conformity.

Brashness defined Rodgers. As a child, he was a tap-dancing prodigy, even performing on stage at Atlanta's Fox Theatre. In high school, he was a three-sport star and played in the marching band, albeit briefly. At Georgia Tech, when asked before his first college game if he could handle the place-kicker duties, he answered, "Coach, I'll never miss." And he rarely did. During his coaching career, he rode a motorcycle to work, spurned socks, wore a permanent in his hair, and hired nubile dancers to lead his team's stretching exercises.

"Playing for Pepper, just being around Pepper, was never dull," said Gary Lanier, a Georgia Tech quarterback between 1976 and 1979.

Rodgers is without question one of the great characters in Georgia Tech history, ranking right up there with Army surgeon Leonard Wood, bear-adopting halfback Stumpy Thomason, and enigmatic Joe Hamilton. That he was a talented player and good coach only adds to the legend.

Rodgers' relationship with Georgia Tech dates to his childhood. Rodgers grew up in Atlanta's West End neighborhood, not far from campus. He sold game programs outside Grant Field in the 1940s and answered Coach Bobby Dodd's recruiting call in 1950. His playing career spanned Georgia Tech's Golden Era. He won the kicking job in 1951 when he assured Dodd and assistant coach Frank Broyles he'd never miss. The Yellow Jackets won 32 games, three bowl trophies, two conference titles, and a national championship in Rodgers' three years in uniform. And he made plenty of kicks, including the game-winner in the Orange Bowl his first season. Rodgers was the nation's "toe-scoring champ" a year later, given to the kicker who scores the most points, and was described by an Associated Press reporter as "the pepper boy with the red-hot toe."

Rodgers' arm proved hot, too, or at least warm. He shared snaps his first two seasons with Darrell Crawford and Bill Brigman

Pepper Rodgers starred as a quarterback and place-kicker for Georgia Tech in the early 1950s. He returned as head coach in 1974 and led the Yellow Jackets to the 1978 Peach Bowl.

and was the Most Valuable Player in the 1953 Sugar Bowl victory, which capped Tech's perfect 1952 season. Rodgers started at quarterback his senior season and capped his career by completing 16 of 26 passes and throwing for three touchdowns in the 1954 Sugar Bowl. "It's not how you start out but how you wind up," was a favorite Rodgers saying.

Rodgers went on a football sabbatical when his Georgia Tech career ended. He finished his degree in 1955 then enlisted in the Air Force to fly fighter jets. He returned to football three years later, finishing out his five-year military commitment as assistant coach at the Air Force Academy. From there, he reunited with one of his Georgia Tech coaches, Ray Graves, on the Florida staff. Rodgers tutored Heisman Trophy winner Steve Spurrier while with the Gators as well as the son of his mentor, Bobby Dodd Jr.

Rodgers' head coaching career began in 1967 at Kansas, and after a stop at UCLA, he returned to his alma mater in 1974. Georgia Tech had tried to hire former assistant and highly successful Arkansas coach Frank Broyles for the job, but he had turned Tech down, telling the athletics director that the school's administration wasn't committed enough to football. Broyles recommended Rodgers, reasoning his personality and option offense could overcome the shortcomings.

Rodgers was "an immediate lightning rod for positive change," said Tech alum and radio broadcaster Kim King in his book, *Kim King's Tales from the Georgia Tech Sideline*. Rodgers had embraced the Southern California lifestyle in his three years in L.A. and brought it home with him. Georgia Tech fans laughed off most of his idiosyncrasies, remembering well the successful days of his playing career. But they disdained his unnaturally curly hair. As Rodgers heard often in his first three seasons coaching on the Flats, "Bear Bryant don't wear no perm."

Rodgers shrugged off the criticism until hearing that his own mother had refused to claim him. Georgia Tech upset Notre Dame without attempting a pass on November 6, 1976, and as Louise Rodgers was leaving Grant Field, she overheard a female fan says, "That was a good win, but I still don't like his hair." Louise initially jumped to her son's defense, but when asked what her relationship was to the coach, she replied that she was his aunt.

"That was the demise of my permanent," Rodgers said. "I cut my hair the next day."

He kept the motorcycle and the strange stretching sessions, though, and in 1978 led Georgia Tech to its first national ranking since the 1971 preseason poll and the program's first bowl appearance since 1972. Tech fired Rodgers following a 4–6–1 showing in 1979 and hired another alum, Bill Curry, as his replacement.

Rodgers' players, even the veterans he alienated in pushing a "youth movement" upon his arrival at the school, can't help but laugh and shake their heads when asked about Rodgers. "Pepper is Pepper," said Randy Rhino, who played for Rodgers as a senior. "He's a great personality and was a great football coach. You never knew what he was going to do next."

56 The Other Rudy

Rudy Allen heard the chant raining down from the stands and thought it was a taunt. "Ru-dy! Ru-dy! Ru-dy!" But the Notre Dame fans weren't calling to the Georgia Tech quarterback that sunny afternoon in 1975. And what Allen thought were jeers were actually cheers for the other Rudy on the field: Notre Dame's Dan "Rudy" Ruettiger.

What happened next made one Rudy a legend and the other a footnote. Ruettiger, a 5'6", 165-pound walk-on defensive end, sacked Allen on the game's final play. What was just another play for Allen turned out to be the climax of one of the most inspirational stories in sports history. Hollywood would make a movie about Notre Dame's Rudy: how he had dreamt of playing for the Irish as a child, how dyslexia held him back academically and

Rudy Allen was the quarterback sacked by Notre Dame's Dan "Rudy" Ruettiger in a 1975 game. Ruettiger was the inspiration for the 1993 film Rudy. *The sack of Allen marks the climax of the movie.*

resulted in his applying for admission to Notre Dame four times before he was accepted, how he spent his playing career on the scout team and didn't dress for a game until the home finale of his senior year. And how Rudy recorded a sack on the last snap of that game against Georgia Tech and was carried off the Notre Dame Stadium field on the shoulders of his teammates.

Allen didn't notice the post-sack celebration—he barely noticed the sack itself. He'd been under pressure from Irish defenders all afternoon and was anxious to escape Indiana farm country and return to Atlanta. The first time Allen saw the Hollywood version of the sack and celebration he let out a triumphant whoop. Never mind that he was the one being sacked. He admits he still gets goose bumps when Ruettiger, as played by actor Sean Astin in the 1993 film *Rudy*, makes the life-defining tackle.

"For him to fulfill a lifelong dream like that, that's special to me," Allen said. "And when you really think about it, we had a lot in common. He overcame tremendous odds, and so did I." Allen was the second African American quarterback in Georgia Tech history. Considering the career of his predecessor, Eddie McAshan, being first might have been easier.

McAshan was a tremendous player. He started three seasons and set several school passing records. Yet his career ended in controversy. A squabble with the school over game tickets for the home finale of his career led to McAshan being suspended for the 1972 Liberty Bowl. The suspension spawned an NAACP protest and a slew of death threats.

Into McAshan's spot stepped Allen in 1973. "By the time I came to Tech, you could look around Division I football and see only a handful of minority quarterbacks," Allen said. "And then for me, after the Eddie McAshan deal, to be the next minority quarterback, it put a lot of pressure on me."

A coaching and scheme change complicated Allen's football life. Georgia Tech replaced Bill Fulcher and his pro-style passing offense with Pepper Rodgers and the wishbone heading into Allen's junior season.

Allen was a 6'4", 200-pound pocket passer, not a running back trained to read defenses and pitch balls to other running backs. Allen lost the starting quarterback job to a converted defensive back. But he still saw plenty of action. The wishbone is not conducive to coming from behind. When Georgia Tech trailed in games, Allen went in to try and pass them back into contention. He rallied the Yellow Jackets to two victories in his junior year and saw significant playing time as a senior in 1975.

The Yellow Jackets fell behind Notre Dame early in the ninth game of the 1975 season. Allen played much of the second half, including the last series. Allen says his offensive tackle threw a "look out" block at Ruettiger on the final play—as in, "We're too tired to block, so look out, quarterback."

Allen didn't get the message. And history will forever remember Rudy for it.

# Marco Coleman

Every sports fan loves the long shot. They love to root for them, bet on them, and ruminate on them. And in the rare instance where the long shot overcomes all the adversity—be it circumstances or obstacles—he becomes a legend.

Marco Coleman is that legendary long shot. Granted, he was a physical marvel at 6'4" and 240 pounds with a quickness and athleticism that made him nearly impossible for opponents to block. But for Coleman to become a two-time All-American and break Georgia Tech's sack records, he had to get on the field first.

Coleman grew up in Dayton, Ohio, the son of a Baptist minister. School was neither easy nor enjoyable for him as a child, which led him to enroll at a vocational high school. The school allowed him to divide his time between the classroom and one of the local factories, where he worked with sheet metal and air-conditioning systems. After hours, he played football for Progressive High School.

Yet a math teacher and a guidance counselor encouraged him to focus on his studies. Coleman began to excel on the football field about the same time one of his teammates, defensive end Derrick Foster, was attracting college recruiters to Progressive's games. The coaches quickly took notice of Coleman, surprising no one more than Coleman himself. "You see, college was an opportunity he never foresaw," his high school coach, Dave Vail, told a newspaper

Marco Coleman recorded 13 sacks and was the defensive catalyst during Georgia Tech's 1990 national title run.

reporter in 1994. The recruiting interest was the nudge Coleman needed to take more of an academic interest. By his senior year, he'd shown enough progress to attract scholarship offers from Purdue, Tennessee, and Georgia Tech. He chose Tech because of head coach

Bobby Ross and the "reputation of the school…the academic reputation more than the athletic reputation."

Coleman spent his first semester at Georgia Tech focusing on
academics. He redshirted for the 1988 season, and as the team
struggled to a 3–8 mark, he started to feel ill. By the time he
returned home for the holidays, he was suffering intense abdominal
pain. His parents took him to the hospital, where doctors discovered his appendix had burst more than a week earlier. He
underwent an emergency appendectomy. He lost 38 pounds during
the ordeal, and the surgeon told his parents he was lucky to be alive.

Coleman gained the weight back by the time spring practice
started and, as an *Atlanta Journal-Constitution* writer cleverly put it,
went from the "top of the death chart to the top of the depth
chart." Georgia Tech lost six veteran linebackers from the 1988
team, and the position was considered a glaring weak spot. It didn't
turn out to be, not with Coleman, Jerrelle Williams, and Calvin
Tiggle stepping in.

Coleman made an immediate impact that fall. With Williams
roaming the field and getting in on nearly every tackle—145 in
1999—Coleman became a pass-rush specialist in defensive coordinator George O'Leary's 3-4 defense. Coleman had the size to line
up as a defensive end and the speed and agility to back off the line
of scrimmage. He did both, and finished his first season with five
sacks and five more tackles for loss.

Coleman became a household name with college football fans
the next season. His five sacks of Maryland quarterback Scott Zolak
in the fourth game of the 1990 season garnered him national attention. The Terrapins refused to double-team him, at least early in the
game, and Coleman "was a monster," teammate Thomas Balkcom
said. "He was Maryland's worst nightmare." Georgia Tech quarterback Shawn Jones said the best part of the win was the fact he plays
with Coleman, not against him. That Coleman was suffering from
a cold that day and struggled to catch his breath throughout the

first quarter only adds to the story.

Coleman finished the season with 12½ sacks and was the defensive catalyst behind the Yellow Jackets' run to the 1990 national title. Coleman added 10 more sacks the next season to break the program's sack record in just three seasons of play. He decided to leave early for the NFL following the 1991 season. By that time, Coleman had found the self-confidence he lacked during his pre-Tech days. Asked at the press conference in which he announced his decision where he thought he would go in the draft, Coleman gave the reporter a funny look. "Where do you think?" he responded. Coleman thought he would go first (he went 12th overall).

He was a long shot no longer.

58 Homered in Steel City

If you can't beat 'em, cheat 'em.

Pittsburgh's Pop Warner used just such an approach against Georgia Tech on November 23, 1918, and snapped one of the longest unbeaten streaks in college football in the process. Georgia Tech arrived in the Steel City more than four years removed from its last loss. Coach John Heisman's Golden Tornado had won or tied 33 straight games, winning the last 18.

Georgia Tech showed no signs of losing anytime soon. The 1918 team had shut out its first five opponents and scored more than 100 points in three of those games, building on the dominance of the 1917 national championship team despite starting eight freshmen. Most of the would-be veterans missed the 1918 season due to military service in World War I.

Pitt featured an equally stout squad. The Panthers went undefeated in 1917 and were on their own 30-game winning streak. Led

About the 33-Game Unbeaten Streak

Georgia Tech's 7–0 victory over rival Georgia late in the 1914 season launched one of the most dominant runs in college football history. Coach John Heisman's team would win or tie 33 straight games, posting 23 shutouts and scoring 50 or more points in 11 games. The streak included the historic 222–0 win against Cumberland in 1916, the 1917 national title run, and the back-to-back 100-plus-point games against Furman and the 11th Calvary in 1918. The stars of those teams included College Football Hall of Famers Bill Fincher, Buck Flowers, Joe Guyon, and Everett Strupper.

by All-Americans George McLaren, Tom Davies, and Leonard Hilty, Pitt would go on to win the national title in 1918.

But talent had little to do with Pittsburgh's success against Georgia Tech. The home team hired the officials back then, and Pitt's Warner brought in a crew he could influence. He convinced the officials that Georgia Tech's pre-snap formation change—the so-called "Heisman shift"—was illegal, and the referee threw penalty flags from the first play on.

Heisman complicated the situation. Too stubborn to adjust his strategy, he instructed his offense to continue shifting. The Panthers won easily, 32–0. In a classic case of what comes around goes around, Pitt lost two games later because of the officiating. The Panthers played their season finale at Cleveland Naval Reserve and were driving for a score late in the first half when the officials discovered the official timekeeper's watch had malfunctioned and whistled the half over. Then Warner and several reporters covering the game alleged the officials granted Cleveland Naval Reserve extra time at the end of the game to score the winning points.

Ironically, Cleveland Naval Reserve's hero was quarterback Judy Harlan—a star on Georgia Tech's 1917 team who ended up playing with the reservists as part of his military service. Pitt would be named consensus national champion anyway. The Panthers 4–1 record was two wins shy of Georgia Tech's—a Spanish flu pandemic and resulting quarantines led to the cancellation of Pitt's first five games that season—but the convincing victory over the Golden Tornado swayed the voters.

Georgia Tech failed to take its revenge in the rematch the next season. In another game played in Pittsburgh, this time with less-impressionable officials, the Panthers snapped a six-game Tech winning streak dating back to the 1918 game between the two teams with a 16–6 victory.

The Golden Tornado would lose two more games late in the 1919 season. Heisman would resign following a 14–7 loss to Auburn in the season finale.

59 Robert Lavette

They referred to him as "Ramblin'" Robert Lavette, and he wrecked everybody and everything in his path between 1981 and 1984, including defenders, record books, and yes, the patches of turf victimized by his celebratory break-dance exhibitions and his tendency to vomit up his game-day breakfast of steak and eggs.

Lavette carried the ball almost 1,000 times for more than 4,000 yards in his career and posted 100-yard rushing performances in nearly half of his games. That so few noticed—and fewer still remember—is not Lavette's fault. He played much of his career in the long shadow cast by the star tailback of the state's other major college team, Georgia's Herschel Walker. And Lavette played on some of Tech's less-heralded teams: the Jackets never won more than six games in a season and failed to reach a bowl game during Lavette's tenure.

Lavette treated every game like a bowl. He posted 100-yard rushing games 18 times, and in few of those did he struggle to reach

Robert Lavette is Georgia Tech's all-time leading rusher. He rushed for 4,066 yards and 45 touchdowns in four years as a starter. He was a workhorse, with 914 carries in his career— 200 more rushes than any other back in program history.

the century mark. He rushed for 145 yards or more in 10 of those games and posted a career-high 203 yards on 38 carries in a head-to-head showdown with Walker in 1982. Lavette's position coach, Rip Scherer, credited Lavette's vision for his effectiveness. "[Lavette] sees things," Scherer told a *Sports Illustrated* reporter for a 1984 story. "I ask him, 'Why did you make this cut?' and he doesn't know."

"What he does," an NFL scout said of Lavette during his senior season, "is make you miss."

And miss and miss and miss. Head coach Bill Curry remembers seeing Lavette play for the first time in a high school game. "He didn't look like Gale Sayers or Walter Payton or those guys, but his results made you feel like you were watching somebody who was great. It was like magic," Curry said. Lavette wowed Curry again in his first practice as a Tech freshman. Carrying the ball in a 3-on-3 drill, Lavette bounced off one defender, caught himself with one hand, ran over a second defender, and kept going.

"Nobody say anything to Lavette about how he should play football," Curry told his assistant coaches that afternoon.

Lavette started all four years and averaged better than 20 carries a game. The 5'11", 190-pounder's conditioning and durability were unsurpassed. He carried 31 or more times in five games and got stronger as games went on. Defensive coordinator Don Lindsey liked to call the leader of his defense at the time, Pat Swilling, the "Bell Cow." To use a similar analogy, Lavette was the offense's workhorse. Consider this: he carried 200 more times in his career than the next closest rusher on Georgia Tech's career rushing attempts list.

"His toughness, it was so intuitive," Curry said. "It was a gift. Like all great running backs, Robert was bow-legged and had great balance. It was really hard to get a shot in on him. He avoided a lot of potential injuries."

Curry liked to talk about Lavette's great "two-yard runs"— defenses were keying on him by the middle of his sophomore year, but he'd grind out yardage anyway and then break long runs late. The only thing that slowed Lavette down at Tech was a sprained ankle that plagued him throughout his junior season. He still rushed for 800 yards that year.

While Lavette could never complain about not getting the ball enough, his career was still marked by frustration. Georgia Tech lost often in his four years. His freshman year, the Yellow Jackets stunned No. 4 Alabama in the opener—with Lavette scoring two touchdowns in his debut—only to lose their remaining 10 games. Failure ate at Lavette's insides in much the same way as his vomit-inducing game-day breakfasts. "I really hated the place," Lavette said. "I considered leaving, and I went in to talk about it to Coach Curry, and he was as frustrated as I was."

Curry's commitment to turning the program around kept Lavette on the Flats. Three years later, Georgia Tech opened the season 3–0, with wins against two ranked teams. The Yellow Jackets briefly moved into the national rankings—their first appearance in the polls since the 1978 season—before losing four of the next six games.

Lavette posted six 100-yard games as a senior, made third-team All-America, and rewrote the school record book.

The Swarm

The pack wears yellow. Matching yellow wigs and yellow body paint. Well, not all Tech students in the Swarm—the unique flock of young fans corralled into special seating sections behind the north end zone of Bobby Dodd Stadium—wear body paint on bare chests. Some where the paint over sports bras (the group is coed, after all) and some eschew the decoration altogether in favor of

The Swarm, a student organization, cheers on the Yellow Jackets from a special section in the north end zone of Bobby Dodd Stadium.

yellow shirts. Those who do sport the paint spell out allegiances to their school, such as "Yellow Jackets," or their disdain for an opponent, such as "To Hell with UGA."

The dedicated cheering section is popular with the television cameramen, not to mention the football team, which emerges from underneath the stadium right next to the Swarm. The team joins the Swarm in singing "Ramblin' Wreck from Georgia Tech" after games. Swarm students gather in the front rows of the north end zone at football games and several hundred are allowed to stand behind the baskets of Alexander Memorial Coliseum during basketball games.

The Swarm was started in 1996 by a female with the Ramblin' Reck Club. She wanted the students to have a more unified presence in the stands. At that time, her request generated 250 followers. The group now numbers more than 1,000.

All Swarm members donate to the Alexander-Tharpe fund, which raises money to pay for Tech student-athlete scholarships. Yet that donation does not guarantee a particular seat. Because all Swarm seating is general admission, members run to secure their seats once the gates open. The tradition is known as "the Running of the Swarm." Once in their seats, they may come face-to-face with Buzz the mascot. The busy yellow jacket often jumps into the section and is passed from person to person above their heads, literally surfing the crowd.

61 "Black Watch" Defense

The culture was broken. Georgia Tech's defense had the talent, it just lacked the attitude. According to no less an authority than head coach Bill Curry, the 1983 Yellow Jackets "couldn't slow down the Little Sisters of the Poor," despite being anchored by game-changers like Ted Roof and Pat Swilling.

Curry needed a culture-changer, and he found one in Don Lindsey. At age 41, Lindsey already wore national title rings on four fingers—three from his years with John McKay and John Robinson at Southern Cal, and one from a stint with Bear Bryant at Alabama. His X-and-O prowess alone didn't account for that fistful of bling. Lindsey was as good a psychologist as he was a tactician.

Lindsey saw a common trait among his Georgia Tech charges. All were competitive, but only one could channel that aggression: Roof. "He was a special kind of leader," Curry said of Roof. "He was such a dominant presence. If we could get more guys to play like him, we knew we'd have something."

So Lindsey employed a tried-and-true technique: helmet stickers, but with a twist. Instead of awarding individual stickers for individual accomplishments, à la Ohio State's buckeye leaves, Lindsey took Roof's headgear and decorated it with a thick black stripe down the middle and a black GT emblem on the side.

Roof became the charter member of the "Black Watch" defense. Lindsey left it to Roof to invite others who demonstrated the attitude of the Black Watch, a famed and feared Scottish military regiment that grew out of a police band charged with watching and protecting the Scottish highlands in the 1700s. Curry learned about the Black Watch while on vacation in Scotland the summer before and recommended the name to Lindsey.

"They were tough ornery guys who wore black tartan," Curry said. "A guide told me the enemy the Germans feared most in World War I was the 'women from hell.' We weren't going to put them in kilts, but it sounded like a good idea."

The legend and the helmet stickers sufficiently motivated Georgia Tech's defenders. And the results were immediate: Georgia Tech opened the 1984 season by holding No. 19 Alabama to six points and The Citadel to three the following week.

The Black Watch's ranks began to swell. Swilling and Riccardo Ingram joined first, followed by linebacker Jim Anderson and defensive backs Mark Hogan and Cleve Pounds and defensive lineman Ken Parker. By season's end, the Yellow Jackets had yielded an average of 18 points a game, down from 28 the year before.

"A thing like that can divide a team, but our guys seemed to be on board with the entire concept," Roof said. "They identified the black stripe with toughness and a physical style of play, and as a defensive football player, those are the characteristics you want associated with the way you play."

A season later, 1985, with Mark White, Mark Pike, and others earning their black stripes, Georgia Tech yielded just 11 points per game, finished with a 9–2–1 record and won a bowl game for the first time since 1972. The defense's attitude finally matched its talent and provided the swagger all great defenses possess. The Black Watch became notorious for its ferocious play. As Roof still likes to say, "Slow guys don't make plays," and Black Watch members never played cautiously. Roof, Swilling, and Pounds all made all-conference teams. "The defense showed they were made of something special," Curry said. "I was proud of that."

As for Lindsey, he nearly was given an opportunity to bring the Black Watch attitude to both sides of the ball. Homer Rice, Georgia Tech's athletics director at the time, considered promoting Lindsey when Curry resigned to take Alabama's head coaching job following the 1986 season. Rice offered the position to Bobby Ross, who had won three recent ACC titles at Maryland. If Ross declined, Rice admitted, Lindsey was his man. But Ross took the job, and Lindsey followed Curry to Alabama. Georgia Tech would be the closest he would come to a college head coaching job. He later coached at Missouri, Hawaii, Southern Cal, and Ole Miss but always in a coordinator's role.

Peter Pund

They called him "Peter the Great," and like the more widely recognized man known by the same moniker, Peter Pund led his people to great success. Georgia Tech's football program slipped from its place as a powerhouse in the mid-1920s. John Heisman was long gone, and his successor, William Alexander, struggled to attract star players like the wizard had.

Yet Coach Aleck snatched Pund, one of Georgia's finest high school players, in 1925. The Augusta native was an aspiring engineer as well as a football player and would go on to work as an aeronautical engineer specializing in dirigibles.

Fittingly, Pund was blimp-like on the football field. He stood 6'2" and weighed 200 pounds, a large player for the day. He played center in an era of two-day football and was as renowned for his play as an interior defensive lineman as he was as a blocker.

Pund's Georgia Tech career spanned the renaissance of the program. A senior and captain on the 1928 national championship team, Pund is considered one of greatest linemen of his day. He cleared running lanes for the Yellow Jackets' great runners of the time, Stumpy Thomason and Father Lumpkin, and controlled the

Peter Pund is considered one of the greatest offensive and defensive linemen of football's early years. Notre Dame's legendary coach Knute Rockne once said of Pund, "Nobody could stop him."

line of scrimmage on defense. Pund so impressed Notre Dame coach Knute Rockne in a 1928 game—a 13–0 Georgia Tech victory—that the legendary coach wrote about Pund in helping sportswriter Grantland Rice pick his All-America team following that season.

"I sat at Grant Field and saw a magnificent Notre Dame team suddenly recoil before the furious pounding of one man—Peter Pund. Nobody could stop him," Rockne wrote. "I counted 20 scoring plays that this man ruined. We were hopelessly beaten, but

I had the thrill of my life to see great fighters go down in defeat before a great fighter."

By virtue of the position he played, Pund elicited little media attention. He failed to make Georgia Tech's "all-time team," selected via fan balloting in 1991. Bull Curry was the center while Rock Perdoni, Larry Stallings, and Pat Swilling were the defensive linemen. Yet Pund has received recognition elsewhere. *Sports Illustrated*'s Dan Jenkins, in picking college football's teams by the decade in 1969, named Pund the best center of the 1920s. Pund is also a member of the College Football Hall of Fame as well as the Georgia Tech Hall of Fame and the Georgia Sports Hall of Fame.

The 140 Rule

Georgia Tech friends and foes long have debated the reasons behind the school's departure from the Southeastern Conference in 1963. Uneducated Tech backers claim officials finally realized SEC affiliation didn't match the school's academic mission. SEC proponents say Georgia Tech couldn't cut it with the big boys anymore. Then there are the side issues, like the falling out between the Yellow Jackets' Bobby Dodd and Alabama's Bear Bryant and the disdain the Mississippi schools had for the Jackets over Dodd's refusal to travel to play them.

Good theories all. But all wrong.

Georgia Tech left the league it helped found in the 1890s because of the conference's passage of the "140 Rule." The by-law limited member schools to 140 scholarship athletes in its football and basketball programs combined. The rule is laughable now, with football's scholarship cap at 85 and basketball's at 13. But it was a controversial move at the time, and not for the reason you might think.

Tech's Dodd opposed the rule because it created a pseudo-tryout system for college football. The 140 Rule failed to change the way coaches recruit; they would continue to bring in the maximum allowed, 45 per year. To meet compliance, they'd simply cut the worst of the lot and revoke their scholarships before the season started—well beyond the point when those players could find other colleges to play for. "It is not the recruit's fault for not making the squad, it was the coach's fault for misjudging their talent," Dodd said in his autobiography, *Dodd's Luck*.

Dodd kept every player on scholarship until the day that student-athlete graduated. He recruited 30 to 32 boys a year, which meant Georgia Tech had anywhere from 140 to 160 on scholarship at a time, depending on how many needed a fifth year to graduate. Dodd wanted the SEC to limit recruiting classes to 32 rather than put an overall cap on scholarships. Such a move would eliminate the need for coaches to cut the players they deemed undesirable.

Dodd almost politicked his version of a scholarship cap into law. The issue split conference presidents, with Alabama's Frank Anthony Rose holding the deciding vote. Dodd lobbied Bryant to convince his president to cast his ballot in favor of Dodd's rule. The Bear agreed but then didn't show up at the voting meeting.

Rose went against Dodd's proposition, upholding the 140 Rule. Georgia Tech's president, Edwin Harrison, announced the school's withdrawal from the conference moments after the voting results were revealed.

Georgia Tech spent the next 20 years as an independent in a failed attempt to become the "Notre Dame of the South." The school's football program joined the Atlantic Coast Conference in 1983. Dodd later acknowledged leaving the SEC was the right move for Georgia Tech from a competitive standpoint, given the school's increasingly stringent academic requirements. Hence the rise of the Tech apologists and the SEC's vocal elitists.

"I just could not compete with those damn state universities that could take these same boys we couldn't take, who wanted to come and play for me," Dodd said in his autobiography. "And it just broke me down. I couldn't beat 'em. You can just outcoach 'em some of the time, brother. Better football players will beat you."

Eddie McAshan

Eddie McAshan polarized the Georgia Tech community when he began his football career, and he divided the Yellow Jackets faithful again on his way out. Unfortunately, all his accomplishments in between often get lost.

McAshan became the first black scholarship player in Tech history when he signed in 1969. He became the first black quarterback to start for a major program in the Deep South a year later. Fast forward to the end of his senior year, when a disagreement over acquiring extra tickets for his family for his last regular season game led to his boycotting practice, a career-ending suspension, and a racially charged protest before and during the 1972 Liberty Bowl.

That McAshan rewrote Georgia Tech's passing records and led the Yellow Jackets on a rare three-season run of success in the post–Bobby Dodd era—not to mention his playing a large role in integrating one of the South's most storied programs—are almost nothing more than footnotes on the story of McAshan's career.

McAshan was going to be a trailblazer somewhere, simply by virtue of his birth date. Kentucky became the first major southern program to integrate in 1967, and by the fall of 1968, most schools were recruiting African Americans. McAshan was a top target. A football and basketball standout in the Gainesville, Florida, school district—which he'd been a part of integrating in 1964—McAshan drew interest from Georgia Tech, Miami, and his hometown college, the University of Florida.

"He had good speed, a great throwing arm, and he was a great leader," Tech's director of recruiting at the time, Jack Thompson, said. "We looked at Eddie as a quarterback rather than a black quarterback."

McAshan's arrival at Georgia Tech did not go unnoticed, but it wasn't until he won the starting job prior to the 1970 season that controversy erupted. Then McAshan led the Yellow Jackets to an upset of 17th-ranked South Carolina in his debut and Florida State the next week. The wins put the Jackets back into the national rankings for the first time since Dodd's last game in 1966. Georgia Tech would finish 9–3 that season, with a victory over rival Georgia and a Sun Bowl win against Texas Tech.

By the time the 1971 season kicked off, McAshan's skin color didn't matter to the Georgia Tech fans much anymore. Another African American, tailback Greg Horne, joined the backfield in 1971. McAshan had another solid season in 1971, cutting down on the interceptions that plagued him his first year. As a senior, McAshan threw for 16 touchdowns in 10 games. "He could really play," said Randy Rhino, a first-year player in 1972. "He was our leader, our quarterback."

McAshan had Georgia Tech on the verge of another successful season going into the finale against Georgia in Athens. His family, not knowing if it would be McAshan's last game, asked him to get as many tickets as possible. McAshan contacted the football office the Thursday before the game and was denied. The game was on the road, and Georgia Tech received a limited number of tickets.

A disgruntled McAshan skipped practice that afternoon and didn't make the trip to Athens with his teammates. He met with coach Bill Fulcher the night before the game and was suspended for abandoning the team.

Georgia Tech lost to Georgia, but the Yellow Jackets still received a Liberty Bowl bid. McAshan believed his suspension would be lifted for the bowl—he practiced with the team leading up to the game. But Fulcher did not lift the ban, and when word got out, the situation took on racial overtones. The NAACP picketed outside the stadium in Memphis. McAshan was prohibited from attending and listened to the game from the back of civil rights leader Jesse Jackson's limousine in the stadium parking lot. Georgia Tech's other black players participated in the game under threat of losing their scholarships but wore black armbands to show their support for McAshan. Jackson would call McAshan the "Jackie Robinson of black college football." But McAshan didn't care about that. He just wanted to play.

Eddie McAshan (1) broke the color barrier at Georgia Tech in 1969 and was the first black quarterback to start for a major college team in the South.

McAshan got his degree from Georgia Tech in 1979, although he didn't patch things up with the football program until 1995, when he was installed in the school's Hall of Fame. Other quarterbacks had broken his records by then. Shawn Jones, an African American, held most of the marks at the time, and another black quarterback, Joe Hamilton, would later surpass Jones. Neither went through what McAshan did, and that, McAshan said, may be his greatest accomplishment at Georgia Tech.

"God's got his blazers," McAshan said. "We just all have a purpose."

65 George P. Burdell

George P. Burdell won three football letters at Georgia Tech, in 1928, 1929, and 1930. Burdell attended classes, took tests, and graduated with a bachelor's degree in 1930. He added a master's a few years later. He lettered in basketball in the late 1950s and registered for every class Georgia Tech offered in 1969.

In between, he served in World War II as both a B-17 bomber crewman in the Army and a seaman in the Navy, married an Agnes Scott College student, and worked for *Mad* magazine.

He's attended nearly every Georgia Tech away football game, if the public-address announcements in his name are any indication, for decades. And he has run afoul of the law in many locales, from Augusta to Lincoln, Nebraska.

Burdell is the most accomplished Georgia Tech alum in history. He also doesn't exist.

Burdell was born in the mischievous mind of a new Georgia Tech student in 1927. Ed Smith enrolled at the school that fall, and the registrar inadvertently gave him two applications. Smith filled

George P. Burdell has racked up numerous varsity letters, degrees, and honors in his lengthy Georgia Tech career, in addition to his various military exploits and philanthropic endeavors.

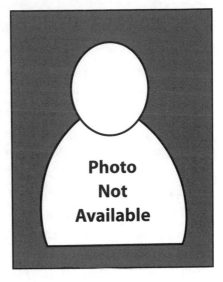

out one for himself and, in what he dubbed a "flippant moment" in a 1977 account published by the *Atlanta Journal-Constitution*, completed the other in the name of George P. Burdell. The "George P." part was a reference to his high school principal at Augusta's Richmond Academy, a former Georgia Bulldogs football player. The surname he stole from a family cat, which had borrowed the name from one of Smith's best friend's mother. Her maiden name was Burdell.

"I rushed out of the registrar's office and down the front steps of the administration building. The first person I saw...I told...about the caper. We both laughed and spread the news," Smith wrote. "That night, a group of us were singing to the accompaniment of the uke and banjo, and between songs we thought up more mischief for George P. Burdell."

Smith and his friends helped get Burdell through school. They registered him for classes and answered for him when professors called the roll. Tests in those days were administered via small notebooks—"blue books"—and Tech's honor system meant instructors rarely spent time in the classroom on test days. Smith or one of his friends would fill out two books, one in Burdell's name. "George

P.'s luck was phenomenal. Invariably, he made better grades than did his master," Smith wrote. "I do not recall his ever making a low grade."

Burdell graduated along with Smith in 1930, and soon after, word of Smith's tomfoolery became public. Other Tech students adopted Burdell and helped him get his master's, basketball letters, and the rest. A Georgia Tech alum listed him on the B-17 flight crew, and another Yellow Jacket, a flight officer, discovered him and forced Burdell to change services and join the Navy.

Burdell even donated money for a room in the Edge Center— the small men's room off the building's lobby, used often by the press and sports communications staff. A simple plastic plaque on the door reads: MADE POSSIBLE THROUGH THE GENEROSITY OF GEORGE P. BURDELL, CLASS OF 1931–1982.

Burdell lives on because as Smith, borrowing from the Ancient Roman poet Horace, wrote, "It is pleasant and proper to be foolish once in a while."

66 Attend the Mini 500

Only at Georgia Tech could a tricycle race upstage a football game. The Mini 500 is the most intense competition on campus during homecoming week. Held annually on the eve of the football game, the Mini 500 attracts teams of seven students—four riders, three pit crew members—from nearly every fraternity, sorority, club, and student organization.

The course is a "modified" oval similar in shape to the Indianapolis Motor Speedway, which is to say it is square. Racers turn laps in the shadow of Bobby Dodd Stadium, using the streets that frame the Peters Parking Deck. Men's teams must complete 15 laps; women do 10. And each team is required to make three pit stops, during which the front tire must be rotated.

The Mini 500 tradition grew out of another Tech tradition: a hazing ritual. Several fraternities in the 1960s forced pledges to ride tricycles around campus. The unusual rite of passage corresponded with an influx of female students, who were first admitted to regular classes in 1952 and couldn't enroll in all programs until 1968. Riding a child's toy to class came with an increased share of embarrassment.

The Ramblin' Reck Club decided to take the idea and ride with it in 1969, organizing the first Mini 500. The race was popular from the start and became a public sensation after the 1984 release of the movie *Revenge of the Nerds*, which featured its own—albeit drunken—version of a tricycle race.

Alcohol is not permitted at the Mini 500, at least not in the pit area. Violating the rule carries a one-year suspension. But since the course is surrounded by fraternity and sorority houses, refreshment is close by. Other rules prohibit spare parts, welding equipment, and power tools and threaten punishment to teams connected to disorderly or unsportsmanlike spectators. Tricycles painted Bulldog red are also taboo.

Crowd control can be a challenge for the Reck Club. Most every year, a handful of spectators show up duct-taped in foam padding and act as speed bumps, lying down in the middle of the course to delay racers.

Racers use various techniques to power their tricycles, as all but the most petite students find it difficult to pedal the small toys. The most popular and effective is to sit side-saddle and use a leg for propulsion.

The Mini 500 is not the only race held during homecoming week. The Freshman Cake Race, a half-mile foot race through campus, dates to 1911. Top finishers receive a baked cake. And the Ramblin' Wreck Parade, featuring classic cars and homemade contraptions and held on the morning of the game, is a take-off on the "Flying Flivver" races of 1929 and 1930. The Flying Flivver was a road race between Atlanta and Athens and featured Dean Floyd Field's original Ramblin' Wreck car.

67 South's Cradle of Coaches

Bill Curry never shies from criticism. As the coach at Alabama in the late 1980s, he returned to his office one day to find the window shattered by a brick. He understood: the Tide had just lost a homecoming game to Ole Miss.

Curry does bristle at false criticism, however, like the accusation that he fired an up-and-coming assistant coach named Steve Spurrier in 1980. Truth is, Georgia Tech dismissed Spurrier and the rest of deposed head coach Pepper Rodgers' staff before hiring Curry as head coach. Spurrier was just two years removed from his NFL career and wasn't yet the wunderkind coach we know today. Rodgers hired him due in large part to a connection between the two: Rodgers was Spurrier's position coach during his playing days at Florida. Curry interviewed Spurrier and the rest of Rodgers' assistants when he arrived at Georgia Tech, but by the time he went to offer Spurrier a job, the not-so-old ball coach had found work as Duke's offensive coordinator and was unavailable. The rest is coaching history.

Spurrier is far from the only coaching legend to cut his teeth on a Georgia Tech whistle. Just as Miami of Ohio was once known as the "cradle of coaches" for producing greats like Paul Brown, Woody Hayes, George Little, Weeb Ewbank, Ara Parseghian, Bo Schembechler, and Jim Tressel, Georgia Tech is the southern equivalent.

Frank Broyles' tenure as Bobby Dodd's offensive coordinator at Georgia Tech in the early 1950s helped launch his illustrious coaching career.

Bobby Dodd, himself a one-time Georgia Tech assistant under another former Georgia Tech assistant, William Alexander, supervised two assistants that went on to build powerhouses: Frank Broyles and Ray Graves. Broyles won a national championship and seven league titles at Arkansas in the 1950s, 1960s, and 1970s, while Graves took Florida to five bowl games in 10 years.

Dodd's successor—and another of his assistants—Bud Carson had two future NFL coaching stars on his staff. Jerry Glanville spent six years on the Flats and would later return to Atlanta to coach the NFL's Falcons. Tom Moore, best known as the glasses-wearing confidant of Peyton Manning as the Indianapolis Colts offensive coordinator, served two seasons under Carson.

A former NFL head coach, Norm Van Brocklin, worked with Pepper Rodgers—and Spurrier—at Georgia Tech in 1979. Van Brocklin coached the running backs. Rodgers' staff at one time also included two future administrators: Floyd Reese, who would go on to serve as the general manager for the NFL's Houston Oilers/ Tennessee Titans; and Dave Braine, who would return to Georgia Tech in 1997 as athletics director.

As for Curry—another one-time Tech assistant—his Georgia Tech staffs included two of the more highly regarded defensive coordinators of the last 35 years. Romeo Crennel coached Curry's defensive line in 1980 before embarking on an NFL career that included Super Bowl titles with the New York Giants and New England Patriots and a brief stint as Cleveland Browns' head coach. Don Lindsey worked for Curry, as well, establishing the "Black Watch" defense. Lindsey was a career assistant who worked for Bear Bryant and Curry at Alabama, Broyles and Lou Holtz at Arkansas, John McKay and John Robinson at USC, Curry at Georgia Tech, Bob Stull at Missouri, Fred von Appen at Hawaii, and David Cutcliffe at Ole Miss.

The 1990s saw five of today's coaching stars don headsets in Georgia Tech's coaching box. Ralph Friedgen and George O'Leary worked as Bobby Ross' coordinators and returned in the mid-1990s. O'Leary worked for and succeeded Bill Lewis in 1995, and Friedgen served as O'Leary's offensive coordinator for three years before landing the Maryland job.

Interestingly enough, another O'Leary assistant and Friedgen coworker, Randy Edsall, replaced Friedgen as Maryland's head coach in 2011 after building a solid program at Connecticut. Former Brigham Young head coach Gary Crowton coordinated Georgia Tech's offense in 1994. And Ted Roof, who worked as the head coach at Duke but found recent fame as the defensive coordinator for Auburn's 2010 national championship team, worked four years for O'Leary.

"I'm not sure you couldn't say a lot of places are cradles of coaches nowadays, with all the moving around coaches do," Curry said. "But Tech has obviously had some terrific guys."

68 Bruin the Bear

Colleges tend to store a bit of everything under stadium grand-stands. Underneath Grant Field in 1929, alongside the spare footballs, goal posts, field maintenance equipment, and concession supplies, lived a 400-pound brown bear.

Bruin was his name, and he belonged to Georgia Tech star half-back Stumpy Thomason. An Atlanta businessman presented Bruin to Thomason and the rest of the 1928 team to honor their Rose Bowl victory over the Cal Bears. Thomason took responsibility for the beast's upkeep, and the two formed a strong bond.

Bruin would often ride shotgun next to Thomason as he cruised the Georgia Tech campus or midtown Atlanta in his car. The bear became as recognizable around town then as Usher or Chipper Jones are today.

Bruin was smart, too. He'd often venture out of his lair under Grant Field's east grandstands and roam the vicinity, poking his snout into trash cans in search of food and his favorite beverages: beer and Coca-Cola. Georgia Tech's dean of students, George Griffin, once said of Bruin, "He is at least as smart as most Tech students, with all the vices of modern youth."

The Atlanta police became so accustomed to calls from alarmed home and business owners citing a bear in their back alley that they would pull up the squad car beside Bruin, coax him into the back, and return him to Grant Field.

Bruin and Thomason grew so close the bear coaxed the football player to postpone a professional career. Thomason's teammate and close friend, Roy Lumpkin, left Georgia Tech following the 1928–1929 school year to play pro ball for the Portsmouth (Ohio)

Spartans, an expansion team in the then-fledgling National Football League.

Lumpkin, a fullback, wanted his backfield mate to join him, but Thomason couldn't stand to leave Bruin in Atlanta. So Lumpkin headed for Ohio, where his refusal to wear a helmet during games made him a folk hero, and Thomason returned to Georgia Tech for his senior season.

Bruin proved far from a lucky charm for Georgia Tech. The Golden Tornado lost more games in the first month of the 1929 season than they had in the previous two seasons combined. They finished with a 3–6 record just one season after winning a national title.

None of the Georgia Tech underclassmen objected when Thomason offered to take Bruin with him as he embarked on his pro career the next spring. Bruin and Thomason relocated to Brooklyn to play for the football Dodgers. Bruin became the Dodgers' mascot, although there's no record of him living under the stands of the Dodgers' stadium, Ebbets Field. Bruin eventually took retirement at a Canadian zoo.

69 Scottish Rite Classic

Thanksgiving in Georgia has always revolved around family, turkey, and football. For three generations, the football attraction was Georgia Tech's and Georgia's freshman teams, not the NFL's Detroit Lions and Dallas Cowboys.

Between 1933 and 1993, Georgia Tech's "Baby Jackets" and Georgia's "Bullpups" met in a charity game at Grant Field. Proceeds went to Scottish Rite Children's Hospital, and the gate receipts covered the hospital's expenses for many years. The *Atlanta*

Constitution's Ralph McGill described the game this way: "Strong legs will run so that weak legs may walk."

The Scottish Rite Classic was one of the biggest football events of the season in Georgia for many years. Between 1933 and 1971, freshmen were ineligible to play varsity football per NCAA rules. That made the Thanksgiving Day game one of the first opportunities for fans to see future stars play. Georgia Tech's Buck Martin, Pepper Rodgers, and Kim King made their Yellow Jackets debuts in the Scottish Rite Classic, as did Georgia legends Charley Trippi, Frank Sinkwich, and Fran Tarkenton.

"We never missed a freshman game when I was a boy; going to it was a tradition," said Randy Rhino, a Georgia Tech legend. "We'd go to the game and then come home and eat Thanksgiving dinner—like most everybody who lived in Atlanta did."

Georgia's Sinkwich, the 1942 Heisman Trophy winner, once called playing in the 1939 Scottish Rite Classic one of the biggest thrills of his career. Sinkwich rushed for more than 200 yards in the Bullpups' 33–0 victory.

The game routinely drew more than 40,000 fans to Grant Field and in its heyday was broadcast across the state on radio. The game's winning team claimed the Governor's Cup trophy, which today goes to the winner of the varsity game played on the Saturday after Thanksgiving.

The Scottish Rite Classic was the brainchild of Georgia Tech coach William Alexander and his counterpart in Athens, Georgia's H.J. Stegeman. Grant Field had hosted a charity college all-star game in 1930, planting the idea in Alexander's head. Three years later, he and Stegeman approached a group of Atlanta businessmen about organizing the game, and the first Scottish Rite Classic was played that Thanksgiving. Georgia won 13–0.

The game was evenly matched throughout the years, with Georgia Tech holding a 30–28–1 advantage. The Baby Jackets won their games in bunches—eight in a 10-year span in the 1940s and

1950s, six in a seven-year span in the 1960s and 1970s, and five in a six-year span in the 1980s and early 1990s—and the games were often close: 29 of the 59 meetings were decided by a touchdown or less.

The Scottish Rite Classic started to lose its appeal once the NCAA lifted its rule forbidding freshman to play in 1974. The freshman game became a JV game featuring benchwarmers and walk-ons rather than up-and-coming stars. By the 1980s, the rosters included volunteer players from the student body. The crowds gradually dwindled, although the game still drew in excess of 10,000 fans.

The last Scottish Rite Classic was played in 1993. The end coincided with the NCAA lowering its scholarship limit to its current level of 85. The two schools attempted to keep the tradition alive with a Legends Game in 1994, but that idea was abandoned after the first year.

70 George O'Leary and Ralph Friedgen

As Georgia Tech assistants, George O'Leary and Ralph Friedgen tackled the rush-hour commute the same way: together. The coworkers and friends were also neighbors—they lived three houses apart on the same street in Marietta—and given Atlanta's notoriously treacherous traffic, they met each morning and car-pooled to work. They talked family and football and gave new meaning to the term "smart car."

By the time they pulled onto campus, they'd swapped enough insights to stuff a new restaurant's comment box. For two coaches who operated largely independent of each other—Friedgen coordinated Georgia Tech's offense, O'Leary the defense—they made each other better. Together, they made the Yellow Jackets a national player during two separate stretches in the 1990s. And that's why you can't separate one from the other in describing their impact on Georgia Tech.

"They approached the game with the same kind of intensity," said Joe Hamilton, who would quarterback under O'Leary and Friedgen in the late 1990s. "They complemented each other very well."

Bobby Ross paired O'Leary and Friedgen in 1987. The Yellow Jackets' new head coach brought Friedgen with him from Maryland, where Friedgen had been Ross' offensive coordinator and developed Boomer Esiason and Frank Reich into quarterbacks defenses feared. Ross hired O'Leary, a hard-nosed up-and-comer, away from Syracuse. Both coaches were schemers, with a penchant for getting the most from their personnel.

Three seasons into their relationship, Friedgen and O'Leary became a dynamic coaching duo. Friedgen took a freshman quarterback named Shawn Jones and molded him into an unpredictable dual-threat player. O'Leary, meanwhile, began to coax a raw toughness from a defense led by two underclassmen, linebacker Marco Coleman and safety Ken Swilling. Three games into that 1989 season—all losses—Ross asked the coordinators to evaluate each other. O'Leary recommended Friedgen incorporate the option more to take advantage of Jones' mobility, while Friedgen encouraged O'Leary to blitz more often to improve the pass rush.

"He's never afraid to speak his mind," O'Leary told a *Baltimore Sun* reporter of Friedgen for a 2004 story. "Ralph is going to tell you what he thinks. I think that's why we get along so well."

Georgia Tech won seven of its remaining eight games in 1989. For the next season, O'Leary added defensive tackle Coleman Rudolph and linebackers Calvin Tiggle and Marlon Williams to his unit, and with Friedgen and Jones putting up 40 or more points in six of 12 games, the Yellow Jackets won a share of the national title.

George O'Leary (background) and Ralph Friedgen twice teamed up to lead Georgia Tech's football program to great success. They first came to Tech as part of Bobby Ross' staff in 1987. O'Leary returned in 1994, became the head coach a year later and hired Friedgen as offensive coordinator in 1996.

O'Leary and Friedgen left Tech, along with Ross, following the 1991 season. Ross had been hired as head coach of the San Diego Chargers, and Georgia Tech decided to hire Bill Lewis rather than take Ross' advice and promote either Friedgen or O'Leary. Hiring one likely would have resulted in the other's staying.

O'Leary returned in 1994 as Lewis' defensive coordinator. Georgia Tech's defense had become atrocious in O'Leary's absence, holding just two opponents under 10 points in two years—and one of those opponents was Division I-AA Furman.

Influential Tech alum and radio color analyst Kim King encouraged athletics director Homer Rice to hire O'Leary back as

Tech's defensive coordinator for the 1994 season. O'Leary was unhappy in the pros, King claimed, and would come back to Tech for the right amount of money. King contacted O'Leary about the job, and after being reluctant initially, O'Leary flew to Atlanta and met with Lewis. O'Leary assured Lewis he wasn't after his job, and Lewis hired him.

O'Leary ended up taking Lewis' job, of course. Rice fired Lewis after a 1–7 start to the 1994 season and named O'Leary interim coach. He proceeded to lose the last three games of the season, prompting an *Atlanta Journal-Constitution* columnist to write, "So, this is what hell looks like."

At the same time Friedgen was coaxing the Chargers offense, led by quarterback Stan Humphries, to Super Bowl XXIX. He stayed one more year in San Diego before rejoining O'Leary at Georgia Tech. He returned to Atlanta for the 1997 season. One season later, Tech won a share of the Atlantic Coast Conference championship. The next year, 1999, the Yellow Jackets won eight games, and Joe Hamilton finished as a runner-up for the Heisman Trophy.

"The No. 1 thing Ralph brings is experience and confidence," O'Leary said in previewing the 1997 season. "He's instilled that confidence back in the offense, that they can strike anywhere with a lot of different players."

Even without Hamilton, Georgia Tech's offense remained potent. George Godsey took over in 2000 and led the Jackets to nine wins. Friedgen's offenses averaged 37 points and 444 yards in the 1998, 1999, and 2000 seasons.

"George O'Leary and Ralph Friedgen were so good together because they would not let you settle for anything less than what they thought was your best. They'd push you past where you thought you could go," Hamilton said. "When you have that on both sides of the ball, you've got something."

The O'Leary-Friedgen combination broke up again following the 2000 season. Friedgen, after 31 years as an assistant, finally landed a head coaching job—at his alma mater, Maryland. Friedgen won an ACC title his first season and 31 games in his first three seasons. He spent 10 years at Maryland but was unable to sustain success. The school fired him following the 2010 season.

O'Leary's career took several strange turns post-Friedgen. Georgia Tech went 8–5 in 2001, a showing that convinced Notre Dame to hire O'Leary away from the Yellow Jackets. His Irish tenure lasted just days, however, as a reporter in New Hampshire discovered O'Leary had embellished his résumé. He was fired and spent the next three seasons as an NFL assistant. He became a college head coach again in 2004 at Central Florida and won two Conference USA titles in his first three years. His Black Knights won another championship in 2010.

With Friedgen now unemployed and semiretired, time will tell if he and O'Leary will team up once again in the carpool lane or on the sideline.

Heisman Hex

The only Georgia Tech man with a connection to the Heisman Trophy is the man the award is named after, coach John Heisman. For all the All-Americans and future NFL stars to play for the Yellow Jackets, none of them won the trophy named in honor of the legend who established Georgia Tech's football program. Quarterbacks Billy Lothridge and Joe Hamilton finished second for the trophy, and halfback Clint Castleberry was third. But all were distant runners-up: Lothridge behind Navy quarterback Roger Staubach in 1963, Hamilton behind Wisconsin tailback Ron

Dayne in 1999, and Castleberry behind Georgia's Frank Sinkwich and Columbia's Paul Governali in 1942.

Some football fans—mostly those with a Yellow Jackets affiliation—claim both Lothridge and Hamilton were robbed by the Heisman voters. Staubach won the award as an underclassman, unheard of at the time, but did post better statistics than Lothridge and led Navy to within a win of a national title.

Hamilton supporters can make a more convincing case: Hamilton threw for more than 3,000 yards, ran for 734 yards, and accounted for 35 touchdowns in 1999, shattering several school and Atlantic Coast Conference records. The winner, Dayne, rushed for 1,834 yards and 19 touchdowns. Dayne's numbers were impressive, to be sure, but many argue Dayne's breaking of the NCAA's career rushing record led to his winning the Heisman as a kind of lifetime achievement award.

Hamilton has never protested the voters' decision. He enjoyed the experience of going to New York City, meeting all the past Heisman Trophy winners, even riding the old-fashioned elevators in the Downtown Athletic Club. "Knowing all the legends who had come up and down the elevator and sat in that room and for me to be in there too...wow," Hamilton said. "You could tell me, 'Joe, you can be invited to the Heisman Trophy ceremony 10 times and

Yellow Jackets in the Heisman Trophy Voting

Year	Player (Position)	Finish
2006	Calvin Johnson (WR)	10th
1999	Joe Hamilton (QB)	2nd
1978	Eddie Lee Ivery (TB)	8th
1966	Lenny Snow (TB)	14th
1963	Billy Lothridge (QB)	2nd
1962	Billy Lothridge (QB)	8th
1943	Eddie Prokop (HB)	5th
1942	Clint Castleberry (HB)	3rd

not win it or only go once and win it,' and I'd take the 10 visits every time. I enjoyed the experience that much."

Several other Georgia Tech players were Heisman contenders. Castleberry's third-place finish came during his freshman year, and those who saw him play say he would have been a Heisman favorite had not his career been cut short by World War II. Castleberry, a bomber pilot, was killed in action.

Castleberry's teammate, Eddie Prokop, finished fifth in 1943 balloting, and tailback Eddie Lee Ivery and wide receiver Calvin Johnson finished in the top 10 in 1978 and 2006 voting, respectively. Lothridge finished eighth in the 1962 Heisman race.

As for Heisman, the trophy was renamed in his honor in 1936. The award was originally known as the Downtown Athletic Club Trophy. Heisman was the club's first athletics director. Neither Heisman nor any of his Georgia Tech players, like stiff-arm aficionado Joe Guyon, were the inspiration for the trophy's famous figurine. Frank Eliscu, a young sculptor commissioned by Heisman to design the award, used a childhood friend, New York University fullback Ed Smith, as the model for the trophy.

Georgia Tech isn't the only program with Heisman ties to suffer a Heisman Trophy hex. Heisman coached at nine schools, including Auburn and Clemson in addition to Tech, and played for two, and only Auburn has ever produced a Heisman winner. Three Tigers—Pat Sullivan, Bo Jackson, and Cam Newton—have won the award.

Notre Dame Draw

The game had none of the makings of an upset: an unbeaten against a team off to its worst start in more than four decades; an offensive juggernaut versus a human sieve; a head coach of 25 years matching wits with a head coach of eight games. Then there was the fact that the underdogs played a tight end at quarterback and a punter with the shanks worse than any weekend duffer.

Yet quite possibly the worst team in Georgia Tech history did upset top-ranked Notre Dame on November 8, 1980...kind of.

The Yellow Jackets and Irish tied 3–3 on what is arguably the most revered football Saturday in the state's history. At about the same time a freshman walk-on tight end named Ken Whisenhunt was quarterbacking Tech to victory—at least from a morale standpoint—Georgia's Lindsay Scott was running away from Florida defenders at a stadium 350 miles to the southeast.

Tech's tie would knock Notre Dame from atop the rankings, and Scott's catch and run would propel the Bulldogs into the top spot. Almost two months later, Georgia would defeat that same Irish team to claim the national title. "We did the Dogs a big favor that day," said Bill Curry, a first-year head coach at the time. "Funny, nobody from over there has ever thanked me."

Curry had inherited a Georgia Tech program on the endangered list. The Yellow Jackets were more than a dozen years removed from Bobby Dodd and had failed in their quest to become the "Notre Dame of the South"—a powerhouse program without a conference affiliation. Tech had recently joined the Atlantic Coast Conference but wouldn't play a league schedule or be eligible for championships until the 1983 season. Some doubted the Yellow Jackets would ever play football as an ACC member, as school administrators contemplated deemphasizing the sport. Hiring Curry, a former player under Dodd who in four years of coaching had never held a position higher than offensive line coach, was a last gasp, and the Jackets seemed to be asphyxiating in his first season. Their one win came against Memphis State, and they'd been beaten by 13 points or more in five of their seven losses coming into the Notre Dame game.

The quarterback situation made a probable loss all but assured. Starter Mike Kelley and backup Ted Peeples were banged up, although Kelley would start and Peeples would play late in the game. Whisenhunt had taken so few snaps at quarterback that when Curry decided to give him some work there during practice earlier that week, Whisenhunt got in the huddle and looked around for the quarterback before realizing it was him.

Curry's quarterbacks coach, Rip Scherer, made sure Whisenhunt knew which position he was to play midway through the first quarter against Notre Dame. Kelley hurt his knee on Georgia Tech's second series, and as a Notre Dame punt rolled dead on Georgia Tech's 5-yard line, Whisenhunt ran onto Grant Field to make his quarterbacking debut. "I was scared to death," Whisenhunt later admitted.

Nerves, not fear, showed in his play. Georgia Tech went three plays and out on the first two possessions with Whisenhunt at quarterback, with his first pass sailing into the grandstands. Then he lost a fumble on his third possession. The miscue sharpened his focus, however, and he led an 11-play drive that culminated in a 39-yard field goal the next time the Yellow Jackets got the ball.

The 3–0 lead stood until the fourth quarter. Georgia Tech made several mistakes, including two short punts that gave Notre Dame good field position and two interceptions, but the Irish answered with miscues of their own. Their kicker missed a short field-goal attempt in the second quarter, freshman quarterback Blair Kiel threw two interceptions, and their running backs lost three fumbles. The Irish needed assistance from Tech, via a 15-yard personal foul penalty, to set up the game-tying field goal with just under five minutes left.

Notre Dame played so poorly Coach Dan Devine elected to punt with 18 seconds left in the game rather than go for it on fourth down. Devine wanted to at least ensure a tie. "I was outcoached," Devine said in the postgame interview. "Tech was more motivated and better prepared."

Word spread quickly. The coach of Notre Dame's next opponent, Alabama's Bear Bryant, telephoned Curry two days after the
tie. Bryant wanted advice, and Curry offered it. Curry's tips helped,
but Alabama still lost to the Irish 7–0.

Georgia Tech returned to losing the next week, too. Navy beat
the Yellow Jackets 19–8 in Grant Field. Then top-ranked Georgia
pounded the Jackets in the season finale. Still, the tie showed
Whisenhunt possessed leadership qualities and that Curry could
coach. Whisenhunt started the next three seasons at tight end and
would later become a successful NFL assistant coach with the
Pittsburgh Steelers and head coach of the Arizona Cardinals. Curry
eventually turned the Yellow Jackets around and eliminated all talk
of deemphasizing the program.

73 Rose Bowl Field

Georgia Tech pockets millions of dollars in bowl money nowadays,
with the cash going toward operating expenses. But the school did
something much more tangible with the football program's first
bowl payout. Tech's take from the 1929 Rose Bowl was never dis-
closed publicly. But Coach William Alexander and his team
returned from Pasadena with enough cash to purchase the large
tract of land on the northwest corner of Fowler and Fifth Street and
turn it into Rose Bowl Field. The deal was arranged by alumnus
George McCarty, the first president of Georgia Tech's famed secret
student organization, the ANAK Society.

The original facility included three football practice fields and
a baseball diamond surrounded by a mammoth stone wall, parts of
which still stand today. The Rose Bowl Field opened in 1930 and

has been the practice facility for every Yellow Jackets football team since.

The site has changed over the years, with one of the football practice fields being sacrificed in the name of the Yellow Jackets track-and-field programs. The track-and-field stadium, located on the north end of the property, opened in 1987.

The baseball section of the property has gradually evolved over the years. The current ballpark, Russ Chandler Stadium, opened in 2002 and provides the football team a measure of privacy by limiting access from Fifth Street.

Even as the baseball and track-and-field teams have made their competitive homes on the Rose Bowl Field site, football has remained the main tenant. The school has gradually upgraded the practice fields, converting one of the two fields to artificial turf in 1980 and erecting an indoor facility over the turf field in 2011.

The indoor practice facility cost $7 million, but Tech didn't need to use any of its recent bowl money for its construction: Georgia Tech alum John Brock, CEO of Coca-Cola, and his wife donated $3.5 million, and the athletics department raised the rest from private sources.

Pranks Aplenty

Pranks play a role in many a college rivalry, be it mascot theft in the Army-Navy series, the defacing of statues on the USC campus the week the school plays UCLA, or the intellectual pranks that make Harvard-Yale so entertaining.

Pranks are likewise a regular occurrence in the Georgia–Georgia Tech rivalry. And the schemes never lack for originality. Consider the first great prank in the series. It involved bovine theft and a touch of hazing. A group of Georgia Tech freshmen, looking to impress their peers, borrowed a milk cow from a local farm and brought him to campus for the game. They slung a hand-printed sign over the cow's back that read: "This ain't no bull. We are going to beat Georgia."

Georgia Tech's football team failed to back up the cud talk, losing 13–0. The halftime and postgame entertainment? On-the-field fisticuffs between students of both schools. The *Atlanta Constitution*'s Ralph McGill described the shiners sported by the combatants afterward as "black-eyed peas."

Tech students took the pranks to Athens in 1945 in perhaps the most storied trick in the rivalry. They put their engineering training to good use, welding the clapper of the Georgia chapel bell to the dome. Georgia was the nation's best team that season, with All-American Charley Trippi in the backfield. Trippi scored all the points in a 33–0 shutout, but the celebration was muted—literally.

The University of Georgia refurbished the bell in 1947, but there is no mention of the incident. The school did allege another bell-related prank, however, noting "remnants of paint reputedly used by Georgia Tech students to paint slogans on the bell in the 1920s."

The Georgia faithful got the last laugh on another clever Tech prank, this one in the midst of the Yellow Jackets' eight-year winning streak against the rivals, a period known as the Drought to Bulldogs fans. A Georgia Tech student launched a remote-control model airplane, decked out in the school's colors, from outside the stadium. After performing a series of aerial acrobatics, the plane landed on the Sanford Stadium turf. At least one Georgia fan sitting close to the landing zone was not impressed with the air show. He jumped from the stands and smashed the plane to bits.

Pranks became less regular after the plane incident. The Georgia Tech band did its part, throwing dog treats at the Georgia sideline and sprinkling foreign grass seed on the Georgia practice

Unsubstantiated Pranks

Rumor has it Georgia Tech fans have stolen Georgia's chapel bell on multiple occasions and the Bulldogs faithful have kidnapped the Ramblin' Wreck car at least twice, but there is no official record of such larceny. Another legend has it that Tech students stole a bronze Bulldog statue from the Georgia campus and buried it under the turf at Grant Field. Again, there is a lack of evidence.

field—in hopes of leaving the initials "GT" behind—during warmups for a game in the 1980s.

The Yellow Jackets band put a less subtle spin on the same idea in 1992. As the band took the field for the halftime show, members rolled out a tarp that covered Georgia's "G" logo at midfield. Painted on the tarp were the letters "GT."

For nine minutes, Georgia Tech's band played, drowned out by the boos of the crowd. The incident was captured on video and uploaded to YouTube, where a member of the Georgia Tech band wrote, "We lost the game, but we won the halftime."

Tech pranksters turned artistic in the 1990s. They painted the Bulldog statue in front of Georgia's Memorial Hall gold one year. In 1999 they adorned the University of Georgia arch with a gold "T." Tech fraternity brothers practiced larceny one year, stealing the bust of former Georgia president Steadman Sanford.

Georgia fans can claim the most noteworthy 21st-century prank. The Bulldogs defeated the Yellow Jackets seven straight years. Georgia Tech's starting quarterback for four of those games was Reggie Ball. Ball was notoriously bad against the rivals, particularly in games at Sanford Stadium. As a sophomore, Ball was driving the Yellow Jackets for the winning score when he lost track of the downs and threw the ball away to avoid a sack on fourth down, thinking it was only third down. And, as a senior, he lost a fumble that Georgia returned for a touchdown and threw a game-sealing interception in the closing minutes.

The prank involved Ball, of course. Late in that 2006 game, a row of Georgia fans sitting behind the end zone lifted up a series of mock jerseys. The uniforms sported the numbers of the four Georgia players to have their numbers retired by the school—Frank Sinkwich's No. 21, Charley Trippi's No. 62, Theron Sapp's No. 40, and Herschel Walker's No. 34—plus a gold jersey with Ball's No. 1 on it.

Funny? Yes. Nice? No. But what else would you expect from fans of the two rivals?

Flunk-Gate

Georgia Tech's football program has suffered its share of humiliations over the years, both on and off the field. Rarely, though, did those embarrassing incidents involve academics. That is, until the spring of 2003.

Ten players, including star tailback Tony Hollings and stud pass rusher Anthony Hargrove, failed out of school that May. Their dismissal triggered an internal eligibility audit that turned up deeper academic issues. A year later, Georgia Tech reported 17 rules violations to the NCAA. A year after that, college athletics' governing body slapped the football program with scholarship reductions and two years' probation for allowing 11 ineligible players to compete over a span of seven seasons. The incidents stained the school's and the program's reputation for high academic standards.

Dating as far back as the 1940s, rivals attempted to use Georgia Tech's rigorous curriculum against the football team. Georgia coach Wally Butts would leave a copy of Georgia Tech's calculus text with in-state recruits, with the message, "Can you pass this?"

Georgia Tech coaches embraced the situation for the most part. Bobby Dodd publicly acknowledged that academic rigors limited the talent on his teams, but only after he retired. George O'Leary, who recruited the eventual flunk-outs, lobbied to get borderline students into school, but did so quietly.

Chan Gailey responded to the news of the 10 ineligible players by encouraging them to continue their educations. "This is a challenging school with high academic standards that will not be compromised," said Gailey, who succeeded O'Leary as Georgia Tech's coach following the 2001 season. "A degree from Georgia Tech is something special."

On the field, the loss of the 10 ineligible players hurt the 2003 Yellow Jackets. They lost three of their first four games while freshman quarterback Reggie Ball learned on the job and former walk-on tailback P.J. Daniels emerged as a rushing threat. Tech improved as the season went on, however, and finished 6–6 to earn a spot in the Humanitarian Bowl. The Yellow Jackets posted a 52–10 win in the bowl game, and the program appeared to have moved past the flunk-gate scandal.

Yet the internal eligibility audit was going on behind the scenes. The 10 players to flunk out revealed the weaknesses in the athletics department's academic advising staff. The audit showed that the advising staff had counted non-degree-applicable courses toward the number of hours student-athletes needed to earn toward graduation to remain eligible. In many cases, the academic advising staff had credited players with nine or more hours that should not have counted toward their degrees. Advisors also credited players with hours in classes related to their majors in which they got D's; school guidelines required a C or better for the class to count toward graduation.

The revelations shamed the Georgia Tech fan base and prompted Dave Braine to turn the introduction of the Georgia Tech Athletic Association's 2004–2005 annual report into an apology: "We deeply regret the mistakes which allowed some of our student-athletes to participate while ineligible. The errors were inadvertent but harmful nonetheless, and we are very sorry."

Georgia Tech would feel the pain of the resulting NCAA sanctions for years to come. Gailey signed a smaller-than-normal recruiting class in 2005 in a sort of preemptive strike in advance of the NCAA's leveling penalties. Yet Gailey issued the unused scholarships to four walk-ons—as a reward for their dedication to the program—and angered the NCAA in the process. Instead of limiting Georgia Tech's recruiting classes in 2006 and 2007, the NCAA cut the program's scholarship maximum from 85 to 79 for those two seasons.

Georgia Tech didn't fully recover from the sanctions until 2009, by which time Gailey had been fired and Braine retired. The hit to the program's academic reputation, however, will never heal, at least in the eyes of some alumni and fans.

76 Joshua Nesbitt

Joshua Nesbitt wanted to play quarterback. Not safety, the position at which Georgia coaches hinted he belonged. Not outside linebacker, where Florida State's brass envisioned him playing. Quarterback. And a quarterback in a pro-style system.

Georgia Tech coach Chan Gailey offered Nesbitt both on signing day 2007. Given that Gailey had started a quarterback similar in style to Nesbitt—Reggie Ball—for four years, Nesbitt knew he would have a chance to play right away. And Gailey's reputation for designing an offense around a dual-threat quarterback, as he did with Kordell Stewart as the Pittsburgh Steelers' offensive coordinator in the 1990s, appealed to Nesbitt, too. So he signed

Joshua Nesbitt came to Georgia Tech to run a pro-style offense only to develop into one of college football's best option quarterbacks in recent memory.

with the Yellow Jackets. Ten months later, he wondered if he'd made a mistake.

Gailey and his pro-style offense were out; Paul Johnson and his triple-option were in. Nesbitt looked like a prototypical option quarterback at 6'2" and 220 pounds, but he didn't want to be a system quarterback. At least not that system. He'd quarterbacked a wing-T offense his first two years in high school. When his coach, Larry Milligan, scrapped the old-fashioned rushing attack in favor of a spread passing attack prior to Nesbitt's junior season, the quarterback rejoiced.

Even before Johnson was introduced as the new coach, Nesbitt let it be known he considered himself a pocket passer who could scramble, not a runner who could throw. Yet he was in line to be the starter as a sophomore, and so elected to give Johnson a chance. The decision turned out to be wiser than the one he made in attending Georgia Tech in the first place.

Georgia Tech has a long history of unlikely greats at the quarterback position. From Wade Mitchell in the mid-1950s and Billy Lothridge in the 1960s to Shawn Jones and Joe Hamilton in the 1990s, the best Yellow Jackets quarterbacks are the ones few forecast as stars.

Nesbitt didn't foresee himself becoming a great option quarterback. He was wrong. Nesbitt finished his career in 2010 as the top rushing quarterback in Atlantic Coast Conference history. He was on pace to become just the eighth quarterback in major-college football history to both rush and pass for 3,000 yards in a career until he broke his arm with four games remaining in his senior season.

His greatest contributions at Georgia Tech had nothing to do with stats, however. His leadership, particularly during the 2009 ACC championship run, was invaluable to the point of being remarkable—so much so that he went into the next season as a Heisman Trophy candidate. Surrounded by future NFL playmakers, Nesbitt took over several games in 2009. He made two of the biggest plays in recent Yellow Jackets history during that charmed season, converting a fourth-down run in overtime against Wake Forest and stripping a fumble recovery away from a defender late in a victory over Florida State.

The season made the humble, unassuming Nesbitt a cult hero around campus and among the Georgia Tech fan base. He attracted national attention prior to his senior season by changing his name from Josh to Joshua—he and his mother thought his full name sounded "more businesslike"—and starring in a unique Heisman marketing campaign that featured Nesbitt in a spoof of a popular beer commercial. Instead of "the most interesting man in the world" as touted in the beer ad, Nesbitt was "the most interesting player in college football." He failed to captivate the country quite to that extent in a season dominated by Auburn's Cam Newton, who did win the Heisman. But he will always be remembered as one of the most interesting players in Georgia Tech football history.

77 Wreck Tech Pajama Parade

The brakes screamed as the train bearing Georgia Tech's football team on its first road trip to Auburn approached the station platform. The locomotive and its load failed to slow, however, and rolled on past and into the Alabama countryside. The train finally stopped several miles down the track. An investigation revealed the rails approaching and leaving the station were lathered with a thick coat of grease. Faced with no alternative, Tech's 1896 team got off and walked to the playing field. When the weary Blacksmiths climbed back aboard for the return trip to Atlanta, they were wincing from a 45–0 loss.

Auburn students later claimed credit for the greased rails. A pajama-clad group of coeds had snuck onto the tracks the night before and done the deed. Two years later, with Tech set to return for the season opener, Auburn's administration threatened railgreasers with expulsion. The brass camped out to guard the tracks only to be overrun by thousands of grease-toting students. The "Wreck Tech Pajama Parade" tradition was born.

Georgia Tech eventually balked at the ritual. The two programs continued to play, due in large part to their close proximity, meeting 90 times in a 96-year span between 1892 and 1987. But every game in the rivalry between 1906 and 1959 was played in Atlanta, and Georgia Tech didn't visit Auburn again until 1974— by which time they rode buses to the game. The two teams met five times at Legion Field in Birmingham in the 1960s.

Yet the Wreck Tech Pajama Parade continued in the form of an impromptu pep rally.

Needless to say, the Georgia Tech–Auburn rally is a colorful one. It is marked by unfathomable streaks: Georgia Tech lost 16 of the first 18 meetings but would lose to Auburn only once in the 16 matchups following that stretch. The Jackets won 13 in a row in the 1940s and early 1950s only to lose seven in a row in the 1970s and nine straight in the 1980s. The swings in the rivalry were so pronounced, one Tigers player who suffered through three losses during the 13-game drought admitted his team was psychologically beaten before the game even started. "When Auburn finally beat Tech [in 1955], we were three-touchdown favorites and won by two points," said Vince Dooley, an Auburn defensive back between 1951 and 1953 and later the coach at Georgia Tech's biggest rival, Georgia.

The Yellow Jackets and Tigers were Thanksgiving Day foes for a time, and the rivalry was once considered as big for the two programs as the annual showdowns with their in-state nemeses, Georgia and Alabama. The schools suspended the series in the late 1980s but played twice in the 2000s. The Yellow Jackets upset ranked Auburn teams in both meetings, snapping the Tigers' 15-game winning streak in the 2005 season opener, after Auburn had gone undefeated in 2004. The 2005 game was in Auburn. Georgia Tech wasn't tired, though. The Yellow Jackets rode motor-coaches, not a train, to the game, and the buses delivered them right outside the stadium.

78 The Bruise Brothers

Joe Hamilton and his Georgia Tech offensive peers abided by the old football adage "keep your head on a swivel" every time they stepped on the Rose Bowl practice field in the mid-1990s. With Ron Rogers and Keith Brooking stalking them across the line, every back, lineman, and receiver knew to keep the linebacker duo known as the "Bruise Brothers" on his personal radar.

"Ron Rogers and Keith Brooking practiced and played the same way: hard and to the fullest, leave nothing out there," Hamilton said. "They brought the lunch pail with them everywhere."

Rogers' and Brooking's intensity produced 902 tackles in their careers and countless more in practice. Their unwillingness to curb their aggressiveness in practice led head coach George O'Leary to often throw one or both of them out of practice to minimize the bruises absorbed by the offense.

"Coach would want me to go easy, but there are just times when it's hard," Rogers said. "You get so excited and you want to hit somebody. I think Coach O'Leary understood and appreciated the effort, but he was trying to control practice."

The Bruise Brothers certainly left a legacy at Georgia Tech. Yellow Jackets history is dotted with great linebacker tandems, from the Morrises—George and Larry—of the 1950s to the anchors of the "Black Watch" defense—Ted Roof and Jim Anderson—in the 1980s to Marco Coleman and Jerrelle Williams in the early 1990s. But no pair changed the culture quite like Brooking and Rogers. Their professed desire to "come with pain" became a point of pride for future tandems, like Daryl Smith and Keyaron Fox and Philip Wheeler and KaMichael Hall.

"When your best players are the ones going hard and finishing the drill and giving the most effort, it's contagious," Hamilton said. "The guys who followed them played the same way, and that got passed on down the line."

Matt Miller, who succeeded Brooking in the Georgia Tech lineup, said the lesson he learned from the Bruise Brothers was, "You can't take one play off. Every day in practice, I mean, it didn't matter what day it was, no matter how tired he was, [Brooking] was always giving 110 percent."

Brooking and Rogers shared a similar approach to football, but they came to Georgia Tech from different directions. Brooking was a well-known football player in his hometown of Senoia, Georgia, where the locals called him "Dick" after Dick Butkus, but was an unknown among recruiters. Georgia Tech's coaches discovered him during the program's summer football camp and offered the rising high school senior a scholarship on the spot.

Rogers, meanwhile, was a blue-chip recruit. His father, Ronnie, played defensive line for Erk Russell at Georgia in the late 1960s and passed on Russell's hard-nosed ways to his son. "He taught me that playing hard is the only way to play," Ron Rogers said of his father.

The Bruise Brothers helped lay the foundation for a turn-around in the Georgia Tech football program. The Jackets went 1–10 their freshman year, a season marked by the firing of head coach Bill Lewis with three games left on the schedule. O'Leary took over, and the defensive guru made Brooking and Rogers the framework of his rebuilding project. They started next to each other in 32 of the final 33 games of their careers and averaged more than 10 tackles per game each in their sophomore, junior, and senior seasons. Brooking finished as Tech's all-time leading tackler. Rogers ranks third on the list, just two tackles shy of finishing second.

"We've had a great time playing together," Rogers said prior to the final game of his Georgia Tech career, the 1997 Carquest Bowl.

"From the first time we met, we knew we were the same type of linebacker. We take our ability and maximize it."

Everett Strupper

The best boxers tend to be those with the most nicknames. By that standard, Georgia Tech halfback Everett Strupper would have been a heck of a pugilist.

Teammates called him "Stroop." His coach, John Heisman, referred to him as "Little Everett Strupper," "Condensed Lightning," and "Apollo." Sportswriters of the day seemingly competed to give Strupper the best moniker: he was referred to as "Lord High Executioner" and a "veritable demon."

Strupper's Georgia Tech career ranks among the best in college football history. He never lost a game in three years. He won a national title. He scored eight touchdowns in a game. He was the first player from a southern college named to a nationally recognized All-America team.

He was also 5'7" and weighed approximately 150 pounds. And he was deaf.

Heisman's first impression of Strupper was that he would never play for the Yellow Jackets. "Too light for the line, I didn't see how he could play in the backfield, because he wouldn't be able to get the signals," Heisman told an *Atlanta Constitution* reporter for a 1923 story on Strupper. "He could have played quarterback fine, but his enunciation wasn't clear enough for him to call the plays."

Heisman's attitude changed once he witnessed Strupper's athleticism. The coach described Strupper as a "star baseball player, a crack at basketball, and the best sprint man we had in the school." And Strupper's deafness was never an issue; he could read lips.

"Little" Everett Strupper stood 5'7", weighed approximately 150 pounds, and was deaf but ran for 100-plus yards in every game during Georgia Tech's 1917 national championship season.

So as long as the signal-caller turned his head and looked in Strupper's direction, Strupper understood the calls.

Strupper first attracted national attention in Georgia Tech's record-setting 222–0 spanking of Cumberland. Then a sophomore, he ran for four touchdowns in the first quarter and eight overall. The performance earned him the "Lord High Executioner" reference from an Associated Press reporter.

The 1917 season would cement his legacy. As part of arguably the best backfield in college football history, Strupper shared carries with Joe Guyon, Judy Harlan, and Albert Hill. Football historian Bernie McCarty would later call the quartet better than Notre Dame's Four Horsemen.

Strupper rushed for more than 100 yards in every game and made Frank Menke's All-America team. Menke, the sports editor for the International News Service, and Coach Pop Warner picked the two most widely recognized All-America teams at the time. The Associated Press, which today is the official All-America selector, didn't pick its first teams until 1925.

Strupper earned the "veritable demon" moniker in a 98–0 victory over Carlisle. Wrote an *Atlanta Journal* reporter, "Everett Strupper played like a veritable demon. At one time four Carlisle men pounced on him from all directions, and yet through some superhuman witchery he broke loose and dashed 10 yards further."

Strupper would have been a Heisman Trophy contender had the award existed at the time. Like the AP All-Americans, the first Heisman wasn't awarded until later, in 1935. The hypothetical 1917 Heisman vote likely would have come down to Strupper, teammate Joe Guyon, Pitt fullback Tank McLaren, Army halfback Elmer Oliphant, and Ohio State halfback Chic Harley. All five of those players would be inducted into the College Football Hall of Fame.

World War I cut Strupper's college career short by a year. He enlisted in the Army prior to the 1918 season. He returned to Atlanta after the war but did not go back to Georgia Tech. He went from halfback to soldier to entrepreneur and started a pair of successful businesses.

Strupper also did journalism on the side. Ironically, the man of many nicknames created a famous one for someone—or something— else. Writing about an Alabama-Mississippi game in 1930, Strupper quoted an excited Alabama fan as saying "hold your horses, the elephants are coming" as the Tide took the field. His sportswriting peers took up the moniker, referring to Alabama as the "Red Elephants." Alabama's elephant mascot would later follow.

Larry Morris

When you're nicknamed "the Brahma Bull," there's no confusion about your playing style. Grant Field was Larry Morris' china shop in the mid-1950s. Morris stalked opponents from his middle linebacker position in the 1952, 1953, and 1954 seasons. The Chicago Bears' rampaging Mike Singletary would later define the position for the masses, yet those who saw Morris play at Georgia Tech or during his decade-long career in the National Football League say Morris set the standard.

Morris treated blockers like a bowling ball does pins and took a ball carrier's desire to gain yardage as a personal affront. His unnatural athleticism combined with uncanny instincts allowed him to contribute on nearly every play, including as a blocker on offense. Sid Luckman, who coached Morris in the NFL, once told reporters Morris could have played every position except quarterback. "And he only knew one speed—full," Luckman said.

Author Gene Asher, in his book *Legends: Georgians Who Live Impossible Dreams*, related a conversation he overheard between two Georgia Bulldogs fans after Morris made 24 tackles in the 1954 rivalry game. "Why did we run all those plays at Morris?" one Dogs fan asked the other. "We didn't. He always was where our ball carriers ran," came the reply. *Atlanta Journal* columnist Harry Mehre, a one-time coach, described Morris as a "human wrecking ball."

Legendary Tech coach Bobby Dodd best summed up Morris' impact on games in his autobiography, *Dodd's Luck*, saying, "If my

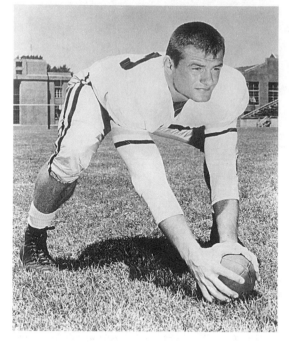

Larry Morris was known as the "Brahma Bull" and lived up to the nickname with his playing style. A 24-tackle performance against rival Georgia in 1954 highlighted his career.

future depended on one game, I would rather have Larry Morris going for me than any other player I ever saw." Notice Dodd said *saw*, not *coached*.

Morris, not to be confused with fellow Georgia Tech linebacker and College Football Hall of Famer George Morris, was a rare underclassman named to the Associated Press All-America team in 1953. He was a repeat All-American in 1954. Morris also starred on the Georgia Tech baseball team. He may have been more skilled at baseball than football—he turned down a contract with the Atlanta Crackers, a Triple A baseball team, coming out of high school.

Morris went on to a storied NFL career. He was the seventh pick in the 1955 NFL Draft and starred as a fullback, center, and linebacker in his 12 seasons as a pro with the L.A. Rams, Chicago Bears, and Atlanta Falcons. He made 12 tackles for the Bears in the 1963 NFL title game. The Pro Football Hall of Fame named Morris to its All-Decade Team in the 1960s.

As for his "Brahma Bull" nickname, Morris earned the label as a senior at Decatur High School. Morris fumbled early in the state championship game, which led his coach, Charlie Waller, to think, *We've got them now. Larry will be a raging bull the rest of the way.* Waller relayed the anecdote to the media afterward, and Morris became the Brahma Bull the next day.

81 Visit the Edge Center

The heart of Georgia Tech athletics has been at the southwest corner of Techwood Drive and Bobby Dodd Way for more than a century. The Arthur B. Edge Intercollegiate Athletics Center's completion in 1982 just made the location official.

Georgia Tech's athletics headquarters is physically attached to Bobby Dodd Stadium, where the Yellow Jackets have been playing football since 1905. The Edge houses Georgia Tech's administrative and coaches' offices, the academic center, sports medicine and training facilities, dining hall, and equipment room.

The Edge Center grew with the demolition of the old Heisman Gymnasium and construction of the north end zone grandstands in 2003 to include a football conference center. The building now measures more than 65,000 square feet.

The Edge Center gained public notoriety in 1996 with the opening of a museum, the George W. Mathews Jr. Athletic Heritage Center. The museum made the Edge Center a popular stop with fans on football Saturdays. The Yellow Jackets' championship trophies are displayed in the museum, including the famed crystal football they claimed in the 1990 season. The museum also features video kiosks, interactive displays, and a theater. The Edge once included retail space, with a Russell Athletic Apparel store and a McDonald's restaurant formerly calling the building home.

What truly makes the Edge Center special is Bobby Dodd's involvement in its creation. Dodd retired as Georgia Tech's athletics director in 1976 and distanced himself from Yellow Jackets athletics. He'd spent 45 years working for the school as an assistant coach, head coach, and athletics director, and the programs slumped following his departure.

Georgia Tech hired Homer Rice in 1980. Among Rice's top priorities were the construction of an athletics administration center and getting Dodd involved with Yellow Jackets athletics again. He enlisted Kim King, the color analyst for Georgia Tech football games and a player under Dodd, to help convince Dodd to return and raise money for what would become the Edge Center.

With Dodd as the frontman, Georgia Tech easily raised the $7 million to build the Edge Center. The facility opened in 1982, and Dodd remained involved as a consultant and fund-raiser until his death in 1988. The school renamed Grant Field in Dodd's honor two months before his passing. It's hard for Yellow Jackets fans to walk past the Edge Center entrance today without thinking about Dodd.

82 Take Part in the Budweiser Bob

Sorry Wisconsin Badgers fans, but the best between-quarters tradition in college football belongs to Georgia Tech. The Budweiser bob is older, better, and less dangerous than Wisconsin's "Jump Around" silliness. The song, played by the marching band, not over the stadium loudspeakers, is better, too.

Georgia Tech's band strikes up the familiar Budweiser jingle, officially titled "Here Comes the King," between the third and fourth quarters at football games. Fans stand and bob to the Oom-Pah beat, alternating knee bends with their neighbors, mimicking the bobbing heads of the Clydesdale horses in the TV ad. The tradition dates back to 1970, predating Wisconsin's "Jump Around" by 28 years. The jingle was the commercial hit of the time, and the band adopted it as a tribute to Georgia Tech's Bud—coach Bud Carson.

Carson was three years into his tenure at Georgia Tech and his unenviable role as the successor to a legend, Bobby Dodd. Carson's first three seasons produced losing records—more than Dodd posted in 22 seasons—but the 1970 team opened with four straight wins that vaulted the Yellow Jackets back into the polls for the first time since Dodd had retired.

The band included "Here Comes the King" in its repertoire because of the chorus, which ends with, "When you say Bud-weis-er, you've said it all." Georgia Tech substituted "Go, Georgia Tech" for the lyrics early in the chorus and capped it with, "When you say Bud...weiser, you've said it all." Why they didn't substitute "Carson" for "weiser" is a mystery, although Anheuser-Busch didn't mind. The brewery sponsored Georgia Tech athletics for years.

Bud's Yellow Jackets finished the 1970 season with a 9–3 record, a No. 13 ranking, and a Sun Bowl win. They went unbeaten at home, and the superstitious fan base made sure to do the Budweiser bob every game.

The superstition quickly became a tradition, even though Carson was fired a year later. Georgia Tech went 6–6 in 1971, and Carson became the first head coach in the 75-year history of the football program to get the axe. Dodd and his predecessor, William Alexander, both retired from Georgia Tech, and John Heisman quit because of his desire to get away from his ex-wife following their divorce.

The Budweiser Bob

The Budweiser bob means something entirely different to the sportswriters who cover Georgia Tech athletics than it does the fans. The timing of the song's playing—between the third and fourth quarters of football games, during the eight-minute timeout in the second half of basketball games, and during the seventh-inning stretch at baseball games—is a reminder to the scribes that deadline is fast approaching. During my tenure covering the Yellow Jackets, the Budweiser bob was my cue to get my mind and typing fingers in gear.

The split from Georgia Tech turned out to be a blessing for Carson. He'd designed and implemented the Cover 2 defensive scheme while coaching the Yellow Jackets, and Pittsburgh Steelers coach Chuck Noll hired Carson to coach the NFL team's secondary. A year later, Noll promoted Carson to defensive coordinator. Carson proceeded to develop the famous "Steel Curtain" defense that led Pittsburgh to back-to-back Super Bowl wins. He spent the rest of his coaching career in the NFL, including two seasons as head coach of the Cleveland Browns.

Carson's greatest contribution to Georgia Tech remains an unintended one—the Budweiser bob. The tradition is now practiced at basketball games during the eight-minute timeout of the second half, during baseball's seventh-inning stretch, as well as between sets at volleyball matches. The band also plays the song at every function and event it attends away from the stadium or gym.

In many ways, the Budweiser song is more like Ohio State's "Hang On Sloopy" than Wisconsin's "Jump Around." It is an alternative fight song, not some gimmick. However it is classified, the Budweiser bob is one of the most enjoyable traditions in college football.

83 Wes Durham

Woody Durham sensed his son, Wes, standing at a career crossroads one summer day in 1988. Wes was a recent college graduate yet a veteran sports broadcaster, at least relative to his age. Wes had literally grown up in a broadcast booth, assisting his dad, the play-by-play voice of the North Carolina Tar Heels. Wes started at age 15 as a production assistant, fetching everything from stats to drinks for the broadcast crew. He moved on to out-of-town scoreboard duties about the same time he got his driver's license.

"I was a sponge," Wes said. "I was trying to learn as much as I humanly could."

Wes applied those lessons as a college undergraduate. He called more than 150 Elon University football, basketball, and baseball games for the student radio station. Elon's athletics director, Alan White, remembers Durham as "pretty polished" for a student broadcaster.

For all his experience, though, Wes couldn't find a job. And the day the rejection letter arrived from Radford University, Woody feared his son was about to give up on his dream. So Woody did what he swore he would never do: he called in a favor. Woody Durham telephoned Radford basketball coach Oliver Purnell. Durham vaguely knew Purnell from the coach's days as a Maryland assistant. He sent Purnell demo tapes and also had North Carolina basketball coach Dean Smith and Tar Heels football coach Mack Brown call on his son's behalf.

Purnell, who would go on to coach in the ACC at Clemson, ultimately recommended Durham for the job. The coach claims the decision had more to do with what he heard on Wes' demos than

221

on the phone from Woody, Smith, and Brown. Regardless, Wes Durham became a professional broadcaster that fall, and today is on his way to legend status at Georgia Tech.

Durham has been the Yellow Jackets' lead play-by-play announcer since 1995. He didn't replace Al Ciraldo, who in 40 years of calling Tech games retired the title of "Voice of the Yellow Jackets." Durham debuted three years after Ciraldo stepped out of the broadcast booth. But Durham has successfully forged his own identity independent of Ciraldo. Where Ciraldo's calls were sharp and pointed, Durham's smooth baritone is akin to that of a disc jockey. Yet both deliveries bring about the same result: the excitement and tension of the game comes through in their voices.

The same can be said in comparing Wes with his father. Woody Durham is more traditional in his style, while Wes is admittedly more "new school," mixing in observations and cultural references. Their voices sound eerily similar—it's hard to tell them apart if you don't know which broadcast you are tuned into—and they share an attention to detail to give an authoritative call and "paint a picture" for the fans.

Woody sensed his son had made a voice for himself back in 2005 when he came to Atlanta to speak to a North Carolina alumni club and was introduced as "Wes' dad." "I'd always been Woody Durham, voice of the Tar Heels," said Woody, who called Tar Heels games from 1971 to 2010. "Now, all of a sudden, I'm Woody Durham, Wes Durham's dad. When I venture out of the Carolinas now, I'm in his territory."

Wes Durham hopes to become the mainstay at Tech his father was at North Carolina. His goal is to finish his career at Georgia Tech, and he also calls Atlanta Falcons games and cohosts a midday sports talk radio show. "I think Wes has great pipes, great delivery," said Ben Sutton of ISP Sports, the network that broadcasts Georgia Tech games. "He's a real pro. He's a Durham."

84 Vince Dooley

Bobby Dodd was pushed into retirement. The shove did not come from dissatisfied administrators or alumni, à la Florida State great Bobby Bowden. Nor was the Yellow Jackets program eroding in Dodd's final years. His last team started 9–0 and finished eighth in the national rankings.

Dodd's exit from coaching was quickened by the success of Coach Vince Dooley at Georgia. Dooley succeeded Wally Butts in 1964 and altered the rivalry's landscape in a way not seen since Dodd implemented two-platoon football at Tech in 1951.

Dooley's Bulldogs won the 1964 meeting 7–0, Georgia Tech's third straight defeat to end the season, after a 7–0 start. Georgia upset the Yellow Jackets again in 1965, a loss that nearly cost Tech a Gator Bowl bid. Then came the 1966 meeting. Georgia Tech was 9–0 and ranked No. 5 in the polls. Georgia boasted an 8–1 record and No. 7 ranking. The Bulldogs won in a rout 23–14, with Tech scoring a touchdown in the final minute to make the score respectable.

Dodd had lost to Georgia three times in a row only once before. He'd owned the rivalry for much of his career, winning eight straight at one point. And Dodd definitely had the advantage in recruiting. Until Dooley succeeded Wally Butts, that is. The youthful Dooley gained a greater foothold with every win in the rivalry and the steady improvement of his program. By 1966 Dooley noticed a difference. "Tech was pretty dominant in a lot of places recruiting back then," Dooley said. "There were pockets around the state where we couldn't sign anybody. Once we beat them a few times in a row, we got on even footing."

Georgia coach Vince Dooley (right) talks with Georgia Tech's Pepper Rodgers prior to a Georgia–Georgia Tech game in the mid-1970s. Dooley won 19 of the 25 games he coached against Georgia Tech.

Dodd's retirement coincided with that evening. He would later admit that Dooley's burgeoning juggernaut in Athens hastened his retirement. Dooley would go on to coach the Bulldogs to 19 victories in 25 meetings with the Yellow Jackets.

Current Bulldogs coach Mark Richt is on pace to top that mark—he won nine of his first 10 games in the rivalry—but his impact will never match that of Dooley's. Dooley made Georgia a power and ran off one of college football's great coaches in Dodd; Richt elevated an already strong program in an era when Tech was mired in mediocrity.

Dooley recognizes the importance of his teams' successes against the Yellow Jackets. He came into the rivalry with a personal losing streak versus Tech. As a player at Auburn from 1951 to 1953, he went 0–3 against the Jackets. Granted, those losses came during a remarkable three-year run by Georgia Tech. Dodd's team went undefeated in 1951 and 1952 and won nine games in 1953. But the defeats stung Dooley nonetheless.

Dooley felt the pressure to beat Georgia Tech from the day he was hired. The Yellow Jackets were on a three-game winning streak going into the 1964 season, and many Georgia fans were still smarting from the Drought a decade earlier, during which the Dogs lost eight straight to the rivals from 1949 to 1956. "They still hadn't gotten over it," Dooley said. "It was a long drought."

Even Dooley's early success failed to win over all the Georgia faithful. He owned an 8–2 mark against the rivals when first-year Georgia Tech coach Pepper Rodgers, who'd quarterbacked the Jackets during the Drought, schemed Tech to a 34–14 victory over the Dogs in 1974. Rodgers' wishbone offense had been so effective against the Bulldogs, one Georgia athletics board member told Dooley, "We'll never beat Tech again." Georgia won 42–26 the next year, and Dooley would lose to Rodgers just once more.

Dooley credited psychology for his overall success against the Yellow Jackets, which included four runs of three or more straight victories and six in a row between 1978 and 1983. "Once you get a streak going, it sometimes takes a couple of years, and one team has to be much better than the other team to break the drought," Dooley said.

85 Graning and Holt

Chick Graning's demeanor made him a great leader but an underachieving football player. Coaches described the 1961 Georgia Tech football team's captain as "basically too gentle to be a truly great football player," even as he went on to play two years in the NFL.

Alabama linebacker Darwin Holt, meanwhile, had a reputation as the meanest cuss in college football. He played past the whistle and would throw cheap shots as randomly as fraternities would parties.

On November 18, 1961, the boy-next-door met the bully. The bully did what bullies do, and the images of two of the South's great programs changed. Holt blindsided Graning with a dirty block on a punt play in the fourth quarter of the Tide's 10–0 victory. Alabama's return man, Billy Richardson, had fair caught the punt. The play over, Graning stopped running and paused before heading to the defensive huddle. He never made it. Holt kept coming and blocked Graning, accentuating the blow by shoving his forearm up into Graning's face. Graning wore the one-bar face mask common at the time, and he had adjusted the bar up to protect his oft-broken nose. Holt's arm connected with cheek and mouth as a result, and fractured several of Graning's facial bones and his sinuses. Graning also lost five teeth and suffered a concussion so severe he didn't remember the play until five days later. Graning's injuries would later be compared to the damage done to NBA player Rudy Tomjanovich by an infamous punch by Kermit Washington. It was "the worst facial injury I have ever seen in my 20 years of association with athletics," Georgia Tech team doctor Lamont Henry said.

The incident's aftermath made the situation worse. Holt threw the block and ran to the sideline to celebrate the blow with teammates. And because the block happened so far away from the play and after the whistle, the officials never saw it. There was no flag.

Georgia Tech head coach Bobby Dodd witnessed the cheap shot, though. He didn't address it after the game out of respect for Bryant. But he would call his good friend and rival a day later and demand an apology and punishment for Holt.

Bryant said he was sorry but refused to discipline Holt, a senior who had played for the Bear first at Texas A&M and then at Alabama. The officials didn't flag Holt for the play, and the SEC chose not to suspend Holt over the incident. SEC commissioner Bernie Moore's lack of action was particularly curious, since he would warn conference coaches to crack down on dirty play prior to the next season. Given the chance to make an example of Holt, Moore passed.

Only then did Dodd go public. He showed the game film on his weekly TV show. Atlanta newspaper columnists took up the cause. Furman Bisher classified Holt's play as Darwinism gone wrong. Bisher wrote a piece for the *Saturday Evening Post* headlined, "College Football Is Going Berserk," and accused Bryant of coaching his team to use dirty tactics. Holt defended himself, claiming he meant to hit Graning in the chest with the forearm but he "slipped" and "accidentally" shivered him in the face.

Graning spent most of the following week in the hospital, and his family allowed photographers to shoot photos of him all bandaged up to run in the newspapers. Holt visited Graning the following April, but the Georgia Tech captain classified Holt's concern as disingenuous. "If I meant to hurt you, I would have killed you," Holt said, according to Graning. "That was his so-called apology," said Graning, who, true to his character, was gracious to Holt and even showed him around the Georgia Tech campus. "I just let it ride. I certainly did not accept it."

Graning admits he should have expected the dirty play. He had seen Holt throw elbows at opponents while studying Alabama game film. "I saw him take a kid's helmet off with an elbow," Graning said. "Those were cheap shots, not missed blocking attempts. It was trying to hurt somebody."

The incident put the spotlight on college football's increasing brutality. With the high profiles of hard-nosed coaches like Bear Bryant and Woody Hayes, the game was going berserk, as Bisher wrote. The incident led to a *Sports Illustrated* investigation of shivering, spearing, and other untoward tactics in the college game and gave officials, college administrators, fans, and media a greater sense of awareness. Incidences of dirty play dropped dramatically in the years that followed.

86 "Bonfire of the Insanities"

The coeds kept feeding the fire. First came tree limbs and leaves. Then unwanted clothing and books, along with pieces of old dorm furniture. Finally, the Bobby Dodd Stadium goalposts. The kindling kept on coming, and the flames kept on growing. Right at the intersection of Techwood Drive and Bobby Dodd Way. The fire was so hot it melted the traffic light above.

The surreal celebration was the nightcap to one of the most surreal days in Georgia Tech football history—November 3, 1990. The Yellow Jackets had upset top-ranked Virginia that afternoon in Charlottesville, Virginia. The win would launch them to an unbeaten season and a share of the national championship.

But the aftermath marked an even bigger victory for the Yellow Jackets football program than the game itself. Georgia Tech became a football school again that afternoon. The campus community that had viewed the program with apathy since Coach Dodd retired more than two decades earlier fell in love with Yellow Jackets football again.

"I figured people would be in their dorm rooms studying as usual," offensive lineman Jim Lavin said. "It was good to see people were excited about football. But you have to give them a reason to be. Give them reasons to get out of the library and out of the study halls."

The only studying done that afternoon, in the words of Tech president John Crecine, involved thermodynamics. "Heat rises," Crecine said of the intersection pyre. The party started seconds after kicker Scott Sisson booted the game-winning, 37-yard field goal in a stadium 500 miles to the northeast of campus. The pandemonium raged on for hours, outlasting the team's postgame celebration, flight home, and bus ride to campus.

The team got a sense of what awaited them as the bus turned onto North Avenue several blocks east of campus. It was near midnight, yet cheering fans lined the street, swamping the sidewalk in front of The Varsity. The team wasn't prepared for the scene along Techwood Drive beside Bobby Dodd Stadium. Approximately 10,000 students greeted them.

"I thought something else was going on," offensive lineman Mike Mooney said. "I was like, *What are all these people doing?*" But they were there for the football team. The throngs reduced the buses' progress to a creep, and before long students were crawling up the sides and on the roofs and hanging from the windows like monkeys.

"It was as if we had just won the Super Bowl," fullback William Bell said.

Ross' youngest son, Rob, was one of the bus-window crawlers. He and Ross' wife, Alice, didn't make the trip to Virginia for the game. They had come to campus to welcome the team home only to get caught up in the chaos. The celebrants chanted, "ACC! ACC!

ACC!" and carried banners that read, "We're No. 1," and, "We're Going to a Bowl."

Perhaps the strangest greeter of all that afternoon stood in front of the football offices, where the team buses eventually stopped. The shirtless, guitar-wielding musician serenaded the team with the Deep Purple song "Smoke on the Water" while the remnants of the bonfire crackled and smoked a few yards away.

Jack Wilkinson, author of the book *Focused on the Top* about the 1990 championship season, appropriately dubbed the celebration the "bonfire of the insanities."

87 The 1934 Michigan Game

The lowest point in Georgia Tech football history can be pinpointed to one day: October 20, 1934. The team was pathetic. They would finish the season with a 1–9 record, the program's worst since the pre-Heisman days when volunteers and players coached the team. But racism, not bad football, is what the 1934 season is remembered for.

Coach William Alexander scheduled a game with two-time defending national champion Michigan. The two teams, traditional powers of the era, had never met. What Alexander failed to take into account was that the Wolverines were led by senior end Willis Ward, an African American. And in the first half of the 20th century, southern prejudice prohibited southern teams from competing against teams that included black players.

The reason behind the oversight is unclear. Ward was a high-profile player, a starter on the 1932 title team and an honorable mention All-American on the 1933 championship squad. He was also a world-class track athlete on par with his Ohio State rival, Jesse Owens.

Georgia Tech was clearly a southern school. The Institute wouldn't admit its first black student until 1961. The football program's color barrier would not fall until 1969. Tech had to have known Michigan had a black football player, and Michigan had to have known Georgia Tech would have a problem with playing against Ward. Yet the game was scheduled, anyway. As Michigan's student newspaper editorialized prior to the game, "If the athletic department forgot it had Ward on its football team when it scheduled a game with Georgia Tech, it was astonishingly forgetful.... If it was conscious of Ward's being on the team but scheduled the game anyway, it was extraordinarily stupid."

Georgia Tech's Alexander at least anticipated the problem. He wrote a letter to the Michigan administration in the fall of 1933 expressing concerns. The game had been scheduled prior to the 1933 season, and Alexander wanted to know well in advance how the Ward issue would be addressed. Alexander's letter stated Georgia Tech would not take the field if Ward was going to play. He insinuated the game should be canceled if Michigan were unwilling to hold Ward out of the game.

Yet one year later Georgia Tech boarded a northbound train. A face-to-face debate ensued almost the moment Alexander and his team disembarked in Ann Arbor, Michigan. Alexander told Michigan coach Harry Kipke the Yellow Jackets would forfeit the game and return to Atlanta before playing against Ward. Michigan athletics officials acquiesced to Alexander's demand, citing a fear for Ward's on-field safety and courtesy for Georgia Tech. Alexander, in the interest of fairness, agreed to bench his best player, end Hoot Gibson.

The situation touched off protests and near-riots on the Michigan campus. Fifteen hundred students and faculty signed a

Tearing Down Barriers

As dark a day as October 20, 1934, was for Georgia Tech and its coach, William Alexander, the Georgia Tech–Michigan game pained Michigan coach Harry Kipke more. Kipke talked Ward into attending Michigan despite racial prejudice among the alumni in the first place. The color barrier had fallen at Michigan in 1890 when George Jewett played for the Wolverines, but the program hadn't included a black player since. Many suspected longtime coach Fielding Yost's heritage—Yost's father served in the Confederate army during the Civil War—had led to the long period between Jewett's departure and Ward's arrival.

Ward came to Michigan in 1931 and joined the football program a year later. Kipke defended Ward's right to play several times during his tenure. According to author John Behee's book *Michigan's Black Lettermen*, "[On] several occasions, Kipke took off his coat and was prepared to fight with those who bitterly opposed having a Negro play for Michigan." Kipke left Michigan and coaching following the 1937 season. He would join the board of regents of the University of Michigan in 1940 and continue to be a champion for black athletes at the school.

petition in support of Ward. Students planned a sit-in on the 50-yard line if the game went forward without Ward. Students lit bonfires in protest on the eve of the game.

The Michigan players showed displeasure, as well. Ward's closest friend and roommate, Gerald Ford, threatened to quit if Ward was held out of the game. Ward talked the man who would go on to become president of the United States out of that decision. The team was not very good and needed Ford to play. Ford played, and Michigan won 9–2 thanks to a punt return for a touchdown. Alexander described it as "probably as poorly played a game between two major-college teams as I've ever seen."

88 The Blue Turf Bruiser

The playing surface looked like a skating rink, Boise's blue turf topped with a dusting of snow. And for three hours on January 3, 2004, Georgia Tech's P.J. Daniels dominated in Eric Heiden–like fashion. Daniels rushed for an NCAA bowl–record 307 yards and four touchdowns in the Humanitarian Bowl. He led the Yellow Jackets to a 52–10 victory over Tulsa in a game in which four Tech quarterbacks combined for just 19 passing yards.

The rushing performance was the second best in Georgia Tech history, behind only Eddie Lee Ivery's 356 yards against Air Force in 1978. And Daniels got his yardage in a little more than three quarters. Head coach Chan Gailey took Daniels out of the game after he eclipsed the 300-yard plateau with 11 minutes remaining—and would have pulled Daniels from the blowout sooner if not for lobbying by his teammates. "Let's try to get P.J. 300," the players told Gailey.

The request was met with bewilderment. Gailey didn't realize Daniels had rolled up that many yards, saying afterward, "I had no clue." Once Gailey learned Daniels was within 10 yards of the mark, he agreed to leave Daniels in and call his number. "Sure, we'll try to do that," Gailey told the players.

Daniels passed 300 with a 10-yard run up the middle for a first down. He was immediately replaced by Jermaine Hatch, who carried on the next four plays and capped the drive with a touchdown run. "Give Daniels a lot of credit," Tulsa safety Shannon Carter told reporters after the game. "He's just a big physical back. He wore us down a little bit."

P.J. Daniels rushed for an NCAA bowl record 307 yards in the 2004 Humanitarian Bowl against Tulsa.

Such was Daniels' style throughout his college career. Georgia Tech's football history is littered with overachievers. From William Alexander and "little Everett Strupper" to "Mouse" Rudolph and Joe Hamilton, putting on the old gold and white seems to coax greatness from unlikely sources. Yet Daniels has to be the unlikeliest of all.

Daniels came to Georgia Tech as a walk-on. College football's factories overlooked him despite his rushing for 1,600 yards as a senior at Houston's Elsik High School. A strong student, Daniels seemed destined for one of the "football Ivys" like Stanford or Northwestern. Daniels didn't fare well on the SAT, however, and failed to qualify in time for signing day. Stanford and Northwestern pulled their scholarship offers, and Georgia Tech coach George O'Leary coaxed Daniels to Atlanta. He redshirted as a freshman and opened his first season of eligibility as a backup—on the scout team. He figured to see action in games as a kick returner, but six other backs were in line for carries ahead of him, including star-in-the-making Tony Hollings.

Hollings was leading the nation in rushing in the fourth week of the 2002 season when he suffered a season-ending knee injury. Backup Sidney Ford was out with a concussion, and the third-stringer, Hatch, was struggling to return from a knee injury. Freshman Ace Eziemefe started the next week and rushed for 136 yards. He shared carries that day with another freshman, Michael Sampson, and veteran Gordon Clinkscale. Daniels played that day, but only on special teams.

Eziemefe wore down over the following two games, and in a lopsided Thursday night loss to Maryland in mid-October, Daniels finally got some carries. The line was not impressive: 10 carries for 23 yards. Gailey saw something in Daniels he liked, though, and made him Clinkscale's backup for the next week's game against Virginia. His first carry versus the Cavaliers was a one-yard touchdown dive, and he went on to rush 20 more times for 94 more yards.

Clinkscale remained the starter the rest of the regular season, but Daniels was the future. Gailey awarded Daniels a scholarship following that season. And when Hollings failed out of school the following spring, Daniels won the job and would lead the Atlantic Coast Conference in rushing the next season, culminating in the Humanitarian Bowl spectacle. He challenged for the league's rushing title his last two years.

Asked late in his career if he had considered giving up football back when he was a mythical "seventh-stringer" (there's no such thing as seventh string), Daniels admitted he had. "I kept asking myself, *Why am I doing this?*" Daniels told *Macon Telegraph* columnist Michael Lough. "When I would get up early in the morning, it would be, *Why am I doing this?* When I would work out with my teammates, it would be, *Why am I doing this?* But it all paid off. I had a goal, and I kept chiseling away at it."

89 Total Person Program

College athletics programs, football in particular, greatly benefit the schools they represent. Good teams attract future students, enhance the campus environment for current coeds, and engage alumni and other financial contributors. Some athletics departments even generate profits.

Giving back to the student-athletes, whose sweat powers the programs, has long been a challenge for schools. Most players get a free or discounted education. Some receive the exposure to pursue professional athletic careers. But as invaluable as scholarships and notoriety are, students-athletes deserve more in the minds of many within the collegiate athletics community.

Enter the NCAA's Life Skills Program, an initiative that helps student-athletes succeed before and after graduation through academic support, career planning and placement, counseling and wellness, and leadership and outreach training and opportunities. The NCAA's CHAMPS/Life Skills Program, currently employed by hundreds of colleges and universities, is modeled on Georgia Tech's Total Person Program. Developed and implemented by athletics director Homer Rice in 1980, the Total Person Program's aim is to help Tech athletics participants gain the skills that will serve them for a lifetime.

"That's important to everybody: the administration, faculty, students, their parents," Rice said. "Stressing that balance really fit what Georgia Tech is about." Finding balance can be difficult for every Georgia Tech student. A popular campus saying goes, "There are three things Tech students want: a social life, good grades, and sleep. And they can only have two." Throw in 20-hours-plus devoted to football, and achieving balance becomes even more difficult for a Tech undergrad.

The Total Person Program is seen as the steadying hand. Freshmen go through the Athletes' Successful Planning in Reaching Excellence (ASPIRE) program, a series of seminars and workshops that address topics from time management to media training. Georgia Tech pioneered the concept of academic support services, which includes a degree-completion program for student-athletes who have finished their athletic eligibility. Yellow Jackets get career help early, with training on résumé and interview preparation, and have access to wellness counselors. Players are given leadership community outreach opportunities. "Some people get out of college and don't even know how to balance a checkbook," former Georgia Tech football player Curtis Hollomon told a writer for Tech's faculty publication, the *Whistle*, in 2000. "The Total Person Program gets you involved in the community and makes you a total person."

ADAM VAN BRIMMER

The Georgia Tech community embraced the program from the start. There was no sense of pride in the athletics department when Rice took over in 1980—the teams were losing, and graduation rates were abysmal. Today, the Yellow Jackets are competitive in nearly every sport, and the graduation rate for Georgia Tech's student-athletes (75 percent in 2010) nearly matches that of the general student body (78 percent). It is well above the national average (59 percent). And Georgia Tech grads typically land well-paying jobs out of college: as of 2009, the median starting salary for a first-year Georgia Tech graduate was $58,900.

But the shepherds of the Total Person Program—Rice, his successor Dave Braine, and current athletics director Dan Radakovich—don't measure the initiative's success in graduation rates or wage scales. "The goal is simple," Braine said, "to give back a better person than we brought in."

90 Eat at Junior's Grill

Of all the Tech memorabilia that hung in the on-campus location of Junior's Grill, owner Tommy Klemis first mentions the football property destroyed in an act of passion. "The kids tore down the goal post when we beat Nebraska in the [1990] national championship," he said. "[I had] the goal post enshrined on the west wall. One of my students presented that to Junior's. He waited until he graduated. He was afraid they might not let him graduate."

Klemis closed Junior's longtime campus location in the Bradley Building in April 2011. But the Klemis family has been serving the Georgia Tech community since 1958, and many suspect the restaurant will reopen near campus sometime soon. And when it does, expect the return of the French toast special and chicken tender basket as well as the makeshift Georgia Tech museum. Diners interested in seeing campus changes need only gaze from their hand-formed burgers and study the aerial photos. One, shot in 1948, shows the campus area before the expressway plowed through the eastern edge. Another, taken in 2002, shows the grounds when Tech started a massive expansion program. "Louis Hiett, from the Class of 1949, gave us an etching of the campus from 1890 that stood in his office for many years," Klemis said. "These walls do talk."

There appears to be an electric current between Klemis and his "students." In the early 1990s, for instance, students protected Junior's Grill when Olympic leaders targeted the property it then occupied as the site for the Olympic Village. "When the 1996 Summer Olympics came to Atlanta, we were torn down," Klemis said. "But the students and alums signed petitions, and we were revived as a Tech tradition and brought onto campus in 1994. So now my family feels as though Junior's belongs to [the students], and that's how we go to work every day."

Klemis supported student events during Junior's tenure on campus. His restaurant sponsored an annual "Georgia Tech Trivia Night," the kickoff to homecoming week. Junior's also served dessert to scholarship candidates the night before their interviews for the presidential scholarship.

In 2004 Klemis and a student organization sponsored a photo contest in the diner. He appreciated the artwork so much he kept it on the south wall. "I have pictures from a student's perspective of the campus. I didn't realize the photographic talent we have in our students," Klemis said. "Our campus from that perspective of photographs is gorgeous."

Local restaurateur Wilber Gold Jr. opened Junior's Grill, then known as Pilgrim's, in 1948 at Techwood Drive and North

Avenue—kitty-corner from Grant Field. In 1958 Greek immigrant James Klemis and his brother-in-law, John Chaknis, bought the business.

James Klemis, Tommy's father, died of a heart attack in 1964. His wife, Lula, kept the grill open and moved it in 1966 when the property that housed the original restaurant was razed. Junior's relocated a few doors down from the old location, leasing space from the Georgia Tech Foundation.

Georgia Tech acquired the property in 1966 and razed the original restaurant and neighboring theater. The brothers-in-law moved their business several doors down into a vacant barber shop and started leasing space from the Georgia Tech Foundation. Tommy Klemis took over the business in the late 1970s.

An Atlanta native, Klemis enrolled in Georgia Tech's electrical engineering program in 1970. He dropped out two years later to work for Western Electric in Atlanta. He took a leave of absence from the electric company in 1975 to help run the family restaurant. He used his Tech education in his business. "When the toaster or anything goes bad, I can fix it," he said.

Klemis' son is a Tech alumnus, and his daughter attended the University of Georgia. Concerning his eight grandchildren: "I'm hoping they'll all go to Tech. I'm afraid my daughter and son-in-law will challenge that."

91 Reggie Ball

The game clock hit zero, and the Georgia Tech students swarmed the field. One group went for the far goal posts, another for the near set. The football savvy among them shunned the uprights, however. They were more interested in picking something up than tearing something down.

The Yellow Jackets faithful carried true freshman quarterback Reggie Ball off the field following his first game at Bobby Dodd Stadium. His play in the upset of Auburn that afternoon was short of spectacular—9-of-21 for 149 yards and a touchdown—but the promise the brash true freshman showed was unmistakable.

Georgia Tech had found the next Joe Hamilton, and he would put the Yellow Jackets on the national scene again. "I bring everything to the table," Ball had said when named the starter a few weeks prior to the game.

The table turned on Ball, however. His career can be considered illustrious, what with his winning the Atlantic Coast Conference Freshman of the Year award, starting 49 games, owning several school records, and leading Georgia Tech to the ACC Championship game as a senior.

Yet in many ways that postgame shoulder ride in September 2003 was the high point for Ball. His improvement in four years as a starter could have been measured with a yardstick, if not a ruler. He choked more often than he excelled in big games, particularly those against the rival Georgia Bulldogs. Then he flunked out of school with one game left in his career. Fairly or unfairly, most Georgia Tech fans agree Ball is the biggest bust in program history.

Reggie Ball started four years for Georgia Tech and led the Yellow Jackets to the 2006 Atlantic Coast Conference Coastal Division title.

Ball is certainly one of the most memorable players in the century-plus they've been playing football on the Flats. He wasn't even supposed to be a Yellow Jacket—he was bound for Auburn until the Tigers backed off late in the recruiting process.

Once he signed with Georgia Tech, no one expected him to quarterback anything other than the scout team as a freshman. Veteran A.J. Suggs had started every game the year before, and sophomore Damarius Bilbo was considered the Jackets' quarterback of the future. Ball wasn't even the most highly regarded quarterback in his signing class—Pat Carter was.

Ball won the starting job in preseason practice, though, with Gailey praising him for—ironically enough—his decision-making prowess. The Ball era only got more and more surreal over time. A week after the Auburn win, Ball reacted to a narrow loss to then–league bully Florida State by guaranteeing the Yellow Jackets wouldn't lose again that season. Clemson hammered them the next week.

Ball came close to getting benched several times his freshman year yet still played well enough to guide Georgia Tech to a better-than-expected finish. Gailey would threaten to bench Ball several more times over the next two seasons, declaring the quarterback competition "open" going into every spring practice. Ball, being the stubborn competitor he was, would always rise to the challenge. Then he'd frustrate Gailey and the fan base with miscues. He threw 30 interceptions as a sophomore and junior. His career completion percentage was 49 percent.

Ball finally showed signs of living up to his hype his senior season. With quarterbacks coach Patrick Nix taking over the play-calling duties and installing a more wide-open scheme, Ball showed a comfort level and self-assuredness that had been missing. He'd always been cocky, but much of that bravado was false, used to disguise an underlying sense of self-doubt that surfaced in pressure situations.

For the first 11 games of 2006, Ball thrived. He played poorly in a blowout loss to Clemson but spent the game dodging pass rushers and searching in vain for open wide receivers. He keyed close victories over Maryland, Miami, N.C. State, and North Carolina that propelled the Jackets to the ACC Coastal Division title.

Ball's dream season became a nightmare on Thanksgiving weekend 2006. He embarrassed himself against rival Georgia in Athens, missing on 16 of 22 passes, throwing two interceptions, and getting sacked four times. He lost a fumble returned for the

Reggie Ball vs. Georgia

To say the Bulldogs were Ball's nemesis is like calling Wile E. Coyote and the Roadrunner friendly rivals. Ball went 0–4 versus Georgia and played so poorly Georgia fans mocked him during his senior year finale, holding his No. 1 Georgia Tech jersey next to the retired jerseys of Bulldogs greats Frank Sinkwich, Charley Trippi, Theron Sapp, and Herschel Walker. Here's a closer look at Ball's four games against the Dogs:

- **2003**: Georgia 34, Georgia Tech 17. Ball completed 8 of 16 passes for 80 yards and threw an interception before being knocked out of the game in the second quarter with a concussion.
- **2004**: Georgia 19, Georgia Tech 13. Ball completed 13 of 31 passes for 141 yards, was sacked three times, and became the ultimate goat in the game's closing seconds. With Georgia Tech driving for a potential game-winning score, Ball lost track of downs and, thinking it was third down, threw the ball away to avoid a sack on fourth down.
- **2005**: Georgia 14, Georgia Tech 7. Ball completed 18 of 35 passes with two interceptions. He nearly redeemed himself by driving the Yellow Jackets the length of the field in the final minutes only to throw an interception on the goal line.
- **2006**: Georgia 15, Georgia Tech 12. Ball capped his career against the rival with perhaps the biggest stinker in series history. He completed just six of 22 passes, threw two interceptions, and was sacked four times. He lost a fumble while scrambling for yardage in the fourth quarter, and the ball was returned for the eventual game-winning touchdown.

eventual game-winning touchdown. He posted another stinker a week later in the ACC title game against Wake Forest. He completed nine of 29 passes with two interceptions in the 9–6 loss.

He flunked out of school two weeks later. His D in a database management class—he blamed a mix-up over his participation in a group project—kept him out of the Gator Bowl and left fans wondering what happened to the next Joe Hamilton between that September afternoon in 2003 and December of 2006.

92 Steal the T

The greatest victory for any Georgia Tech student—football player or otherwise—is to steal the east-facing T off Tech Tower. The crown of Tech Tower is emblazoned with the letters T-E-C-H on each of its four sides. The signs have been a campus landmark since the 1920s, when the class of 1922 crafted the letters as a symbol to "light the spirit of Tech to the four points of the campus." The original signs were made of wood and painted gold and white.

The T didn't become sought-after signage until four decades later. A group of fraternity brothers, dubbed the "Magnificent Seven," scaled the tower and removed the sign in April 1969. They took the east-facing T because it was the one most visible from the interstate that marks the campus' eastern edge. The Magnificent Seven later presented it to President Edwin Harrison during his retirement ceremony "so that he would have what every Tech man needed—his own glowing yellow T for a conversation piece."

Stealing the T became the student body's favorite challenge. A T theft and its subsequent return was as much a homecoming tradition in the 1970s and 1980s as the Mini 500 and the football game. John Crecine, Georgia Tech's president from 1987 to 1994, approved of the practice, telling the student newspaper, "I think stealing the T off the Tech Tower is among the all-time greatest rituals."

Georgia Tech's administration eventually grew tired of the thefts, however, and took steps to protect the signs. The school wired alarms connected to the nearby Georgia Tech police headquarters to the sign in the 1990s and has added spot welds, fiber-optic cameras, and motion sensors over the years. Maintenance crews even grease

Tech Tower stands in the center of campus. Stealing the T off the façade is a favorite student prank.

the drain pipes that pass near the signs to discourage climbers. Those measures have secured the Ts. One of the last successful assaults came in 2001, although the perpetrators were caught in their getaway attempt. The sign was quickly replaced.

Yet stealing the T remains part of Georgia Tech lore. The tradition is outlined in the *T-Book*, a guide given to incoming freshmen during orientation. Instructions note that tower schematics and layouts of the security system are available "if one knows where to look" and go on to advise the freshmen on T theft etiquette: "Once stolen, put the letter in public location easily accessible to the president of the Institute."

93 Find Dean George Griffin

Name the only Georgia Tech football player immortalized in a campus statue. (Here's a hint: he's less known for his gridiron exploits than for his contributions to the school in the six decades following his graduation.)

George Griffin played quarterback for Coach John Heisman in the mid-1910s, scoring two touchdowns in the Yellow Jackets' infamous 222–0 rout of Cumberland in 1916. Yet it was his compassionate side that led Georgia Tech to commission and install a statue of Griffin—in a business suit, not football gear—outside the Ferst Center for the Arts.

Griffin worked in the school's student dean office from the early 1930s through 1964 and became known as both "the best friend of all Tech men" and "Mr. Georgia Tech." He was known never to forget the name of a student he'd met, started the "hip pocket fund" to issue interest-free loans to students struggling financially, and founded the Georgia Tech Placement Center and the Alumni Career Services Program.

"He was a team player, willing to do just about anything Georgia Tech asked him to do," Georgia Tech president Bud Peterson said during the 2010 Dean Griffin Day luncheon. "But he was best known for his passion for students and would do anything he could to help them succeed. If he had just invested in programs, we probably wouldn't be celebrating him today. His real legacy is about the people he touched, and specifically, students."

Griffin's legacy reaches into every corner of Georgia Tech's campus:

- He's remembered by the mathematics department because he served as an instructor there.
- His name adorns the Yellow Jackets' track and field complex—he coached the school's track-and-field and cross-country teams for parts of five decades, won 10 conference titles, and coached Olympians Homer Welchel (javelin, 1924) and Ed Hamm (long jump, 1928). Hamm won a gold medal and set a world record. Griffin also coached tennis—his 20–1 mark is the best in Tech history—as well as the freshman football team.
- He served as the executive secretary of the Georgia Tech Alumni Association.

Yet for all his other contributions, Griffin will forever be known as "Dean Griffin." Parts of his "Look to Your Left, Look to Your Right" speech during orientation are relayed to freshmen today. During Griffin's years as dean, only one in three entering freshmen went on to graduate. The message was to make a commitment to your studies and stick to it, and Griffin would do all he could to help, both before and after graduation.

Griffin's statue sits outside the facility that hosts freshman orientation, known to Tech students as Familiarization and Adaptation for the Surroundings and Environs of Tech, or FASET for short. The upperclassmen who participate in FASET dress up the Griffin statue so he will be immediately noticed by the new students and be an impetus for conversations about campus life. "It's a simple, neat way to welcome our new family to Georgia Tech," FASET veteran Kelly Sokowski told the student newspaper, the *Technique*, in 2009.

Griffin's football career, meanwhile, was far from statue-worthy. It is best remembered for a telling exchange Griffin once had with his coach, Heisman. Walking along North Avenue one day, Heisman saw Griffin across the street and waved him over. "Griffin, you are a great disappointment to me," Heisman told him. "I always expect you to get away for a long run, but you never do."

Griffin would use Heisman's quote as the title of his 1971 autobiography (*Griffin—You Are a Great Disappointment to Me*).

94 White Uniforms

Wearing white after Labor Day breaks a fashion commandment. College football has its own spin on the edict: no wearing white after Labor Day in your home stadium. Georgia Tech favors tradition over fashion, however.

The Yellow Jackets are one of only two major-college teams—LSU is the other—to claim white jerseys as part of their home uniforms. The white tops date back to the program's beginnings: the 1892 team wore white shirts and pants and dark socks.

Georgia Tech mixed and matched for the program's first 50 years or so. Head coach John Heisman's teams wore two-toned jerseys for a period, and Heisman's successor, Bill Alexander, put the Yellow Jackets in navy blue shirts late in his coaching career.

Georgia Tech became instantly recognizable by its white home jerseys during the Golden Era of the early 1950s. Head coach Bobby Dodd's Yellow Jackets were a power at the time, winning the 1952 national championship and finishing in the top 10 in the rankings five times in six seasons between 1951 and 1956.

That success coincided with the advent of televised college football. Telecasts were in black and white, so teams had to dress in contrasting light and dark colors. Most schools chose to wear their signature color—like Alabama crimson or Tennessee orange—at home, making white the de facto road color.

Georgia Tech wore white most Saturdays as a result. Wearing light-colored jerseys was an advantage in the sweltering South, particularly early in the season. The Yellow Jackets went so far as to don white helmets for a brief period in the 1960s.

Once Dodd retired following the 1966 season—by which time color television had supplanted black-and-white—Georgia Tech began experimenting with gold jerseys. The Jackets would go back to white in the early 1970s. The NCAA eventually forced Georgia Tech to switch. College athletics' governing body established a uniform policy in the mid-1970s. Home teams had to wear dark jerseys.

The Yellow Jackets took the new rule to the extreme: they adopted black as the home jersey color. The uniforms were made famous in the 1984 and 1985 seasons by the "Black Watch" defense led by Ted Roof and Pat Swilling.

Bobby Ross lightened the jersey shade to navy blue when he took over in 1987. Georgia Tech finally went back to the white home jerseys when the NCAA lifted its ban in 1995. The NCAA did so at the behest of new LSU coach Gerry DiNardo, who so wanted to restore the white jersey tradition at his school he personally petitioned every member of the NCAA's football rules committee. The committee relented.

White jerseys also fit the desire of first-year Georgia Tech coach George O'Leary to draw inspiration from the program's past. The Yellow Jackets' theme for that season, printed on all the football team's marketing materials, was "Getting Back to our Roots" and heavily referenced the Dodd era.

O'Leary's successor, Chan Gailey, left his own mark on Georgia Tech's uniform history. His teams wore gold shirts to match their helmets. Naturally, Gailey's replacement, Paul Johnson, went back to the white jerseys.

Georgia Tech still wears dark jerseys at home on occasion. In relaxing the jersey rule in 1995, the NCAA still allowed visiting teams to retain the right to wear light jerseys. Conference rules can trump that guideline—the Southeastern Conference allows the home team to pick the uniform color, which is why LSU wears white for every SEC home game—but the Atlantic Coast Conference refuses to legislate jersey colors.

Georgia Tech has been forced on occasion to wear dark jerseys at home as a result. N.C. State chose to wear white in visiting Atlanta in 2010; the Yellow Jackets wore gold jerseys. Johnson, for his part, doesn't gnash his teeth over uniform colors. "They were here when I got here," Johnson told a writer for the school's website prior to his debut in 2008. "I don't worry about stuff like that."

95 Founding the SEC

For those who despise the concept of major conferences, blame Georgia Tech. Georgia Tech and six other schools formed what would become college football's first major conference on December 21, 1894. Tech, Georgia, Vanderbilt, Alabama, Auburn, North Carolina, and Sewanee established the Southern

Intercollegiate Athletic Association (SIAA) one year prior to the start of the Big Ten.

The formation of the SIAA allowed for a league track-and-field meet and a basketball tournament. The founders also established eligibility rules to limit, or at least curb, the inclusion of ringers— players like Army doctor Leonard Wood, who enrolled at Georgia Tech in 1893 strictly to play football. The SIAA was as much a fore-runner of the NCAA as it was the SEC. Seven more schools joined the league in 1895. By 1900 the conference had grown to 19 schools. By 1915 membership reached 30 schools. The NCAA, formed as the International Amateur Association of the United States in 1906, did not establish its divisional structure until 1956.

The SIAA quickly changed the college athletics landscape in the South, although it remained more a loose collection of pro-grams than a power conference, at least in football. The teams played each other, and league titles were awarded. But the programs operated independently of each other, and in 1915, a disagreement over freshman eligibility shook the SIAA's stability. The league numbered close to 30 members by then and included both large public universities and small private schools. The majority of the big programs wanted the "one-year rule" observed while the small teams preferred players be eligible immediately.

The one-year rule failed to pass a league vote in 1915, and Georgia Tech and several other of the larger schools established the Southern Intercollegiate Conference. First-year players in SIC pro-grams were ineligible, although the schools remained part of the SIAA. The hope was the SIAA would eventually relent and adopt the one-year rule.

Yet the eligibility vote continued to fail. SIC teams finally split from the SIAA following the 1920 season, with the presidents of 14 schools meeting in Atlanta in February 1921 to organize a new league. The Southern Conference began play in the fall of 1921. Organizers originally planned to cap membership at 16, but four

The SEC: In the Beginning

College football's power league, the Southeastern Conference, dates back to the 1890s, although it didn't always go by the SEC name. A look at the conference and its forebearers.

Southern Intercollegiate Athletic Association (SIAA), established 1895

Alabama*	LSU
Auburn*	Ole Miss
Georgia*	Mississippi State
Georgia Tech*	Tennessee
Sewanee*	Texas
North Carolina*	Tulane
Vanderbilt*	Clemson
Cumberland	Kentucky

Southern Conference (SoCon), established 1921

Alabama*	Virginia Tech*
Auburn*	Washington & Lee*
Clemson*	Florida
Georgia*	LSU
Georgia Tech*	Ole Miss
North Carolina*	Vanderbilt
Kentucky*	Sewanee
Mississippi State*	Tulane
Tennessee*	VMI
Maryland*	Duke
N.C. State*	South Carolina
Virginia*	

Southeastern Conference (SEC), established 1932

Alabama*	Mississippi State*
Auburn*	Sewanee*
Florida*	Tennessee*
Georgia*	Tulane*
Georgia Tech*	Vanderbilt*
Kentucky*	Arkansas
LSU*	South Carolina
Ole Miss*	

Denotes founding members

more large state schools plus Vanderbilt and Tulane expressed interest in joining the league in 1922. The league expanded to 20 teams
for the 1922 season.

Growth would be the Southern Conference's undoing. The
league numbered 23 schools by 1928, and the man who originally
organized the Southern Conference, University of Georgia president S.V. Sanford, informed his peers at the 1932 SoCon meetings
he would lead the formation of a new conference. Sanford had
already formulated his plan: the 13 schools located west and south
of the Appalachian Mountains, including Georgia Tech, would
leave the SoCon and establish the Southeastern Conference.
According to the meeting minutes, Florida's president told the
group the withdrawing schools regretted the move but felt the
SoCon's size necessitated it.

The SEC's first football season kicked off in the fall of 1933.
Interestingly enough, many of the schools that remained in the
Southern Conference after the split would become Georgia Tech's
peers again 65 years later. Clemson, Duke, Maryland, North
Carolina, and N.C. State left the SoCon to establish the Atlantic
Coast Conference in 1953. Georgia Tech left the SEC in 1964 and
joined the ACC in 1978.

Joining the ACC

Georgia Tech fans may be too proud to admit it, but the athletics
programs needed rescuing in the late 1970s. The Yellow Jackets left
the Southeastern Conference in 1964 over a controversial scholarship cap, known as the 140 Rule. The football program was a top 10
fixture at the time and couched its move from the SEC to independent status as a chance to become the "Notre Dame of the South."

Georgia Tech failed to become even the Hawaii (another independent at the time) of the South. Coach Bobby Dodd retired following the 1966 season. The program slipped toward mediocrity. Scheduling became difficult. Attendance gradually decreased.

The situation was twice as dire for the other programs as it was for football. Scheduling and travel had the athletics department operating in the red. So in 1975 Georgia Tech and five other schools formed the Metro Conference. The members were all located in metropolitan areas: Georgia Tech (Atlanta), Cincinnati, Louisville, Memphis State, St. Louis, and Tulane (New Orleans). Georgia Tech administrators knew the Metro Conference was far from a permanent solution. The league didn't sponsor football, and rivalries were nonexistent.

Georgia Tech's powers-that-be desired a league better suited geographically. They approached the SEC about rejoining the league and received support from the conference's most influential figure, Alabama coach Bear Bryant. But several other schools—including rival Georgia and the Mississippi schools, which Dodd had refused to play for years for travel reasons—balked.

The major conference alternative to the SEC, at least in terms of geographic practicality, was the Atlantic Coast Conference. The ACC numbered eight members at the time. South Carolina had left the league in 1971, and aside from Clemson, the conference's other schools valued basketball ahead of football. Conference leaders wanted to boost the football profile. Inviting Georgia Tech would give the ACC a traditional football power and exposure in the fast-growing Atlanta market. Plus, the ACC schools had history with Georgia Tech dating back to the days when all were in the Southern Conference. Yet the negotiations were tense. Administrators at the league schools knew Georgia Tech would have preferred to rejoin the SEC and wanted Tech to demonstrate its commitment by paying a six-figure entry fee. Doug Weaver, Georgia Tech's athletics director, initially refused and was holding out until N.C. State's athletics director approached him and offered to pay the entry fee in exchange for five year's worth of ACC men's basketball tournament tickets. Each ACC school gets several thousand tickets to sell for the popular tourney, and N.C. State wanted Tech's seats. Weaver did the math, then politely refused N.C. State's offer. Then he paid the ACC's admittance fee.

The Yellow Jackets programs officially joined the league in 1979. But football's long-term scheduling practices meant the program couldn't compete in the league until 1983. Georgia Tech played one ACC opponent in 1979, two in 1980 and 1981, and four in 1982 before playing a full conference schedule in 1983.

For a time, it looked as if Georgia Tech would renege on its ACC commitment, at least in football. The budget deficit and back-to-back one-win seasons led then-president Joseph Pettit to talk openly about deemphasizing football and moving the program into Division I-AA. Dodd and several prominent alumni lobbied against such a move. Meanwhile, Coach Bill Curry was rebuilding the program. The Yellow Jackets went 3–8 in their first ACC season, but all three wins came against conference foes. Two years later, Tech won nine games, finished second in the ACC, and went to a bowl game. The basketball program was on the upswing as well, winning the ACC tourney in 1985 and advancing to the Elite Eight.

Georgia Tech had found a new home.

97 Frank Kopf Game Charts

William Alexander mentored under John Heisman, a coach ahead of his time. Heisman pioneered concepts like the forward pass, pre-snap motion, and the pulling guard, all in the name of finding an edge. Alexander found his advantage in scouting.

Alexander would send assistants to the games of future opponents. Coaching in an era before every game was filmed from at least two angles and teams changed their game plans each week, scouting allowed Alexander to gain valuable insights. He wasn't alone, of course. Many other coaches scouted.

Where Alexander lapped his rivals, though, was in the practice of self-scouting. He and his staff could analyze the Yellow Jackets' performance, identify tendencies, and make adjustments. Their scouting data came from an unusual source: a sportswriter.

Frank Kopf was a chemistry teacher and coach at Tech High School, located adjacent to the Georgia Tech campus. He moonlighted as a sports columnist for the *Atlanta Journal* on the weekends. His scientific mind led him to take notes during games via a series of play diagrams, which the newspaper then printed.

Kopf diagrammed every play and included pertinent information like when the play was run, the down and distance, and the result. He also noted weather conditions in some cases. Kopf charted most of Georgia Tech's games between 1927 and 1934. Alexander or one of his staff members would clip the diagrams out of the Sunday newspaper and paste them to lab sheets from Kopf's Tech High School. Alexander would pour over the charts and plan strategy for subsequent games. Kopf also charted the occasional Georgia game, giving Alexander an edge in the rivalry matchups.

Alexander's efforts made scouting Tech futile for opponents. But then the Yellow Jackets needed every advantage in those days. His 1927 and 1928 teams were outstanding, with the 1928 Yellow Jackets claiming a national championship. But Georgia Tech failed to post a winning season in the six years that followed.

Kopf continued to teach at Tech High School through 1940 before joining the Army during World War II. He retired from the Army as a colonel and achieved the rank of brigadier general in the National Guard. He worked at Georgia Tech as a professor of chemistry following World War II.

Kopf the writer was direct and analytical, much like a game chart. But he was witty, too. Writing about a Georgia-Kentucky basketball game in the 1922 season, Kopf described the Wildcats' Bob Lavin as "no doubt the fastest streak of lightning that ever graced the scorebook in the position of guard."

98 Dustin Vaitekunas

The premise seemed sound: if the quarterback's protector doesn't seem to grasp the importance of his task, show him what failure looks like. But somebody, be it Georgia Tech coach George O'Leary, two defensive linemen, or a combination of those three, decided offensive tackle Dustin Vaitekunas needed to *feel* what an unprotected quarterback feels.

So when the coach called Vaitekunas before his teammates at the end of a practice in September 2000, flipped him a football, and told four defensive linemen to rush Vaitekunas as if he were an opposing quarterback, the lesson was sure to go horribly wrong.

Two blitzers pulled up. Two didn't. Even at 6'7" and 314 pounds, Vaitekunas couldn't absorb the impact. He spent 15 minutes on his back. As Georgia Tech's training staff tended to him, the team left the field. Practice was over, after all. The trainers got Vaitekunas back to his dorm room and gave him some painkillers.

Chronic pain for the program followed. Vaitekunas left school the next day, surrendering his football scholarship. O'Leary didn't try to talk him out of it. The coach didn't apologize. Neither did anyone else associated with the program or Georgia Tech. As Vaitekunas told *Sports Illustrated*'s Adrian Wojnarowski a year later, O'Leary "was never held accountable for anything. That's the big issue I have with the whole thing. Nobody told him that this can't go on, that this isn't how you run a program."

O'Leary would answer the public outcry over the incident by saying it was blown out of proportion, that he expected all four linemen to break off the run before hitting Vaitekunas. They weren't permitted to hit the quarterback in practice, anyway, so they wouldn't hit Vaitekunas, O'Leary argued. Vaitekunas was a quarterback for the purposes of the drill.

Exactly what the blitzers were or were not supposed to do that afternoon is unknown. O'Leary's hard-nosed approach to football is well-chronicled, however, and many who played for him admit they wouldn't be surprised if he ordered the football version of a Marine Corps "code red." One of O'Leary's players, Georgia Tech safety Michael Dee, summed up the affection O'Leary elicited from his charges in an interview with *Sports Illustrated*'s Gary Smith: "If he was on fire, I wouldn't walk across the street to piss on him."

Yet O'Leary could coach them up. Even with the Vaitekunas' controversy swirling around the program, Georgia Tech went 9–3 that season. The Yellow Jackets won seven games in a row following the incident.

The aftermath polarized the Georgia Tech fan base. Some found the incident inexcusable. Others chalked it up to an unfortunate miscommunication between coach and players. Still others labeled Vaitekunas as soft and trumpeted his quitting as good for the program—it freed up a scholarship, after all. Regardless, Vaitekunas never played football again. He enrolled at Cleveland State following his departure and finished his education. But he remains a footnote in Georgia Tech football history, and a sad one at that.

99 A Colorful First

The Hall's Furniture store was the most populated building in Dalton, Georgia, on the afternoon of September 17, 1955. Local football fans packed the showroom in advance of Georgia Tech's game against Miami at Grant Field. They gathered around a handful of special television sets and saw the Yellow Jackets like they never had before, at least not on TV.

The Jackets actually looked yellow.

The Georgia Tech–Miami game was the first televised nationally in color. NBC broadcast the game on 100 stations in 100 cities—and probably about 100 televisions sets, given the newness of the technology.

Color TV in the mid-1950s received the same reception from consumers as the Internet did in the early 1990s—everybody had heard about it, but few had access. CBS debuted color television broadcasting in 1951. The technology was complex, however, and color sets sold for the equivalent of more than $10,000 in today's money. And with networks transmitting little color programming, even the wealthy struggled to justify the expense.

NBC's parent company, RCA, was among those electronics manufacturers pioneering color TVs. Hence, RCA used NBC to market the technology. NBC's color broadcasting debut came on New Year's Day, 1954, with the Tournament of Roses Parade. The network gradually added more and more color programming that year, eventually offering 12 hours a week of color television. By September of 1955, the network was ready to show sports in color. NBC chose Georgia Tech's season opener as its foray into the field.

Seeing Georgia Tech's players in their gold helmets flash across the screen left the crowd at Hall's Furniture dumbstruck in the game's opening minutes. Hall's was home to the only color TVs in Dalton at the time, so most of the town turned out to watch the game. Adding to the excitement, Georgia Tech tight end Don Ellis was a Dalton native, and his young wife had given birth to twin girls earlier that day. The furniture store finally started to resemble today's sports bars when Ellis sacked Miami's quarterback midway through the first half. Georgia Tech went on to win 14–6 and jumped eight spots in the rankings to No. 2.

The color telecast was far from an unqualified success, however, at least from a broadcasting perspective. The action moved quickly, making the players a blur at times. And the production costs were exorbitant. Almost 10 years would pass before the next college football game was shown nationally in color. By the time CBS televised the 1965 Rose Bowl in color, consumers had embraced color TVs.

100 RAT Caps

Once upon a time, you didn't need to check the media or ask a friend how Georgia Tech's football team was faring. All it took was a walk around campus between classes.

Every Georgia Tech freshmen receives a gold-colored, beanie-like cap during convocation, Georgia Tech's version of orientation. Between 1915 and the early 1960s, every "RAT"—which stands for either Recently Acquired Tech student or Recruit at Tech, depending upon whom you ask—wore the cap whenever he or she was outdoors during the fall semester. Inscribed on the side of the cap were the results of every Georgia Tech football game: wins written right-side up, losses logged upside down.

The RAT cap is one of Georgia Tech's oldest traditions, predating even the Ramblin' Wreck. Established in 1915 by the ANAK Society, a secret club reserved for upperclassmen who "show both exemplary leadership and a true love for Georgia Tech," the RAT cap originally distinguished the freshmen from the upperclassmen in the school's ROTC program.

The RAT cap quickly grew into a kind-hearted hazing ritual. Or at least it was kind-hearted until a freshman challenged the tradition. Forgoing the cap could result in a freshman getting a "T-cut"—a buzz haircut with only the initials "GT" left on the scalp. Female students who shunned the caps could be made to rat their hair and tie on ribbons. But few women faced such a penalty, as Georgia Tech didn't admit its first female until 1952, and the tradition faded away when hazing was abolished a decade later.

Freshmen did get a reprieve from wearing the RAT cap if Georgia Tech's freshman team defeated Georgia in the annual Scottish Rite game, played each Thanksgiving Day. If Tech lost—and in the 30 games played during the RAT cap era, the Jackets lost 14 times—freshmen had to wear the caps until the end of the school year.

RAT caps can still be seen on campus today, at least during home football games. Many freshmen, including all of those in the marching band, wear the caps at Bobby Dodd Stadium. Every cap-wearing RAT wears it "smart," and football scores are just one piece of decoration. Using a black magic marker, freshmen write the word "RAT" on the underside of the cap's bill, which is to be worn turned up. The upturned bill should also include the student's name and hometown as well as the major and projected graduation year. The major, name, and grad date are to be written on the curve of the bill's edge.

The back should read "To Hell with Georgia" and co-op students circle the top button of the cap. The football scores go along the sides and across the top. Tech's score is always listed first, no matter the outcome of the game.

Acknowledgments

The Georgia Tech sports communications staff, both past and present, and especially Dean Buchan, Mike Stamus, and Allison George, deserve more gratitude than can be expressed in one run-on sentence. Thank you. So many Georgia Tech greats submitted to interviews for this book or for other pieces I have done over the last decade. Sessions with the late George Morris, Rudy Allen, Eddie Lee Ivery, Randy Rhino, Bill Curry, Kim King, Gary Lanier, Wes Durham, and many others made writing this book not only easy but fun. So too did some of them damn Dogs, particularly Theron Sapp, Dan Magill, Loran Smith, and Vince Dooley. Thanks to Simit Shah, Richard Reynolds, and Jack Wilkinson for research assistance and to my wife, Ann, for chipping in to help when called. Perhaps the greatest thrill of writing this book was the chance to break bread and share stories with Homer Rice, whose 750-word foreword captures the essence of Georgia Tech football better than I did in 70,000 words.

Bibliography

Media

Alexander of Georgia Tech, by Edwin Camp

Auburn Football Media Guide

Bear: My Hard Life and Good Times as Alabama's Head Coach, by Paul Bryant

The Blueprint, 1918

Clean, Old-Fashioned Hate, by Bill Cromartie

College Football Historical Society newsletter

Dodd's Luck, by Bobby Dodd and Jack Wilkinson

Engineering the New South: Georgia Tech 1885–1985, by Robert McMath

Focused on the Top, by Jack Wilkinson

Georgia Media Guide, 2004 edition

Georgia Southern Football Media Guide

Georgia Tech Alumni Magazine (http://gtalumnimag.com)

Georgia Tech Athletic Association newsletter

Georgia Tech Basketball Media Guide, 2004 and 2010 editions

Georgia Tech Football History database

Georgia Tech Football Media Guide, 2004 and 2010 editions

Georgia Tech game notes, reports, and interview transcripts

Georgia Tech game programs

The Georgia Tech Trivia Book, by Tim Darnell

The Georgia Tech Vault, by Jack Wilkinson

Georgia Tech vs. Notre Dame play-by-play recap

Georgia Tech's Living History program

Georgia Trend magazine

The Glory Years: Georgia Tech, by John Heisman

Great Moments in Georgia Tech History

Gridiron Grudge, by John Chandler Griffin

The History of Georgia

The Jingle Man, by Steve Karmen
Kim King's Tales from the Georgia Tech Sideline, by Kim King and
   Jack Wilkinson
Legends: Georgians Who Live Impossible Dreams, by Gene Asher
*Leonard Wood: Rough Rider, Surgeon, Architect of American
   Imperialism*, by Jack McCallum
Lessons for Leaders, by Homer Rice
Memphis University School Today magazine
Michigan in the Olympics: 1936 Berlin, University of Michigan's
   Bentley Historical Library
Michigan's Black Lettermen, by John Behee
Missouri sports information department, Colorado-Missouri 1990
   statistical report
National Football Foundation newsletter
NCAA Graduation Success Report, 2010
NCAA infractions committee reports
OU Insider (oklahoma247sports.com)
Our Georgia History, the Georgia Historical Society
Principles of Football, by John Heisman
Ramblin' Wreck, by Al Thomy
Rudy, from Rudy International
Sports Illustrated's Encyclopedia of College Football
Stadium Stories: Georgia Tech, by Adam Van Brimmer
T-Book (www.tbook.org)
Whistle, faculty newspaper

Archives
ACC teleconference archives
American Football Monthly archives
Associated Press archives
Athens Banner-Herald archives
Atlanta Journal-Constitution archives
Atlanta Magazine archives

Baltimore Sun archives
Buzz magazine archives
Collier's Weekly archives
Concordia Sentinel archives
ESPN.com archives
Florida Sun-Sentinel archives
Gainesville Times archives
Georgia Bulletin archive
Georgia Tech Library, archives, and records
Golf Styles Atlanta magazine archives
Life magazine archives
Lincoln Journal archives
Los Angeles Times archives
Macon Telegraph archives
Michigan Daily archives
New York Times archives
Orlando Sentinel archives
Playboy magazine archives
San Francisco Chronicle archives
Savannah Morning News archives
Sports Illustrated vault
St. Petersburg Times archives
Technique archives
Tennessee Football Coaches Association archives (www.tnfca.org)
Time magazine archives
USA Today archives
Washington Post archives

Websites
The Bobby Dodd Foundation website
    (www.bobbydoddfoundation.com)
Campaign for Free Enterprise website
    (www.freeenterpriseland.com)

From the Rumble Seat (www.fromtherumbleseat.com)
Georgia Sports Hall of Fame website (http://gshf.org)
Georgia Tech ANAK Society website
    (www.cyberbuzz.gatech.edu/anak)
Georgia Tech Band website (www.gtband.net)
Georgia Tech website (www.gatech.edu)
Heisman Trophy website (www.heisman.com)
Limestone County Sports Hall of Fame website
    (www.lcshof.com/index.html)
LostLettermen.com
Lou Groza Award website (www.lougrozaaward.com)
NASA website (www.nasa.gov)
Notre Dame Football website
    (www.und.com/sports/m-footbl/nd-m-footbl-body.html)
Oversigning.com
Payscale.com
Ramblin' Reck Club website (www.reckclub.org)
RamblinWreck.com (Official Home of Georgia Tech Athletics)
Reinhardt University website (www.reinhardt.edu)
Scout.com
Southeastern Conference website (www.secdigitalnetwork.com)
Southern Conference website (www.soconsports.com)
The Varsity website (www.thevarsity.com)